BUDDHISM
PRIMITIVE AND PRESENT
IN MAGADHA AND IN CEYLON

BUDDHISM
PRIMITIVE AND PRESENT
IN MAGADHA AND IN CEYLON

BY

REGINALD STEPHEN COPLESTON, D.D.

SECOND EDITION

GYAN

Published by

GYAN

Gyan Publishing House
5, Ansari Road
Daryaganj, New Delhi-110002
Phone: 011-47034999, 9811692060
E-mail: books@gyanbooks.com

Distribution Network
gyanbooks.com
India, USA, Canada, UK, Australia, France

ISBN : 978-81-212-3169-5 (PB)
First Published, 1908

2nd Impression 2020

Printed at: Gyan Press, Delhi.

Buddhism Primitive and Present in Magadha and in Ceylon
Author: Reginald Stephen Copleston

BUDDHISM

PRIMITIVE AND PRESENT

IN MAGADHA AND IN CEYLON

BY

REGINALD STEPHEN COPLESTON, D.D.

BISHOP OF CALCUTTA

SECOND EDITION

LONGMANS, GREEN, AND CO.

39 PATERNOSTER ROW, LONDON

NEW YORK, BOMBAY, AND CALCUTTA

1908

CONTENTS

PART IV. THE ERA OF ASOKA

PART V. BUDDHISM IN CEYLON: THE PAST

PART VI. BUDDHISM IN CEYLON: THE PRESENT

INDICES

PREFACE TO FIRST EDITION

THE scope of this work is limited to the history and description of that particular stock or branch of Buddhism which has been established and continued in Ceylon.

I have tried to treat this subject in a way at once popular enough to interest the general reader, and accurate enough to be of value to the scholar. With a view to the former purpose I have avoided as far as possible the use, in the text, of Pali words and technical terms; with a view to the latter purpose I have given references for every statement which professes to be drawn direct from the Pali books.

The notes which stand at the end of some chapters, the chapter on the literary history of the Texts, and the Appendix on Sirivaddhanapura, may, I hope, be found contributions to scholarship or history. In the interest of all readers I have suppressed, as a general rule, the marks of quantity and the diacritical points in proper names after the first occurrence of each. The reader who wishes to refresh his memory as to the pronunciation of a name can find it in the index.

Originality, or at any rate independence, I do not disclaim. My statements and opinions are not derived at second-hand from translations or manuals. I have read a large part of the original "sacred books" of which I speak—almost all that has been published, and a good deal that has not—and I have had access to competent Sinhalese authorities.

But while I claim to have been in this sense an independent student, I am glad to say I am not advancing strange or startling views, but adding, in most points, the slight weight of my confirmation to what has been written by those who have gone before me.

In regard to the history, the reader of this book will be invited to a conclusion midway between scepticism and credulity.

Starting with a strong inclination to believe ancient records rather than to set them aside, I have been compelled to doubt whether we have evidence which can be called historical for the centuries before B.C. 260, and to assign to the era of Asoka an immense importance, as that in which Buddhism and Buddhist literature took the shape in which we know them. At the same time, I see no reason to doubt that the literature which has come down to us contains material which is nearly or quite contemporary with Gotama, or that what it tells us of his life and work is, in its main features, true.

In regard to the contents of the sacred books and the moral value of their teaching, as well as in regard to the description of modern Buddhism in Ceylon, I have aimed at not merely an impartial but a generous treatment. Impartial, in a sense, it was impossible for me to be. The questions raised are not for me open questions: I start with immovable convictions about the main principles of truth and goodness. But heartily to welcome all that agreed with those principles, and favourably to interpret in their light all that was not opposed to them—this is what I have desired to do. If I have blamed many things and pointed out many defects, I hope I have earned the right to do so by candid and ungrudging acknowledgment of much which I could praise.

Even in the defects and errors which distress him, the Christian sees the traces of longings and instincts, exaggerated here or misdirected, yet implanted by that Heavenly Father, from Whom His children have been so far estranged; while in many a noble aspiration or passage of beauty and truth he thankfully adores the teaching of that Divine Word, Who has ever been everywhere the Light of the world, and of that Holy Spirit Who has never ceased to move, with life-giving influence, over the chords of human thought.

It would be an affectation to attempt to enumerate all the writers from whom I have derived help; but I must make special acknowledgment of the obligation which I am under, as is every student of Pali, to Professor Max Müller, and the translators of the *Sacred Books of the East*; to Professor Rhys Davids, and the editors of the Pali Text Society; to Dr. Hermann Oldenberg, the editor of the *Vinaya Pitaka*; and Dr. Fausböll, the editor of the *Jātaka*. Most of these scholars are also authors of independent works, among which I owe most to those of Professor Rhys Davids and Professor Oldenberg.

The work of George Turnour and of Professor Childers deserves to be respectfully called to mind, whenever Pali studies are spoken of, especially in Ceylon.

In the chapter on Asoka I am under special obligation to the *Corpus Inscriptionum* of General Cunningham, and the *Inscriptions de Piyadasi* of M. E. Sénart.[1]

Although I have aimed at exercising an independent judgment, I have been helped and influenced by the various manuals and treatises, such as those of the scholars above-named, of Sir Monier Williams, and others. I have made great use of Mr. C. Vijesinhe's important translation of the Mahavansa, with its analysis of contents and chronological tables. My obligations to friends in Ceylon, both English and Sinhalese, for information verbally given, are both too numerous, and from the nature of the case, too indefinite to be separately recorded.

The translations which occur in the following pages I have borrowed, in a great many cases, from the *Sacred Books of the East* and other English versions. I have done this, not so much to save myself trouble as to give my readers security. But whenever the source of a translation is not acknowledged, I am myself responsible for it. For all the more important among the passages which I have translated myself, I had the advantage of reading them over in proof to the late lamented D. A. de Silva Batuvantudāvē, Pandit, a teacher for whom I had a high esteem. The help which he gave me in this—and he saved me from several mistakes—was among the latest acts of his life. He died in April, 1892, and his remains were cremated with great pomp. He was a really learned scholar, and an upright man. He had been the teacher of generations of European students, and the author of valuable works.

The writings of one very important author, the learned Spence Hardy, I purposely avoided consulting during the preparation of this work, though I had read parts of them sixteen years ago. His information was to so great an extent derived from Sinhalese sources, and his studies were likely to have run so parallel to

[1] To these should now be added Professor Führer's monograph on his discoveries in Nepal, and Vincent A. Smith's *Asoka* (2nd ed.).

my own, that I thought there would be more value in comparing my results afterwards with his, than in using his help to obtain them. Since this book has been in the press I have read his *Eastern Monachism* and *Manual of Buddhism*, and have been astonished at the accuracy with which he obtained, through Sinhalese channels, the contents of the Pali texts and commentaries. The fact that he was able to do so shows how untrue it would be to say that the Sinhalese had entirely lost the knowledge of the Pali books before European scholars recovered it for them. I have not been led by the perusal of Hardy's works to alter anything that I had written; but I have become more convinced that I have given too small a place, in comparison with the Pali texts, to commentaries and later works. Under this conviction I have somewhat enlarged my twenty-fourth chapter, and still acknowledge that my treatment of that part of the subject is incomplete.

The conditions under which I have had to work—writing different parts at widely different times—have led to my repeating myself in several instances; but I have not always corrected this, because, though it is a blemish on an author's work, it is not altogether an injury to a reader. Besides these defects of which I am aware, I cannot hope entirely to have escaped more serious errors, and I shall be grateful to any one who will point them out.

To Him Who is alone the Way, the Truth, and the Life, I humbly commit what I have done.

COLOMBO, *July*, 1892.

NOTE TO REVISED EDITION

THE book has been entirely re-written. Notice has been taken of such recent discoveries as have become known to the author; but the alterations are chiefly for clearness and better arrangement. In several cases information which, though important, seemed to burden the text, has been relegated to a note at the end of the chapter. These notes, it is hoped, will be found to be among the most interesting parts of the book.

The tone in which that part is written which deals with Ceylon is that of one who was living (when he wrote it sixteen years ago) in the easiest and happiest intimacy with that beautiful island and its people. It is a tone which the writer could hardly now assume, but which he has not thought it necessary to alter or disguise.

The writer is much indebted to his friend, Mr. Harinath De, M.A., the accomplished Librarian of the Imperial Library, Calcutta, who has kindly corrected the proofs and has made several valuable suggestions.

June, 1908.

PALI TERMS, SPELLING, AND PRONUNCIATION

Pali Words.—In this book, which moves on Pali ground, the Pali forms of names and terms are generally used in preference to the Sanscrit. Several of the laws under which Pali differs from Sanscrit can be observed in the names of the three castes; which are in Sanscrit, Kshatriya, Vaishya, Shudra; and in Pali, Khattiya, Vessa, Sudda.

Pali terms, introduced into the text, are explained on their first, or on their first important, occurrence; and a reference to that explanation may be found in the Index of Pali Words.

Spelling.—The system of the Pali Text Society has been followed; but it has not been thought necessary, in proper names, to repeat the marks of quantity or the diacritical marks of consonants after the first occurrence, or to mark the quantity of "e" and "o," which in Pali are always long, or of final "i," where the quantity scarcely affects the pronunciation. With these exceptions all vowels not marked long are short.

The termination of proper names is usually modified according to custom: e.g. Buddha, not Buddhā; Gotama, not Gotamo: as we write Herodotus, Plato, Virgil; not Herodotos, Platon, Vergilius.

The reader who wishes to remind himself of the correct form of a proper name will find it, subject to the above modification, in the Index of Proper Names.

Pronunciation.—*E* and *O* are always long, and are pronounced as *a* in "pale" and *o* in "pole." Short *A* as in "woman"; long *A*, as in "father." Short *I*, not as in "fill," but as *e* in "elicit"; long *I* as *ee* in "peel." Short *U* as in "pull"; long *U* as *oo* in "pool."

C is pronounced before all vowels as it is in Italian before *i*, i.e., as *ch* in "church." The symbol ṃ represents a sound nearly equivalent to *ng* in "sing"; thus Siṃhalā, a Sinhalese man, is pronounced nearly as "sing-hala." (There is no such word, for an inhabitant of Ceylon, as Siṃhalī, or "Cingalee.") Double consonants are pronounced doubly; thus, "mettaṃ" is pronounced nearly as "mate-tongue."

BUDDHISM

PART I

INTRODUCTORY

CHAPTER I

THE SUBJECT DEFINED

THE interest which the study of Buddhism has aroused of late years in Europe has not been unreasonable, though it has been supported, in too many cases, by very little information. The important literature in which this system is embodied, and the immense number of those who have professed it, justly give it a strong claim on men's attention. It is a stupendous fact, which no thoughtful man can contemplate without emotion.

It will no longer be asserted, by any one who is well-informed, that Buddhism reckons at the present day more adherents than any other creed.[1] But once it probably was so, and for many centuries. While Greeks and Romans, Jews and Christians, were few in number, and before Islam had arisen, vast multitudes in India and China, and the countries adjacent to these, professed to find refuge in the Buddha. It is very possible —and it is a startling thought—that more men and women may have owned the Buddha than have owned, as yet, any other teacher.

Truth is not measured, nor even is significance, by numbers. The small nation, for instance, of Jews, the little cities of Greece, and Rome while she was still confined to Italy—these have made contributions to the development of mankind compared

[1] See Note A, at the end of this chapter.

with which what has hitherto been done by the multitudes of India or of China is as nothing. But the spectacle of human multitudes is always an impressive spectacle, often a most pathetic one; and we cannot but ask, with deep interest, what is the nature of that teaching which has attracted so many of our fellow-men? What are the elements of truth, and the tendencies consonant with the Creator's purpose for man, which have given it a hold on so many hearts?

In such an inquiry we shall be much misled if we start either with the assumption that what so many have believed must be true, or even with the assumption that what has given it a hold on men is that part of it which differs from other creeds. It is quite possible in regard to any system, and I think it will be found to be the case with this, that the elements of good and truth which it contains are to be found, not in the dogmas which are peculiar to it—its characteristics—but in what it has in common with other systems.

The dogmas peculiar to Buddhism are the least true, and, I cannot but think, the least winning part of it. The secret of its attraction must lie in some felicity in its presentation of certain truths, from among those to which human nature everywhere responds. Which those truths are, and what is that way of presenting them by which Buddhism has gained access to the Indian heart, the reader of this book will be, I hope, in a position to judge for himself; so far at least as concerns the limited field over which I purpose to conduct him.

For whereas the question is complicated by the great variety of shapes which Buddhism has taken, in the present work, out of all that variety, one clearly-marked form will be treated of alone. That form has strong claims to be considered the most genuine one; and so, I suppose, is the form in which the essence of Buddhism is most sure to be discovered. I purpose to describe the primitive stock and one of its existing branches; to show what Buddhism was in Māgadha, the land of its origin, and what it is now in Ceylon. The Buddhism of Ceylon belongs to what is called the Southern School[1]; and in treating of it we

[1] Professor Rhys Davids, in the Preface to the Revised Edition (1903) of his *Buddhism*, has pointed out that the nomenclature, "Northern" and "Southern" Buddhism, is misleading. "The oldest books," he says, "whether Pali or Sanscrit, were neither Northern nor Southern, but were alike composed in the

leave on one side not only the highly developed system of the Lamaism of Tibet, but also the less widely divergent branches which are to be found, for instance, in Nepal, in China, and in Japan. Nor even of the Southern School do I undertake more than what concerns Ceylon. If the Southern School has had a different development in Burma or in Siam, such differences lie outside the scope of this book.

In this narrowing of the field there are, I think, advantages. For if the vast extension of Buddhism has roused interest in it, the variety of its forms has been a prolific cause of confusion and mistake. Travellers and readers have been bewildered by statements apparently contradictory, made by authorities, each of whom was speaking about a different thing. Towards the clearing up of these confusions a step has been taken whenever a writer, though treating of Buddhism at large, has distinguished with adequate emphasis between the different systems which bear the same name. I hope to emphasize the distinction even more effectually by admitting nothing within the cover of my book that is not part of the description or of the history of one particular branch.

Such an entirely separate treatment of the Southern Buddhism could not of course be justified, unless it were certain both that the Southern School was independent of the Northern in its origin, and also that in its subsequent history it had been unaffected by that system. Both these points may be asserted with perfect confidence. Buddhism was carried to Ceylon (about 250 B.C.) before the original institutions and teaching of the Buddha had undergone those changes which constituted the Northern School. When the religion in its "Northern" form was introduced into China (about 70 B.C.) the Buddhists of Ceylon had for nearly two centuries preserved unaltered the traditions of that earlier date. Nor is there any trace, either in the records or in the monuments, of any intercourse between Ceylon and any of the countries in which the Northern developments prevailed.

From that point of view in which the lover of his kind looks

valley of the Ganges. The use of the terms in question had its origin in the fact that our MSS. of those books had come respectively from Ceylon and Nepal; and the term 'Northern Buddhism' was extended to the very different systems prevailing in Tibet, China, and Japan, notwithstanding the fact that there is no such unity as 'Northern Buddhism.'"

out with emotion on the teeming myriads of his Buddhist fellow-men, the range of our present study is small indeed. Out of the hundreds of millions of men who, if not all Buddhists, are yet all in some degree affected by Buddhism, the whole Southern group counts only some thirty millions, while the Buddhists of Ceylon are less than two millions.

But from the point of view of that student to whom Buddhism is primarily a moral and philosophic system, the Ceylon branch of it, though small, is perhaps the best he could study, or at least the one to study first. For while it is confessedly among those which have least diverged from the primitive stock, it has a far longer continuous history than any other branch.

It is a historical method that we propose here to adopt. We shall pursue the same course as was pursued by the Pali chronicles, first in Magadha, from Gotama's time to that of Asoka, and then in Ceylon from Asoka to the present day. The epochs of our historical sketch will be the dates—here given in round numbers—of

Gotama himself, founder of the religion, about 500 B.C.

King Asoka, its most powerful patron, and his son Mahinda, its founder in Ceylon, about 250 B.C.

Buddhaghosha, its greatest commentator, about A.D. 400.

Parākrama Bāhu, the greatest Buddhist king of Ceylon, about A.D. 1200.

Sumangala Terunnānse, the most distinguished leader of the present "Community" in Ceylon.

In the next chapter I propose to give a brief summary of this history, and afterwards to treat the several sections of it in detail.

NOTE A

THE NUMBER OF THE BUDDHISTS

It is not many years since even the name of Buddhism was unfamiliar, and its nature and extent unknown in Europe. And when first Europeans became vaguely aware of its importance and its vast extent, it is not surprising that there was a tendency to overstate a fact so startling. In many countries of the populous East, including China, the temples of Buddhism and its professors were found. These countries were set down as Buddhist; and it was computed that the aggregate of their populations exceeded the aggregate population of the countries known as Christian.

But this computation was misleading. In each of those vast areas of Asia, which Europeans know by a single name, there are many different elements of population and of culture. China, uniform and homogeneous as it is in some respects, is by no means all one in the matter of religion. Yet if the reader looks at any of the lists which show how the number of Buddhists in the world is made up, and observes the large part which is played, in making up the total, by the number assigned to China, he will see that the conclusion mainly depends upon the question: Is China entirely Buddhist?

In such lists, towards a total of somewhat less than five hundred millions, China contributes more than four hundred millions. But if the whole of China is reckoned to Buddhism, where—one necessarily asks—are the Confucians and the Taoists? Is it a mistake to suppose that these are numerous in China? Or are they not religions? Or can the same man be both a Confucian and a Buddhist?[1]

To the question whether Confucians are numerous in China, the answer may be given in the words of Dr. Legge: "Confucianism is the orthodoxy of China. . . . The mass of the 'learned class' and the masses under their influence are preponderatingly Confucian, and in the observance of ancestral worship . . . an overwhelming majority are regular and assiduous."[2]

There is some truth in the explanation that is suggested by the question: Is Confucianism not a religion? It is thought by many not to be such in the fullest sense; to be rather a social and political than a spiritual system.[3] But it might be plausibly urged that Buddhism too is

[1] This, however, was fully recognized by Max Müller in his *Selected Essays*, vol. ii. 224 f., and by Professor Rhys Davids in his *Buddhism*, p. 4; where such lists are to be found.

[2] Legge's *Fa Hien*, Introd., p. 7. Elsewhere he speaks of Confucius as "reigning supreme, the undisputed teacher of this most populous land."

[3] But see the title of Confucianism to be called a religion defended by Dr. Legge, *Religions of China*, p. 5 f.

rather a philosophy than a religion; and if the comparison between the numbers of the adherents of the different "religions" is to be made at all, the term must be taken in its widest and conventional sense.

Can then a man be at once a Confucian and a Buddhist? No doubt he can. Professor Max Müller says: "It is very difficult to find out in China to what religion a man belongs, because the same man may profess two or even three religions."[1] Dr. Edkin says: "The mass of the people believe in them all." "It is not too much to say," says Dr. Eitel, "that most Chinese are theoretically Confucianists, but essentially Buddhists or Taoists. But fairness requires us to add that, although the mass of the people are more or less influenced by Buddhist doctrines, yet the people as a whole have no respect for the Buddhist Church, and habitually sneer at Buddhist priests."[2]

"In Japan," writes a well-qualified observer, "Buddhism is everywhere mixed up with Shintoism, and Buddhist temples and Shinto temples exist everywhere."

In short, while there are insincere professors within the pale of every religion, it is peculiarly difficult in the case of Buddhism to define its pale at all. Dr. Legge, after carefully stating the case, sums up thus: "My own opinion is that its adherents are not so many as those even of Mohammedanism; and that, instead of being the most numerous of the religions (so-called) of the world, it is only entitled to occupy the fifth place, ranking below Christianity, Confucianism, Brahmanism, and Mohammedanism, and followed, some distance off, by Taoism."[3]

But it has become sufficiently clear to the reader that the reckoning of numbers—in no case of any value as a test of truth—is peculiarly inapplicable to this case. I may conclude this note by quoting what I have written elsewhere: "No such numerical estimate can be of the slightest value; for this important reason, that Buddhism differs from the religions with which it is thus numerically compared—notably from Christianity and Mohammedanism, and, to some degree, from Hinduism—in not claiming exclusive possession of the ground. . . . While the facts about China make it no less than false to say that the Buddhist religion is the sole refuge of five hundred millions of mankind, they show the futility of any positive statement at all about its numbers."[4]

The number of Buddhists in Ceylon, by the census of 1901, is 2,141,404; that of Hindus, 826,826; and that of Mohammedans, 246,118; while the number of Christians is 349,239.

[1] l.c., p. 226.

[2] Quoted by Dr. Legge, l.c., p. 7.

[3] *Ib.*, p. 8.

[4] *Nineteenth Century*, July, 1888, p. 121.

CHAPTER II

GENERAL HISTORICAL SKETCH

BUDDHISM began by the teaching of Gotama, towards the latter part of the sixth century B.C. The date 500 B.C. must coincide pretty nearly with the middle of his career.

To the question, What was at that time the condition of India? the answer must be gathered chiefly from other sources than the Buddhist books. For these books were not compiled —it is practically certain—till a period from one hundred and fifty to two hundred and fifty years after the Buddha's death; and those who compiled them must have described the customs and surroundings, not of Gotama's day but of their own. As to a few definite historical points, names of persons, tribes, and places, and as to the leading facts in the history of the religion itself, the books have probably preserved a true tradition, but the setting must be mainly that of their own day. It is unsafe to infer, for instance, from the incidental mention of writing in the books, that writing was known in Gotama's time; or from the mention of monasteries, that these existed before Gotama introduced them. If these are facts they must be learnt from other sources.

But India had an unwritten literature, though it had no history, long before the Buddhist books were composed; and from that older literature something like a picture of Indian life in the sixth century B.C. has been constructed. Such knowledge as we can obtain is almost confined to the Aryan race which had settled in the Panjab and the Ganges valley.

There was then no vast empire: small tribes or clans still divided or disputed the land, but were beginning to be amalgamated by the increasing power of particular princes. The Pitakas[1] indicate this in their tradition of the wars of Ajāta-

[1] The collection of the Buddhist sacred books is known by this name, which it is convenient often to use.

shattru, and of the foundation and growth of the city which was afterwards Patna.

Among these Aryan clans was spoken a great variety of dialects of the one common language, closely akin to Latin and Greek, which had not yet a name, but to the central or ideal form of which the name "Sanscrit" (the "perfect") was afterwards given.

The Vedas were already echoes from a far antiquity, and the memory of their authors (the Rishis or saints) was already a mysterious tradition. The old sky-worship, and the high simplicity and daylight freedom of that word, were gone; on the other side, the innumerable idols and the elaborate systems of caste and law, which make up Hinduism, were only beginning to appear. The "Laws of Manu," the famous code of developed Brahmanism, was not drawn up as a code till centuries later; but most of the customs and rules which it embodies were probably already in force, though with nothing of the rigidity which was afterwards given to them on the supposed authority of Manu. The six philosophical schools were not yet developed, but the spirit of metaphysical and psychological speculation was at work. Those strange struggles of thought by which, out of inquiry into the meaning of the old Vedic words and rites, were gradually wrung, during two centuries of bewilderment, the ideas of personality and of the unity of being, had already attained to comparative clearness in the best of the Brahmanic Sutras.[1]

The tendencies which we still recognize as characteristic of the Indian mind were in full play. Social and political interests belonged only to a few; but the air was full of intellectual effort and of earnest search for deliverance from the ills of life: the sage or teacher was more than either priest or king.

But the specific results in art and science were still to come, or barely beginning. The earliest recorded astronomical calculations appear to date from this time or earlier. The astonishing feats of grammatical analysis of language which culminated (probably many centuries later) in Pānini's Grammar, may already have begun. Medicine may have already been studied, and the sacrificial system led necessarily to some knowledge of

[1] See Oldenberg on the Shatapathabrāhmana, in his *Buddha*, p. 25, f.

anatomy; but the development of Indian medicine was due to Buddhism.[1]

At such a time it was that the rumour began to spread from district to district, and from town to town, that a distinguished teacher had arisen among the Sakyans. The Sakyans were neither a central nor a very powerful people. Their home was far northward, on the outskirts of the Aryan land. Their city, Kapilavastu, lay near the root of the Himalayas, and (as recent discovery has shown) within the borders of what is now Nepal. It was about a hundred miles north-east of the great city of Benares, and at a greater distance from what were then the rising states of Magadha on the east, and Kosala on the west. The exact position of Kapilavastu was ascertained, and its ruins identified, by Professor Führer in 1896, being located with certainty by the discovery of a Pillar erected by King Asoka about 243 B.C., to record his visit to what was then the reputed birthplace of the Buddha.[2]

Not only did the reputation of the Sakyan teacher spread to the neighbouring towns, but he went himself on foot to Benares, the sacred city, and then to Rājagaha, the city of the Magadhans, and soon Buddhism became known to Bimbisāra, its king.

There is no reason to think that any of those who saw the wandering teacher, or who heard that a son of the Sakyan chief had left his home on such a mission, felt any surprise or admiration at his choice of life. The custom that a well-born man, when he had fulfilled for a time the duties of a householder, should leave them for a life of ascetic contemplation—this custom, so strange to us, though not yet formulated as a rule, was already at least a familiar, probably a very frequent incident. That Gotama, the son of Suddhodana, had left his native Kapilavastu, and at Benares had announced himself as the teacher of truths hitherto unknown, all the interest of this report lay in

[1] The story of Jīvaka, in Maha Vagga, viii., is interesting in this light; especially the test of his progress, viii. 1, 7. See Chapter X, p. 106. For a description of the India of the sixth century, see Hunter, *Indian Empire*, pp. 78–114, and Monier Williams, *Hinduism*, p. 54.

[2] The Pillar, which bears Asoka's inscription, is not on the site of Kapilavastu itself, but on that of the neighbouring "Lumbini Grove," where the actual birth of Gotama is said to have taken place. That being identified, the position of the city was easily inferred from it.

the question: What is the new method which Gotama professes?

But to those who came in contact with the young mendicant there was much to attract attention. His youth—he had not waited, as most men did, till the bloom of life was rubbed off; the dignity and grace of deportment, which the tradition, probably with truth, assigns to him; his singular courtesy and readiness; the wealth of illustration with which he set forth his tenets; these things, as well as the commoner gift of intense belief in his own convictions, secured for him hearers and followers, and soon installed him in the favour of the Magadhan king.

Gotama lived, we are told, to extreme old age, and passed his long life in teaching, as he travelled about from town to town and from village to village. He saw the number of his followers grow till they formed a very large body, or community; for which he had to provide, step by step as occasion suggested, rules of life and the outline of a constitution. Not only had many attached themselves to him from among those who were already ascetics, finding in his doctrines what satisfied them better than their own, but the movement became popular; the enthusiasm for a "homeless" life became infectious, and multitudes, many of them as young as he had been, pledged themselves to his rules. And before his death a marked position among his disciples had belonged, and had even been expressly assigned, to some who were nearest to him by personal affection, or by insight into his doctrine, or as most perfectly fulfilling his ideal.

But Gotama nominated no successor, and left behind him no writings. He had urged his followers to depend upon themselves; and although he had impressed upon them that when he was gone his principles would take the place which he had occupied as their teacher, yet he left it entirely to themselves to apply those principles: "You must be your own refuge, your own light."[1]

Here ends the first stage in our history. Gotama's death must be placed, at any rate, between B.C. 500 and B.C. 450, and there are strong reasons for fixing it at B.C. 477. From this date to that of Asoka, which we may call B.C. 250, is the second

[1] Mahāparinibbāna Sutta, p. 112.

period, the period during which the sacred books, which form the Pitakas, were compiled, and in which, according to tradition, the Councils were held. The Buddhist tradition—obviously on a hundred grounds incredible—is that the Pitakas were edited, fully and finally, at a council held immediately after the decease of the Buddha, and that nothing more was done between that day and Asoka's than to guard them from the slightest alteration. The first council, at the outset of the period, established the Canon; the third, in Asoka's reign, reaffirmed it; while the second, half-way between the two, vindicated the received rules of monastic life against certain minute innovations. It is easier to set this tradition aside than to ascertain what is true. But we shall have no difficulty in deciding that during the whole of these two centuries the compilation of the Pitakas was in progress; our doubt will be, whether even by the end of the time the compilation was completed. Of the literary work of this period, part was no doubt the record from actual memory of what Gotama had said and done; a larger part was the composition, by generation after generation of his followers, of discourses and arguments based upon his principles; another was the development in detail of such rules of life and organization as he had established; while no inconsiderable part was the collection, and appropriation to Buddhist use, of older or extraneous poems, folk-lore, and religious treatises.

During the two centuries, or two centuries and a half, which saw the formation of this mass of literature, an event occurred of incalculable importance—the invasion of India, and the partial occupation of its north-western regions, by the Greeks. Before that event—that is, before B.C. 327—a movement had been taking place towards the establishment of powerful monarchies. The Greeks gave their support to the leader whose star was in the ascendant, and the result was the erection of an empire which extended in some sense all over India and even to Ceylon. The centre of this empire was at Pātaliputra (now Patna), the capital of that state of Magadha in which the Buddha had been welcomed by Bimbisara; so that leading Buddhists must have been among those who came into closest contact with the Greek influence. The Greek historian Megasthenes, who lived at the court in Pataliputra (which he writes "Palibothra"), uses language which seems to refer expressly to the Buddhist monks; and in the Pali books themselves there are traces of Greek legends, and perhaps of Greek philosophy. In any case, the presence of the Greeks must have stimulated the growth of a Buddhist literature. When the great Emperor, at the height of his power, became not only a Buddhist, but a zealous patron and propagator of Buddhism, it attained on its own native soil the climax of its vitality. This was the era of Asoka.

Among the fruits of Asoka's zeal is said to have been the conversion of Ceylon; and if it be his work at all, it is the part of his work which has had most enduring result. That Buddhism was established in Ceylon by Mahinda, and during the time of the Ceylon king who was contemporary, or nearly contemporary, with Asoka, cannot, I think, be seriously disputed. But that Mahinda was Asoka's son, as the historians say, and came to Ceylon direct from Magadha—this some critics doubt. They think it more likely that the religion, having spread by this time to the southern coasts of India, found its way to Ceylon from thence; [1] and the desire of the native chroniclers to connect their island with the famous Asoka is thought to be explanation enough of the tradition. I shall give reasons hereafter for believing the historians: for the present it is enough to note that the third scene of our drama is to be played in Ceylon, and dates from Mahinda, in the latter part of the third century B.C.

Of the condition of Ceylon in the last two centuries before our era, and the first three centuries after it, the historians give us only occasional glimpses; but on the whole we may say that during the earlier part of that period Buddhism was growing, and becoming more and more established in the island; and that in the latter part, from B.C. 50 to A.D. 300, it was less flourishing. Still, throughout the country to this day, especially in the north-central and north-west-central regions, many a carven pillar and many dome-like "dagabas" (or relic-shrines), and a few inscriptions, in characters not far removed from those which Asoka used, bear witness to the activity of the Buddhist kings in those six centuries. The fourth century A.D. saw great advances made in literature and in art, both devoted to the service of the national religion.

[1] For this view, see Oldenberg, *Vinaya Pitaka*, vol. I, p. xlix, *sqq*.

The next epoch is that of the decisive impetus given to Buddhist learning by Buddhaghosha.

Mahinda, whoever he was, or in whatever sense he was Asoka's son, introduced the Pitaka texts into Ceylon. With them he brought also—the historians tell us—the Pali Commentaries, and translated them into Sinhalese. The originals of these were soon lost sight of, but the Sinhalese versions were scrupulously preserved. Six centuries later Buddhaghosha came from Magadha—so the story goes—to inquire after these Commentaries. He translated into Pali what he found, and composed more. He certainly gave his name to voluminous and important works, by which the Ceylon school of Buddhism has been moulded ever since. They are considered in Ceylon as absolute authorities on the interpretation of the sacred text; and although the European scholars, who have made the Buddhist books known in Europe, have occasionally set aside the authority of the Commentaries in one detail or another, yet in general it may be said that the European translations represent the traditional interpretation as it was left by Buddhaghosha. His date may be roughly stated as A.D. 400.[1]

The scene of this work was Anurādhapura, in (what is now) the North Central Province of Ceylon. This city was the magnificent seat of the Buddhist kings for several centuries. From the ninth century onward, they made their capital for the most part at Polonnaruwa, somewhat further to the east.

In the earlier part of this period there was little, except the quarrels of members of the reigning family, and occasional invasions, to interrupt the course of official patronage of the national religion, and the erection of splendid "vihāras" (dwellings) for the monks. But from the tenth century onward, constant invasions from South India of peoples who were hostile to Buddhism, led to the destruction of many shrines and vihāras, to the expulsion of monks, and even to the persecution of Buddhists. The religion seems to have languished, till the victories of Parakrama established him in undisputed power, which he used for the reformation and promotion of Buddhism and for the erection of innumerable buildings for its service. He

[1] Buddhaghosha is not known to the Northern Buddhists, but the Burmese tradition agrees with that of Ceylon.

was first the great national hero, and then the Augustus of Ceylon.

The brilliant epoch of Parakrama was followed by troublous times, in which famous shrines were destroyed, and the chief relics had to be hidden, till another conqueror and reviver of religion arose. Such vicissitudes continued during the rest of Sinhalese history. When Europeans first settled in the country, about A.D. 1500, the native religion was not flourishing; and it appears to have continued to decline, in spite of efforts made at different times, as the Mahāvaṃsa (the chief national chronicle) relates, to revive it by getting monks and books from Aracan and Siam. During the pressure of the Dutch wars it fell so low that the historian more than once says, "there was not one monk in Ceylon."

From A.D. 1500 onwards, Portuguese and Dutch authority—and in the latter case, to some extent at least, persecution—had gone far to extinguish what remained of Buddhism, and it had but little internal vitality, when the British occupation began in 1796. From that time all hostile pressure was removed; but the influence and example of the English, and of the most educated and enlightened of the Sinhalese themselves, necessarily operated in favour of Christianity. Buddhism became more and more the religion of the less civilized and the less prosperous. It had no royal patrons, and few respected professors; and by the middle of the nineteenth century even intelligent observers thought that it was all but extinct.

The last quarter of the last century saw a remarkable revival. It was due, in its origin, mainly to external influence, and was more academic than national; but it has had a few leaders of high character, and has taken, I believe, considerable hold of the people.[1] In Burma, where Buddhism was already at a

[1] Here I added in 1892: "The wave has, however, as I think, already reached its highest point. As a phase of educated thought it may be traceable for some time to come; but as a popular force it is already passing by." I have now omitted this sentence, not because I am sure that it was incorrect, but because I am not now in a position to judge. Two Sinhalese friends, however, have kindly written for me statements on the Buddhist Revival, and I find in them nothing that would require any alteration of what is written in Chapter XXVIII. The character of the movement appears to be unchanged. Meanwhile, if the figures in both censuses are correct, the number of Buddhist priests in Ceylon decreased between 1891 and 1901 by about one-fourth.

higher level of practical efficiency than in Ceylon, there has been a similar movement; indeed, these are both results of wide-spread causes, through which, in most Asiatic countries, there has arisen an increased interest in the national religions, together with a disposition to emphasize whatever in them is in accordance with the latest phases of European thought.

PART II

THE FOUNDATION OF BUDDHISM

CHAPTER III

LIFE OF GOTAMA

TO the English student of Buddhism no part of the subject is more interesting than the character and the doings of its founder. I propose, therefore, to set these forth as fully as possible. But since a thoughtful reader will especially desire to be helped to discriminate between the original records of Gotama's life and the embellishments with which these have been encrusted, I must first of all ask his attention to some account of the sources from which our knowledge is derived.

In the oldest collection of Buddhist writings, that is, in the Three Pitakas, or " threefold collection," there is no express biography of the Buddha. There are, it is true, embedded in the earliest of those books fragments of a biographical nature, which must be older than the books in which they are quoted ;[1] but it is difficult to think that any complete Life of Gotama existed before the Pitakas were compiled; for surely it would not have been lost.

It was the teaching of their leader, more than the person—the teaching primarily and the person only secondarily—that interested the early Buddhists. They did not call themselves Gotamists[2]—it would have been alien to the whole spirit of their founder—nor even did they call themselves Buddhists. Even when they said, " I take refuge in the Buddha," it was not Gotama's acts, nor his character, nor his surviving influence,

[1] These are in verse; and even among these some show evidence, in metre, language, and contents, of being older than the rest. See p. 53.

[2] They would seem to have been popularly called, during the Buddha's lifetime, Sakyans (Sākyaputtā), as if they belonged to his clan.

that they placed their trust in, but the doctrines of "all the Buddhas," of which, in this age, Gotama was the teacher.[1]

Such biographies as do exist are only partial and supplementary. The oldest is that which forms an introduction to one of the Commentaries, and professes to give a complete life of Gotama up to the date at which his Buddha-hood began. This has no external claim, in its present form, to an earlier date than that of Buddhaghosha, and bears the undisguised marks of compilation from older sources. The *Lalita Vistara*, a production of the Northern School, which, having been early translated, has been much followed by European writers, is later still.

But though the Pitakas contain no connected biography of Gotama, they do contain material for considerable portions of his life. At two points in Gotama's life, namely at the opening of his career as a teacher, and at its close, his movements and words are narrated in minute detail. Besides these two chief portions of biographical material, there are many passages in which, as occasion has arisen, have been preserved records of events in his earliest life (before he became Buddha), or incidents of his travels or conduct as a teacher. Into these three groups —the entrance on Buddha-hood, the approach of the end, and the scattered notices—we may divide the elements of biography which the Pitakas supply.

The detailed account of Gotama's assumption of Buddhahood and entrance on his career as the Buddha, forms the introduction to the Rules of the Community which he founded. For that Community is represented as growing out of the truths which he discovered, and the circumstances under which he was led to disclose them. This forms the main contents of the first book of the Mahā Vagga, or principal section of the Vinaya, or Rule of (monastic) training.

The record of the last days forms a Sutta, or discourse, by itself,[2] in the Sutta Pitaka, or collection of sermons. Parts of

[1] Even within the Pitakas a progress may be observed from earlier writings, in which the individual Gotama is only venerated as the teacher of a certain doctrine, to later writings, in which he is beginning to be the object of the believer's devotion for his own sake. Contrast the language of the Maha Vagga with such a passage as that in Maj. Nik. 22, where Gotama says: [Those who have not even entered the Paths] "are sure of heaven if they have love and faith towards me."

[2] The Mahāparinibbāna Sutta, or Great Sutta of the Decease.

the same story are found also, in no very clear connection with their surroundings, in the fifth book of the same Maha Vagga.

The third division includes a multitude of scattered passages. In the Vinaya, or Rule, the formulation of certain rules is assigned to certain occasions, and in connection with these we read of Gotama's interviews with kings, with disciples, with members of his own family, and others. Allusion is also made, here and there, to what took place before he became Buddha, and in such cases the allusion is made in such a way as to suggest that the incidents were well known, and perhaps that they had been recorded (as has already been hinted) in some earlier narrative.[1] In the Sutta Collection, also, the reader meets every now and then with references—placed in the lips of Gotama or of his disciples—both to such events as the Vinaya has already mentioned, and to other details or events.[2]

Of these three groups, into which we have thus divided the biographical data of the Pitakas, we may say with confidence that the account of the opening of the Buddha's teaching career, given in the Maha Vagga, is the oldest;[3] that the description of the closing scene, in the Parinibbana Sutta, is much later;[4] and that of the scattered notices some are as old as the former, and some more recent even than the latter.

But it is impossible at present to discriminate these dates with certainty. The oldest material may have been composed immediately after the Buddha's death, or even in his lifetime; the latest was almost certainly recognized by 230 B.C. I shall therefore place before the reader the biography which would be constructed out of the Pitakas by one who supposed all parts of those collections to be of equal authority. In the first section I shall distinguish by italics those portions which are drawn from the Vinaya; and I shall not refrain from indicating from time to time what I think to be the traces of a variety of date in my sources. The Life may conveniently be divided into five sections.

[1] The chief are M.V. i. 21–24, 54; v. 28; and C.V. vi. 4, vii. 3, xi. 1.

[2] Such are especially Ariyapariyesana S. (Maj. Nik. 26) and *ib.* 4, 35, 36, etc.; Sāmaññaphala S. (Digh. Nik. 2) and in the same Nikāya, 4 and 6; in Sutta Nipāta, Nālaka S. (iii. 11).

[3] "Bears unmistakably the stamp of high antiquity."—Oldenberg, *Buddha*, p. 113.

[4] "Probably later," l.c., p. 115, but see below, p. 169.

§ 1. In the days of Bimbisara, king of Magadha, or shortly before his time, *Gotama was born, the son of Suddhodana, of Kapilavastu, in the Sakyan country.*[1] *His mother died in his infancy, and he was nursed by his aunt, Pajāpati.* The Sakyan clan was a noble and very proud one, and Gotama was of the purest Khattiya[2] race on both father's and mother's side.[3] His birth was made known by rejoicing deities to a hermit named Asita, who thereupon repaired to Suddhodana's palace, saw the infant in his glory, surrounded by deities, etc., and announced to the Sakyans that the child would be a Buddha.[4] The young man grew up in the midst of wealth and ease;[5] he had (according to the conventional description of luxury) three palaces, one for each of the seasons.[6] But he sometimes considered the sadness and the inevitable approach of old age and death,[7] and under the influence of such thoughts, while still in the prime of youth and beauty, *he left his home*[8] (as many older than he, but few so young and happy, had done), his father (and mother) weeping as he went, *his father's heart pierced with excessive grief,*[9] *leaving his wife and his son Rāhula behind.*[10]

He became the pupil of two wise teachers, Alāra Kālāma and Uddaka Rāmaputta;[11] *and afterwards the companion in austerities of five mendicants in the neighbourhood of Benares.*[12] The details of his austerities are given, in conventional descriptions, as of unexampled severity; he starved himself, remained in one position, held his breath, etc., till his frame was attenuated to the utmost imaginable degree, and his strength was entirely exhausted.[13] *At last he saw the uselessness of such austerities, and, to the indignation of the five mendicants, gave them up.*[14] We are not told what led him to the more successful method; but so it was, that *sitting one night under the tree which thenceforth*

[1] M.V. i. 54, 1. Only one reference is given for each event or detail, though as a rule each is mentioned in several or in very many places. The visit of Asita is an exception, being mentioned, as far as I know, only in the passage referred to (Sutt. Nip. iii. 11). The Sutta, however, in which it occurs bears every mark of an early date.

[2] Digh. Nik. vi.

[3] His feet were marked with a mystic wheel (Angut. iv. 36), and he had the thirty-two marks of a "great one" on his person.

[4] Sutt. Nip. iii. 11.

[5] Digh. Nik. iv. 6.

[6] Maj. Nik. 75.

[7] Saṃyut. Nik. xii. 10, 2.

[8] Maj. Nik. iv.

[9] M.V. i. 54, 5.

[10] M.V. i. 54. 2.

[11] M.V. i. 6, 1.

[12] M.V. i. 6, 10.

[13] Maj. Nik. 12.

[14] M.V. i. 6, 10.

was called the Buddha tree[1] (of this age, other ages and other Buddhas having other trees), and there practising meditation according to the method which he afterwards taught, or asking himself, as all Buddhas had done before him, whence is death, etc.[2] *he arrived at perfect insight into the nature and cause of sorrow and the way of destroying it. He was then Buddha, the Buddha of the age. He had attained, unaided, and by direct insight and conscious realization, the saving truth for the benefit of gods and men.*

This is the first chapter of the life. It may be observed that the story, as thus extracted from the oldest group of authorities, contains, so far, no point of likeness to the recorded life of Jesus Christ. The nearest approach to any such thing is the prognostication by Asita of the child's future career. This belongs to the familiar class of stories which tell of signs accompanying the birth of famous men ; and it takes its particular shape from the custom of the astrologer's visit—a custom still almost universal not only among Hindus but also among the Buddhists of Ceylon—to prepare the horoscope of a new-born child.

All the elaborate details of the "Great Renunciation" (as Europeans have called it) are wanting; the four signs, the sleeping babe, the flying horse, and the rest. One feature which has been woven into that legend does occur in the Mahā Vagga—the scene of the sleeping women in their uncomely disorder—but it occurs in reference not to Gotama, but to another person. Further, the temptation by Māra, in the shape and meaning which it bears in the later story,[3] is altogether absent. There is no hint of any appeal made either to the lust or to the fears of the hero; there is neither tempest nor siren. The crisis through which Gotama is represented as having passed, is one of intellectual insight, not of moral choice.

The materials that have been used up to this point, though all from the "canonical books," have been brought together from many different passages in them. The events of the second period of Gotama's activity, the founding of his Community, are more systematically recorded in the first book of the Maha

[1] *Passim.* The account in Maj. Nik. iv. differs a little from others.

[2] Saṃyut. Nik. xii. 4, 9, varying a little from Angut. iv. 21, etc.

[3] The contrast between the poetical development and the prose of the "canonical" books is well drawn out by Prof. Oldenberg, *Buddha*, pp. 102–105.

Vagga.[1] I give the substance, and in important places the actual language, of its chief contents.

§ 2. For seven days the newly "enlightened" one, the blessed Buddha, sat under the tree of enlightenment, the Bodhi-tree (in Sinhalese, "Bo-tree") enjoying the bliss of emancipation—thoroughly experiencing it and penetrating its meaning. During each night of these seven days,[2] the series of causes which leads to suffering was clear to him in its details. During each of the three watches of the night he reviewed the series, and pronounced his solemn sense that all doubt was dispelled, and the true nature of things was clear.[3] The hosts of Māra were scattered, as clouds are scattered by the sun.[4] Next, for seven days, he sat in like trance under another tree, where he pronounced, in answer to an arrogant Brahman who accosted him, the characteristics of a true Brahman—purity, self-control, knowledge, and holy life. For a third seven days he sat under a third tree, sheltered from a seven days' storm of rain and wind by the coils and hood of a mystic serpent, who at the end of the time appeared as a young man and did reverence to the Buddha, and elicited from him this declaration of the nature of happiness: "Happy is the solitude of him who is full of joy, who has learnt the Truth, who sees (the Truth). Happy is freedom from malice in this world, self-restraint towards all beings that have life. Happy is freedom from lust in this world, getting beyond all desires; the putting away of that pride which comes from

[1] As introductory to the Rule, this book contains a detailed account of the events from Gotama's attainment of Buddha-hood down to the conversion of his two chief disciples, Sāriputta and Mogallāna (i. 24). "Among the elements of historical or legendary character with which, in the Vinaya Pitaka, the discussion of the monastic discipline is interwoven, this account occupies by far the first place, both in extent and in importance, for it contains the oldest version accessible to us now, and most probably for ever, of what the Buddhist fraternity deemed to be the history of their master's life in its most important period." Rhys Davids and Oldenberg, *Sacred Books of the East*, xiii. 73 n.

[2] Or, "at the end of these seven days."

[3] It was in the first watch that he uttered what is really the first Buddha-utterance (as Buddhaghosha admits "some said"): "Verily when things as they are become clear to the Brahman in ardent meditation, then all his doubts depart, as he knows things in their reality and in their causes." The famous verse, "Anekajātisaṃsāraṃ," etc., is a later composition.

[4] This is the only reference here to Mara, and he is evidently here an opponent rather than a tempter; but here is the germ of the later legend of his elaborate attack.

the thought, 'I am'! This truly is the highest happiness."[1] A fourth period of seven days was passed under a fourth tree, and there the Buddha received his first disciples. Two merchants, Tapussa and Bhallika, acting on the suggestion of a deity who had been their kinsman in a former life, offered to Gotama rice-cakes and honey. The four great gods, guardians of the four quarters of the world, provided four stone bowls, and in these the Buddha accepted and ate the offering. The two merchants then enrolled themselves as his disciples, "taking refuge" in the Buddha and in the Doctrine. There was as yet no "Community"—the third "precious object" of faith—so their peculiar form of profession, the "two-fold," marked the first stage in the erection of the system.

Gotama then arose out of that state of meditation in which he had passed these four weeks, and returned to the second of the four trees. There, we read, the thought occurred to him,[2] "I have acquired this knowledge, but it is deep and difficult, and mankind are shallow and given up to desires; they will not understand me: why should I weary myself with teaching it?" For a while this idea possessed him, and he gave utterance to it in a stanza which was *anything but inspired*.[3] There is no reference in the Maha Vagga to Mara as having suggested this idea; it was "only too natural," and arose of itself in the mind of Gotama. He was "feeling discouraged,"[4] as he soon afterwards acknowledged. But in the later Sutta, which describes Gotama's last days, he is made to say that at the time of his attaining Buddha-hood Mara tried to tempt him instead of preaching to enter Nirvana at once—to be, what another development of the idea called, "a Buddha for himself alone."

For a moment the hopes of the world's blessing hung in suspense. But the great lord of all the gods, the mighty Brahmā,

[1] M.V. i. 3, 4. This, and all translations marked S.B.E., are quoted from *Sacred Books of the East*, etc.; for the rest the author is responsible. But most of the quotations for which no exact reference is given are freely abridged: when the quotation is literal the reference is generally given.

[2] Cetaso parivitakko. He was not in any of the Jhānas, but his mind was at work.

[3] Anacchariyā. The Commentary explains this by "anu-acchariyā," which the Sinhalese interpret as "non-supernatural."—M.V. i, 5, 3.

[4] "Vihiṃsasaññi," "from a sense of weariness or discouragement," M.V. i. 5, 12.

saw the danger, and came himself, adopting a special attitude of homage on one knee, to entreat the Buddha not to withhold the doctrine. "There are," he urged, "some beings with eyes so purged from the dust of desire as to be able to apprehend it: open the door to them; look down from the height of truth on the perishing multitude and pity them." Thrice he urged his petition before the Buddha could be persuaded; but at last Gotama, moved both by Brahma's earnestness and by compassion for beings, looked abroad with his Buddha-eyes, and saw that it was so. There were some beings like lotus-flowers, emerging in different measures from the water, on the petals of some of the uppermost of which not a drop of water hangs—beings clear in different degrees from the dust of desire; and he granted the great deity's prayer. Brahma did homage and disappeared.

In spite of the supernatural embellishments of this story, what strikes one most in it is its human naturalness.

The same *naïveté* characterizes the next event. "To whom," thought the new Buddha, "shall I preach first? Who will be able to understand?" And he thought at once of his two old friends, Alara Kalama and Uddaka Ramaputta, his guides in his earliest religious efforts, both men of noble nature. But deities informed him that they had lately died.[1] Next his mind turned to the five mendicants who had been his companions in austerity, and who had done much for him; and perceiving, by supernatural vision, that they were living in the deer-park at Benares, he started thither.

This was a moment, as later Buddhism looked back to it, of central importance. For to those five mendicants in the deer-park called Isipatana, the first sermon, or exposition of the law, was to be addressed. This reckons, along with the moment of Buddha-hood and the moment of final Nirvāna, as one of the three great epochs of every Buddha's career. It is in accordance with this view of the expedition to Benares, that the episode which follows finds place.

[1] I cannot sympathize with those controversialists who urge this ignorance of the death of these two men as fatal to the Buddha's claims. It is of course an admission that he was not literally, at all times and of all matters, omniscient; but an admission more creditable than damaging. It is characteristic, that the Lalita Vistara represents the deities as only echoing what the Buddha had already perceived and stated! (L.V. p. 524.)

On the road to Benares Gotama fell in with a member of one of the sects of naked ascetics, Upaka by name, himself a hermit and a seeker after truth; and Upaka said to him, "Your countenance, friend, is serene; your complexion is pure and bright. In whose name, friend, have you retired from the world? Who is your teacher? Whose doctrine do you profess?"[1] The reply was a proud one: "I follow no teacher; I have overcome all foes and all stains; I am superior to all men and to all gods. I am the absolute Buddha. And I am going now to Benares to set in motion the Wheel of the Law, as a king the triumphant wheel of his kingdom. I am the Conqueror." Upaka replied, "It may be so"; but he shook his head and went his way.[2]

Gotama went on to the deer-park. When his five former companions saw him coming they agreed among themselves to show by their way of receiving him that they regarded him as one who had fallen away from his high aspirations and ascetic efforts, and had returned to the pleasures of an easy life. They would not, they agreed, salute him, or rise or take his bowl. But as he drew near an overmastering impulse led them to break their compact. They rose to meet him: one took his bowl, another brought water to wash his feet, and so on. But they addressed him by his old name in the old way. When they spoke to him thus he replied: "Do not address the Tathāgata[3] by his name, and with the appellation 'Friend.' The Tathāgata, O Bhikkhus,[4] is the holy absolute Sambuddha. Give ear, O Bhikkhus! The immortal (Amata) has been won by me. I will teach you: to you I preach the doctrine. If you walk in the way I show you, you will ere long have penetrated to the truth, having yourselves known and seen it face to face; and you will live in the possession (even in this life[5]) of that highest goal of the holy life, for the sake of which noble youths fully give up the world and go forth into the homeless state." To this the five replied: "By austerities such as you practised with us you did not obtain this insight; how much less is it likely

[1] M.V. i. 6, 7. S.B.E.

[2] Lalita Vistara makes him take his leave politely.

[3] A title of the Buddha, which is variously explained. In these pages it is frequently represented by "Buddha."

[4] i.e. mendicants.

[5] Diṭṭheva dhamme. M.V. i. 6, 12. The phrase is omitted in S.B.E. viii, whence the rest of the passage is quoted.

that you have done so in a life of ease?" Gotama repudiated the charge of having returned to a life of ease, and repeated his proud assertion. The hermits replied as before, and a second time the Buddha made the same answer. They repeated their doubts a third time; and then Gotama challenged them to say whether he had ever, in old days, spoken to them in such terms of self-assertion. They admitted that he had not. He then proceeded to lay down his fundamental principles. Neither the extreme of indulgence nor the extreme of austerity, but the middle way between these two has led him to insight and wisdom. This Middle Way, which leads to calm, to knowledge, to Nirvana, is the holy Eight-fold Path of right belief, right aim, right speech, right conduct, right livelihood, right endeavour, right recollectedness, right meditation.

Next he propounds the "Four Noble Truths."[1] "This, O Bhikkhus, is the noble truth of Suffering: birth is suffering; decay is suffering; illness is suffering; death is suffering; presence of objects we hate is suffering; separation from objects we love is suffering; not to obtain what we desire is suffering; briefly, the five-fold clinging to existence is suffering.

"This, O Bhikkhus, is the noble truth of the Cause of Suffering: thirst, that leads to re-births, accompanied by pleasure and lust, finding its delight here and there. (This thirst is three-fold), namely, thirst for pleasure, thirst for existence, thirst for prosperity.[2]

"This, O Bhikkhus, is the noble truth of the Cessation of Suffering: (it ceases with) the complete cessation of this thirst—a cessation which consists in the absence of every passion; with the abandoning of this thirst; with the doing away with it, with the deliverance from it, with the destruction of desire.

"This, O Bhikkhus, is the noble truth of the Path which leads to the cessation of suffering; that holy Eight-fold Path—that is to say, right belief, right aim, right speech, right conduct, right livelihood, right endeavour, right recollectedness, right meditation.[3]

[1] For the explanation of these and for a discussion of the Eight-fold Way, see below, Chap. VII, note.

[2] See below, p. 75.

[3] M.V. i. 6, 19–22. S.B.E. In the rest of this quotation I have ceased to follow S.B.E. exactly. The two sentences which follow are an abridgment.

"The first principle, the fact of suffering, must be *understood*; the cause, desire, must be *abandoned*; the third principle, that of the cessation of suffering by the cessation of the cause, must be *seen face to face*: the Path must be *practically realized*.

"Now these things," said Gotama, "I have done: I have realized these truths and passed along this path. When I knew myself to have done so, I knew that I was free; that my freedom could never be lost; that this is my last birth; that I cannot be born again."

The five hermits were delighted; and one of them, Koṇḍañña, gained at once a clear view of the principle that "whatever has a beginning tends necessarily to an end." The lower deities of the earth shouted in applause, "The Kingdom of Truth has been founded"; the four great deities and all their train shouted. The shout was passed on from one world of divine beings to another, till it reached the Brahma world; and then the whole ten thousand worlds were shaken with a mighty shock, and a light, greater than that of the deities, filled the universe.

So was the Wheel of Doctrine set revolving.[1] Although Tapussa and Bhallika, the two merchants who offered the first food to the new Buddha, were the first persons to take refuge in him and his teaching, they were only lay hearers. Koṇḍanna (now called Aññātakoṇḍañña, from his "recognition" of the doctrine) was the first to attain full knowledge, and to be associated with Gotama in his Order. Koṇḍanna was at once received to both steps, initiation and full profession, his application for them being welcomed with the formula, "Come, mendicant: the doctrine is well spoken: lead the religious life for complete extinction of sorrow."[2]

The rest of the five ascetics were soon converted, and grasped the fundamental principles, and were fully convinced of the unreality of "self," and arrived at complete detachment from desire and from identifying themselves with anything; thus

[1] In this favourite phrase there is probably a union of two allusions. The Wheel had probably long been a symbol of doctrine. The Buddhists associated with this the idea of a universal monarch, whose kingdom was symbolized by his royal chariot-wheel rolling through the world. See Rhys Davids, *Hibbert Lectures*, p. 129 *sq.*

[2] This formula, expressly welcoming an application, has been considered parallel to the *call* of Christ's disciples by the words, "Follow Me." This is a fair specimen of such parallels.

reaching the state of Rahats, or perfect beings, who had no other existence to look forward to, who had indeed (though the phrase had not yet made its appearance in the system) secured Nirvana—were already possessed of it in a partial sense, and were secure of it in the full sense at death. There was thus a Community of six, and they all Rahats; for Gotama himself was reckoned as one among the rest.

At this point ends, in our books, the first section, or recitation-portion, of the Maha Vagga. The division of such portions is made as a rule, no doubt, with a view to their length, not to their contents; but in the present instance, the break corresponds with a well-marked point in the narrative. Thus far the narrative has been, as the reader must have observed, connected, progressive, and uniform in literary tone. It has been marked by picturesqueness and simplicity, and by the absence—except for obvious embellishments—of the improbable. The steps by which the Thinker came to find himself the centre of a Community, have been so far clearly traced.

From this point, though not with any marked transition, the narrative loses these characteristics. The order is henceforward chiefly that of the Rules of the Community; and such biographical fragments as occur are introduced, without note of time, to account for them. The next three recitation-portions have reference to events which must have followed close upon those we have related—the conversion of a number of distinguished laymen, and of some women; of a number of fire-worshippers; of the king; and of two chief disciples—but even in these we no longer find the consecutiveness, or the freedom from exaggeration; and from the end of the fourth recitation-portion the narrative order is lost altogether.

Of the distinguished laymen whose conversion is now to be recorded, the first is Yasa; and his story deserves to be somewhat fully quoted, for a peculiar reason. Whether it was first told of Yasa or not, or whether it was already a conventional episode, we cannot say; but it has been adopted by the later biographers as model for part of the history of Gotama himself.[1] Yasa was a noble youth, delicately nurtured, with the extreme of luxury—a palace for each of the seasons, and so on. In the

[1] It occurs, of course in quite a different connection, in the Ramayana (Sundarakāṇḍam).

four rainy months he never stirred from the palace in which he enjoyed the society of a number of female musicians. One night, however, he happened to be restless, and arose and looked into the hall where these ladies were sleeping. The scene revolted him. One had her hair in disorder; another had spittle flowing from her mouth; others were muttering in their sleep: all their charms were gone—it was "more like a cemetery." The worthlessness, the dangerousness of that life came home to him. He felt that sacred "disgust" which is the spring (according to Buddhism) of religious endeavours; and thereupon he left his home, and entered on the homeless state. His departure was facilitated by supernatural agencies; the gates of the palace and of the city were opened by no human hand.

Yasa found his way straight to the deer-park, where the Buddha was; and was welcomed by him; and soon grasped the great fundamental principle—that whatever has an origin must necessarily tend to decay. His father, coming to seek him, came also under the Buddha's influence, and became a lay disciple, "taking refuge" in the Buddha, the Doctrine, and the Community (the full "threefold profession"); while Yasa himself became a full member of the Community, and the seventh Rahat. His mother and his wife became the first female disciples.

This story differs in some significant details from those which have preceded it; it is evidently, I think, a later composition. It is full of technical expressions: the instruction given to Yasa is on the conventional lines of instruction to laymen; and a rather irrelevant miracle is introduced—the Buddha rendering Yasa invisible while his father enters.

The devotion of Yasa was followed by that of four other noblemen, who were converted by precisely the same course. They were followed by fifty more; to all of whom exactly the same instructions were addressed, with exactly the same results. All became Rahats, of whom there were now sixty-one.[1]

The dispersion of these sixty members of the Community is next recorded. Using the formula which became the conventional description of his own purpose, the Buddha said to them: "Go forth, mendicants, on your rounds, for the good

[1] The wooden dullness of all this is in striking contrast to the variety and probability of the earlier section.

of the many, for the welfare of the many; for the good, the gain, and the welfare of gods and men. Let no two go the same way.[1] Gotama himself took a course of his own.

This dispersion of the Community is represented as the cause of a great many men coming from different countries and from great distances to Gotama, to be received into the Order, by the lower and higher stages, of admission and of full profession. It was the inconvenience of this that led to the Regulation by which members of the Order were empowered, without coming to Gotama, themselves to admit candidates to the two steps of Pabbajjā (entrance on religious life) and Upasampadā (perfect membership); and the exact ceremonies and words to be used were then appointed, though not (it is important to notice) in the final form.

Whether it is due to the importance of this event, or only to accident and to the compiler's awkwardness, the chapter which records this Institution of the Form of Admission is preceded and followed by two passages which narrate, almost in identical terms, a sort of attack made by Mara, the adversary, upon the Buddha. Mara approaches him and says, "Thou art bound by fetters, and canst not escape me." Gotama replies, "I am delivered from all fetters, from all desires: thou art defeated."[2]

The next incident in the book, though there is no note of time to mark its chronological position, is the conversion of a thousand Jatilas, or fire-worshipping ascetics. It took an immense number of miracles to convince these people; and of these miracles some account must be given. The number of them, or rather of the final batch, is summed up, at the end of the passage, as having been three thousand five hundred: they can be classed in three groups.

Gotama went to the chief Fire-worshipper's abode, and begged to be allowed to pass the night in the building where the sacred fire was kept. It was with difficulty that his host was persuaded to allow this, because there was a very powerful and poisonous serpent in the chamber. The Buddha, however, assured him

[1] This has been considered parallel to Christ's sending the Seventy, two by two.

[2] In my opinion, these passages are quite irrelevant, and were suggested to a compiler by the reference to "fetters" in M.V. i. 11, 1. The story of the Jatilas also evidently comes from a source different from that of the first Bhānavāra.

that there would be no danger, and entered. During the night the fire-room was seen filled with blaze and smoke. The serpent was sending forth all the fiery influence that he could, and the Buddha was emitting counter-blaze—that radiance, or radiant influence, symbolized by the rays which surround the head of some images of the Buddha, and to which appeal is still made in the Buddhist chants.[1] In the morning the serpent was found a senseless form, and the mighty power of the Buddha was acknowledged. "Still," said the Jatila to himself, "he is not equal to me."

The second group of these miracles touches another field of fable more familiar to Western readers. When the Jatila summoned his guest to breakfast the Buddha said, "Go in, and I will follow you," and straightway went to the spot where grows the mighty Jambu (rose-apple) tree, which gives name to Jambudvipa (the Indian world), and brought back a fruit of it, and was in the breakfast-room before the Jatila got there. Another time he brought such and such a mystic flower from such and such a heaven.

The third group is trifling. The Buddha wanted to wash some rags which were to form his robe; and forthwith a tank to wash them in, a stone to beat them on (here, at least, is a touch of nature only too familiar to dwellers in Indian lands), and other conveniences for washing were supernaturally provided. And when five hundred of the Fire-worshippers were trying to split five hundred sticks, or to light five hundred fires, and the like, they were supernaturally prevented from doing so, or enabled to succeed, according to the will of the Buddha. It is by reckoning the number of sticks and fires in each case that the number of miracles is made so large.

These wonders induced the Fire-worshippers, who were in three companies, each led by a great teacher, to betake themselves to the Buddha and join the Community of mendicants. To them he is said to have preached a sermon on "Burning": "Everything is burning; all the objects which strike the sense, and all the processes of sensation are burning with the fire of desire, and all other accompaniments of decay and death. The wise man sees this, feels the religious "disgust" for all such

[1] The range of meaning of this word "tejo," from "fire" and "splendour" to something like "moral influence," suggests an interesting inquiry.

objects, and enters the path which leads to freedom from the passions and from re-birth." This discourse was the means of advancing the one thousand new mendicants from the position of mere members of the Community to that of Rahats.

Now follows in proper sequence an important event, which is probably in substance historical, however absurd some of the exaggerations which adorn it. The fame of Gotama reached the king of Magadha, King Bimbisara. The report of the Buddha's person and preaching is expressed in words which recur constantly throughout the sacred books. It is by this description that most of those who came to learn of him or to argue with him were attracted; it must therefore be quoted in full (M.V. i. 22, 2):—

"The ascetic Gotama, the Sakyan, having gone out from the Sakyans to a religious life, has come to Rājagaha, and is dwelling there in the Laṭṭhivana garden, at the Supatiṭṭha shrine. Of this blessed Gotama a glorious fame is come abroad, to this effect: That he is a blessed, perfect, absolute Buddha, of full attainment in knowledge and conduct, in the perfect state of being, knowing all worlds, the unsurpassable trainer of man, the teacher of gods and men, a blessed Buddha: he it is who has seen face to face and fully learnt by his own insight (the nature of) this world of Devas, and Maras, and Brahmas, and the whole population of Brahmans, ascetics, gods and men, and makes it known; he who proclaims a doctrine lovely in beginning, lovely in midst, lovely in end, with[1] its meaning and its expression, and makes known a religious course in every way complete and pure."

The king said, as all are reported to say who hear the great announcement: "Good is the sight of perfect beings (Rahats) like that!" So with twelve myriads of Brahmans and householders (as a rule householders means cultivators) Bimbisara repaired to the presence of the Buddha; and in due course, the process of instruction and conviction taking place as in former instances, eleven myriads, with the king, obtained complete insight into the principle, that "all that is formed must be in turn dissolved"; and one myriad enrolled themselves as lay disciples.

[1] Lalita Vistara reads here "su" for "sa," and this possibly is the true text—"excellent in meaning," etc.

The king announced that his wishes were now fulfilled. His great wishes from boyhood had been, first, some day to be a king; next, that an absolute Buddha might come to his kingdom, that he might wait on the Buddha, might hear his teaching, and finally that he might understand it.

Having formally asked to be admitted, " From this day forth, while life shall last, as a follower who has gone for refuge " to the Buddha, the king begged for the honour of entertaining Gotama and his monks the next day. It was graciously granted; and on the morrow, attended by the thousand monks who had lately been fire-worshippers, the Buddha entered the royal city. This entrance of Gotama into Rajagaha is a celebrated epoch in Buddhist history, and later writers exhausted the resources of Oriental hyperbole in describing its magnificence. The Maha Vagga is content with telling us that Sakka (Indra), king of the (lower) deities, assumed the form of a Brahman youth and headed the procession, reciting certain verses in celebration of the event. Bimbisara, to secure the residence of the Buddha near him, made over to him the Bamboo-grove garden, for the use of his Community. The form of words he used was the regular formula for such presentations; and the Buddha took occasion from the royal donation to lay down the rule: " I allow you, monks, to receive the donation of a park."[1]

King Bimbisara had considerable influence on the Buddha, and it is said that it was upon his suggestion that the institution of Uposatha (Poya days), now one of the most conspicuous customs of popular Buddhism, was adopted. This dependence on, and readiness to be moulded by, royal patronage, has always been—in Magadha and in Ceylon—a characteristic of this religion. It has always thriven best as an " established " religion; and the eagerness with which any appearance of government patronage is even now caught at, is very curious. Buddhism is now the only religion which is in any political sense "established" in Ceylon.

The Great Teacher has now collected a vast crowd of followers about him, has made provisions for the continual extension of his Community, and has obtained the patronage of the king.

[1] The name, "ārāma," "park," is of constant recurrence, and enters into many names of Buddhist properties in Ceylon; as Thūpārāma, "Dome-park"; Tissamahārāma, "great-Tissa-park," etc.

Only one thing is wanting to the complete organization of the system—the conversion of the Two Great Disciples. To these two, Sāriputta and Mogallāna, tradition assigns a part only second to that of the Buddha himself, and they are, in fact, the reputed authors of considerable portions of the "words of Buddha."

These two friends were members of a large train of wandering ascetics, who followed a religious leader called Sanjaya. The two had agreed together that whichever should first attain to "Amata"[1] should tell the other. Sariputta happened to fall in with one of Gotama's monks, and was convinced by his dignified and restrained deportment that he must be a saint. He chose a proper time for speaking to him, and said (just as the Brahman, who saw Gotama when he first became the Buddha, had said to Gotama): "Whence have you this bright countenance? Who is your teacher? What is the doctrine you have adopted?" Assajī (for this was the young man's name) told him who his teacher was, and stated very briefly the general drift, without the detailed expression, of the doctrine; repeated to him, in fact, the favourite lines—

> Whatever things proceed from a cause,
> Of them the Buddha has stated the cause;
> And what their dissolution is,
> This is what the Great Ascetic teaches.

Sariputta grasped with perfect insight the principle: "All that has a beginning must have an end," and thus congratulated Assaji: "If but that be the doctrine, you have already reached that state where there is no sorrow; that which hath not been seen by many myriads of ages of bygone ages hath come near to us."[2]

Mogallana soon saw in Sariputta's face the same proof of clearness and gladness, and asked, "Have you then attained to Amata?" "I have," he replied, and told him exactly what he himself had heard from Assaji; and, exactly as he had done, Mogallana recognized the principle. They went together to the Buddha, and as he saw them come, he said, calling them by

[1] This word, Sanscrit "Amrita," has a wide range of meaning: "immortal" and "immortality"; ambrosia, the food of immortality; and in Buddhist language, "the bliss of final emancipation from re-birth."

[2] Abbhatitaṃ. So Oldenberg, *Buddha*, p. 126.

their common names, not by those which became attached to them in Buddhist usage: "There come two friends, Kolita and Upatissa: these will be of my disciples the noblest, the happiest pair!" They were admitted, on their own application, to both grades—Pabbajja and Upasampada. The two hundred and fifty comrades followed their example; but the leader, Sanjaya, was greatly annoyed.

So numerous were now the adherents of the Buddha that people began to complain: "Gotama is breaking up family life; he is leading away all Sanjaya's followers. Whom will he take next?" The monks told this to Gotama, but he replied: "This will soon pass over; reply to their stanza of complaint by this stanza: 'The great heroes, the Tathagatas, lead men by sound doctrine. Who will murmur at the wise, who lead men by sound doctrine?" So the people were convinced, and the complaints soon died away.

§ 4. Here ends that part of Gotama's history—the history of his foundation of the Community—which can be called in any sense continuous. At the end, as has been said above, we have again a continuous record of his last days. But for the long period of forty-five years which, the Commentaries tell us, intervened between the first preaching and the death, we have only a few scattered incidents.

It would naturally have been in the earlier part of this period[1] that Gotama paid the visit to his native place, of which we have a short but somewhat touching account in M.V. i. 54. In the course of his wanderings he came to Kapilavastu, and went for alms to his father Suddhodana's house. There the lady, the mother of Rahula,[2] said to her boy, "This is your father, Rahula, go and ask for your inheritance." The boy obeyed, and, addressing his father, said, "Your shadow, sir, is bliss." His father rose and went out. The son followed, crying, "Give me my inheritance, reverend sir!" Gotama ordered Sariputta to admit the lad (by Pabbajja), and Sariputta, when he had

[1] If the story is consistent, it must have been within some seven years of the Bodhi-tree, for Rahula was young enough to be the first novice; i.e. probably under fourteen. He was born before Gotama set out for the homeless life, and in that life Gotama spent at least seven years before becoming Buddha.

[2] Gotama's wife is so described, instead of being named, because Rahula became a monk: her title in the Community was therefore "Mother of Rahula." There is nothing more said of her in the Pitakas.

inquired what was the proper way of admitting a novice (sāmanera), and the rite had been duly instituted, admitted Rahula to the Community. Rahula's hair was cut, he was clothed in the yellow robe, and was lost to his family. His grandfather, Suddhodana, came to the Buddha; and describing his own grief when his two sons, first Gotama himself, and then his half-brother Nanda, had entered the religious life, he begged that it might be made a rule that no son should be admitted without his parents' consent. "Lord," he said, "when the blessed one went forth it was no small grief to me, so when Nanda did; very great is it now that Rahula has done so. The love of a son cuts the skin, having cut the skin it cuts the hide, it cuts (in like order) into the flesh, the sinews, the bones, the marrow! It would be well, Lord, if their reverences admitted no son without the consent of his father and his mother."[1] And the Buddha made it a rule accordingly.

Of incidents said to have occurred in the course of the Buddha's teaching the texts as well as the Commentaries are full, since almost every discourse has to be prefaced with some account of the occasion on which it was delivered. In the Commentaries and Jātaka stories these incidents are numerous and varied, and some of them are interesting; but they do not come within our present scope since there is no evidence that they were attached to Gotama till many centuries after his death. To this class belongs, for instance, the story of his sympathy for a young woman to whom he recommended, as a cure for grief, some mustard to be obtained from a family which had suffered no bereavement.[2] In the Pitaka texts the introduction to a discourse is usually short and commonplace, oftenest simply: "At that time the Buddha was residing at Sāvaṭṭhi," or the like. But here and there we meet with incidents which display traits of character.

There are several which represent Gotama as behaving with generosity towards rival teachers and alien sects. In the case of the Jatilas, already mentioned, he was reluctant to let the leader act without consulting his followers. When Siha, the Licchavian Commander-in-Chief, had been converted, and

[1] M.V. i. 54. S.B.E.

[2] See Arnold's *Light of Asia*, p. 124. The story of Kisagotami is in the Commentary on Dhammapada.

applied to be received as a disciple, the Buddha said: "Consider well, Siha, before you act: well-known men like you ought to consider well before they act." This delighted Siha, and increased his confidence in the Buddha. "Any of the other sects," he said, "if they had got me to join them, would have been carrying banners round all Vesāli, crying, 'Siha, the commander-in-chief, has come over to us!'" His admiration culminated when the Buddha said: "For a long time, Siha, your house has been one in which the Niganthas have always found food, so you should make a point of giving to them when they come on their begging rounds."[1]

The influence of Gotama's personal attraction and kindness is everywhere implied in what is recorded. In a few cases attention is drawn to it, as when it is said of Roja the Mallian, that Gotama—on the suggestion of Ānanda that this Roja was an important person to secure—poured out such an effluence of love upon him, that he could not but follow the teacher, as a calf follows the cow.[2] This exertion of influence was confessedly dictated by policy, but the story shows what was the tradition about Gotama's attractive power.

Of special acts of kindness on the Buddha's part, there is only one, so far as I know, recorded in the Pitakas; but that is a beautiful illustration of the character which was attributed, no doubt justly, to the Founder of Buddhism. A monk was very ill, and was neglected by the others both because he was—as he said—of no use to them, and because, as is evident from the story, his condition was repulsive. Then the Buddha said to Ananda, "Fetch some water: you and I will bathe this monk." The Buddha poured the water over him and Ananda wiped him: the Buddha lifted his head, and Ananda his feet; and so they laid him on the bed.

The terms in which the Buddha rebuked the monks for their neglect of this poor man, and the last words of the sentence I am about to quote, reach higher, I think, than anything else in the Pitakas, into the levels of Christian teaching. "You monks have no mothers and no fathers to wait on you. If you do not

[1] M.V. vi. 31, 11. S.B.E.
[2] M.V. vi. 36.

wait on one another, who will wait on you? Whosoever would wait on me, let him wait upon the sick."[1]

A large class of stories record gifts made to the Buddha and the Community. It is chiefly among the wealthy and high-born that the conversions are recorded, and gigantic are the presents, especially in the way of cartloads of food—five hundred cartloads of sugar, for instance—of which we read. But a strange gift is mentioned on the part of a devout woman: she could get no meat, when meat was particularly necessary, for a monk who was ill; so she cut off a piece of her own flesh to send him. This led to a stringent order against the eating of human flesh; but her wound was healed by the Buddha.[2]

A certain Meṇḍaka, though only a "householder," was a donor whose gifts cost him little, for his family possessed extraordinary advantages. He himself was able, if he bathed his head and sat down by his granary, to fill it by making showers of grain fall from the sky; his wife had only to sit down by a dish to ensure its being filled with a supply which was inexhaustible; his son had an inexhaustible money-bag; and his daughter a rice-bag of similar quality. It was a small thing for such a man to supply 1250 cows, each with her keeper, to supply the 1250 monks with fresh milk continually.[3]

Several gifts consisted of parks, such as Bimbisara had presented at Benares. Of these the most celebrated is the Jetavana, near Sāvatthi, which was the gift of Anāthapiṇḍika, the prince and model of all donors. The conversion of this person, and the circumstances of his great donation, are related with unusual distinction.[4] He was the brother-in-law of the treasurer of Rajagaha; and the first intimation he received of the existence of a Buddha in the world was derived from the excited state in which, on a certain day, he found his relative and all his house. "Have you a wedding going on?" he asked, "or is the king coming?" "No," replied the treasurer, "the Buddha is coming with his Community to eat at my house." Hardly able to believe that he had been so happy as to have been born

[1] M.V. viii. 26, 3. At present, I feel bound to say, the degree to which the Buddhists of Ceylon—speaking generally—are wanting in the character here attributed to their Teacher, is shocking, and all but incredible to persons who have lived only in Christian countries.

[2] M.V. vi. 23. [3] M.V. vi. 34. [4] Culla Vagga, vi. 4.

in a Buddha's days, Anathapindika determined to go the next morning to visit Gotama. Celestial beings opened the gates for him. Supernatural voices encouraged him; and strange alternations of light and darkness excited his expectations. He was received with unusual solemnity, and with some striking verses from the Buddha's lips, and was instructed and enlightened in the usual method. He invited the Buddha to take a meal with him on the morrow, and the invitation was accepted. The treasurer, the mayor, and the king all offered to assist him in providing the entertainment, but he declined their offers. The meal passed off as usual, but at the end of it Anathapindika invited the Buddha to spend the rainy season at Savatthi. Gotama replied, "The Tathagatas love solitude." This was an intimation that a park would be required. Anathapindika made search in every direction, and decided that a garden belonging to a certain prince Jeta was exactly what was wanted, being accessible but not crowded or exposed. But it was not to be bought for less than such a number of pieces of gold as would cover its surface. The price was paid—though not accepted without reluctance on the seller's part—the gold was brought in carts, and the Jetavana was covered with coins. Dwellings and halls of every kind, baths and bathing tanks were erected, and the park was handed over to the Buddha and the Community; as may still be seen and read on one of the bas-reliefs of the Bharhut Tope (erected probably 200–150 B.C.), which is figured in Cunningham's *Stupa of Bharhut*, plate lvii, and of which there is a model in the Museum at Calcutta.

Before closing this section we must say something of two important members of the Community, about whom from scattered notices we learn a good deal—the good Ananda, whom we have already met, and the wicked Devadatta. We have seen the two chief disciples, Sariputta and Mogallana, brought upon the scene with a careful record of the circumstances of their conversion; but most of the other persons of whom we hear appear, as Ananda does, suddenly upon the stage.[1] But Ananda is a very prominent figure in the story. The Commentaries tell us that he was Gotama's cousin; in the Pitakas we find him,

[1] Much of the tradition is taken for granted, even in the Vinaya. The later Pitaka books contain classified lists of the monks (and nuns) who were distinguished in different ways.

from first to last, in closest attendance on the Buddha. He nurses him in sickness; is often consulted about his movements; is the medium of many of his communications with monks and laymen. While others are represented as more learned and of higher attainment—in fact, Ananda was one of the last to become a rahat—no other was so near to the person and to the affection of the leader.

Another important personage was the guilty Devadatta. It would be possible, I think, almost with exactness to trace, within the Pitaka books themselves, the growth of the tradition about him. In the Maha Vagga he is mentioned only once, as having been the occasion, by reciting the Form of Confession in the presence of laymen, of a rule forbidding such a practice. But in the Culla Vagga, a second part of the history of the Rule, Devadatta's crimes are narrated in great detail. He had acquired, in former births, a great amount of merit, and in this life was far advanced in Buddhistic attainments; and was a great master of supernatural powers. But pride and honours were too much for him; he coveted the first place, and set to work to obtain it. He cultivated the friendship of Ajātasattu, the young son of King Bimbisara, and aroused in him the same envy against his father the king, as he himself indulged against the Buddha. "You kill your father and be king, and I will kill Gotama and be Buddha." The young prince's attempt to murder his father was happily discovered and averted for the time (though he carried out his evil purpose later), and the king, acting on true Buddhist principles, voluntarily surrendered the kingdom to him. Devadatta persisted in his attacks on Gotama, once sending men to kill him, who, instead of killing him, were subdued and converted by his influence; once hurling down a rock, which failed to strike him, but brought on Devadatta the greatest of all possible guilts, that of shedding a Buddha's blood; for a splinter of the fallen rock pierced Gotama's foot. Foiled in these attempts, Devadatta set to work to introduce dissension into the Community, and for this purpose invented five points of greater strictness than the existing rules required. He persuaded a good many monks, Vajjians of Vesali, to support him in demanding of the Buddha that these five points should be made rules. On Gotama's refusing this, he led away a train of five hundred monks; but these were soon induced to return by the preaching of Sariputta. Devadatta was most generously treated by Gotama, and warned again and again; but when he persisted in his determination to divide the Community, his doom was solemnly predicted.

Several references to Devadatta may be gathered from other parts of the Pitaka, but they are all in obvious reference to this account in the Culla Vagga. We read in the Majjhima Nikāya[1] that Prince Abhaya was stirred up by N̄ātaputta to tax Gotama with having used unkind language about Devadatta, calling him "damned," "doomed to hell for a Kalpa" (age), "past cure," and the like; and the Buddha explained that a word which is true, and intended to do good, though it give pain, is right. The condemnation was uttered out of the Buddha's compassion for all beings.

It is as an illustration of the horrible evils of schism, and of the great dangers which arise from being praised and made much of, that Devadatta's story is elaborated; and all the references to him, except the first, belong to the later portion of the Pitaka cycle of traditions. They lead us, therefore, fitly on to the concluding portion of the biography we are constructing, which is to be found in the Sutta of the Decease.[1] For the mind of the compiler of that Sutta was evidently occupied with the thought of dissensions and schisms, and with the desire to prevent or heal them. He had brought together a variety of topics, but this is the dominant one. His aim has been—with special reference, as I believe, to the circumstances of his own time—to represent the last thoughts of the Buddha as having been directed to the great purpose of unity.

§ 5. The throne of Magadha was occupied in these later days of Gotama's life by Ajatasattu. This monarch was anxious to overcome the Vajjians, and sent his ministers to inquire of the Buddha whether he would succeed or not in his enterprise. The Buddha turned to Ananda, and asked whether the Vajjians were in the habit of meeting in large numbers; whether they met and acted in unity; whether they were keeping their laws and making no innovations in them; whether they honoured the old; whether their women were well conducted; whether they were keeping in repair and treating with reverence the shrines which existed in their country; and, finally, whether

[1] Maj. Nik. 58. See Sanyut. Nik. vi. 2, 2, xvii. 35, and Angut. iv. 68.

they were maintaining due provision for the support of the Buddhist saints (rahats) in their country. To all these questions Ananda replied in the affirmative; and then the Buddha told the minister that as long as these seven conditions of prosperity continued the Vajjians would prosper. When Vassakāra was gone, the Buddha summoned his monks together to give them a corresponding instruction as to the conditions on which the permanent prosperity of the Community depended. In five sets of seven and one of six, these conditions of permanence are stated; and they embrace—in no very logical order—nearly all the leading principles of Buddhism. (It is easy to see that the first set of seven, which really corresponds to the seven qualities commended in the Vajjians, is the original part of this collection.)

Then follows a curious account of Gotama's rebuking Sariputta for a rash compliment. Sariputta had professed his conviction that there never had been, nor ever would be, any one greater or wiser in absolute knowledge than Gotama. "Brave words, Sariputta; but can you see into the minds of all past and future Buddhas, and estimate exactly their characters and powers? Can you see into me, the Buddha of the present?" Poor Sariputta admitted that he could not; and that all that he was entitled to assert was, that all Buddhas, past and present, must have obtained Buddha-hood by the same course of extinction of lust, and of active self-training, by which Gotama had attained it.

The Sutta has next some sections which are in the main identical, though with some differences of arrangement, with certain sections which I passed unnoticed in the Maha Vagga. One of these is important as possibly affording a means of ascertaining the date—or at least the relative date—at which the Pitakas were compiled.

With a view to the war against the Vajjians, the Magadhan chiefs were building a fortified city at Pāṭaligāma.[1] It was a spot haunted by thousands of those local deities which haunt trees, ponds, houses, and the like, and (as the Buddha saw, though no one else did) the Magadhan authorities were in un-

[1] Parinibb. S., p. 12. Pāṭaligāmam nagaraṃ māpenti. They were making a city out of what had been but a "gāma" or country district. As a city it was called Pātaliputra (Greek, "Palibothra"), and is represented now by Patna.

conscious but auspicious sympathy with (what a later phraseology would call) the genius of the place. Where the local deities of highest power haunted, there the mightiest nobles were planning their dwellings; where the deities were those of middle or lower dignity, there Magadhans of corresponding rank were settling. The Buddha revealed this auspicious fact to Ananda, and said: " It is as if the Magadhan ministers had taken counsel with the Tāvatiṃsa gods. Of all the dwellings of noble men (or, " of the Aryan world "), of all places of traffic, this will be the chief city —Pataliputta, the central town. But there will be three dangers for Pataliputta, from fire, or from water, or from breach of friendship."

The Buddha was of course entertained there, and he is represented as having expressed his satisfaction in some lines which inculcate the cult of local deities in a way inconsistent with the strictest Buddhism, and which belongs to the region of the astrologer and the house-charmer.

> In what spot soever the wise man takes up his abode,
> There let him give food to good and self-controlled men of religion:
> To the deities that belong there let him offer an offering:
> Thus served they serve him, honoured they honour him;
> So dealt with they feel for him as a mother for her own dear son:
> He always sees good luck whom the local deities love.[1]

The builders of the city resolved that the gate by which the Buddha went out should be called the Gotama gate, and the crossing at which he should cross the Ganges should be called the Gotama ferry. He did not cross, however, by the ferry, for the river was in flood; but miraculously disappeared from the one side, and stood, with his train of monks, on the other.[2]

Many a comprehensive discourse was delivered as the Buddha went from place to place in the neighbourhood of Vesali; but it was after he had entered on the retirement of the rainy season at Beluva, near that city, that the symptoms of his approaching end appeared. He became very ill, and suffered much, but he would not pass away till he had bidden his monks farewell. So

[1] See Rhys Davids' notes, S.B.E. xi. pp. 19 and 20. Many stanzas have been pressed into the service of Buddhism, even in the Pitakas, which are thoroughly alien to its spirit. Such is that about the snakes, translated on p. 105.

[2] Parinibb. S., p. 14., and M.V. vi. 28.

by an effort of will he turned back the sickness, and retained his hold on life. On his recovery Ananda asked for some last instructions. The reply is very striking.

"What is it the Community expects of me? I have preached the doctrine, making no distinction therein of inner and outer: the Buddha has not reserved the teacher's perquisite.[1] If there is any one who thinks, Ananda, 'I will be the leader of the Community of monks,' or, 'The Community is dependent upon me,' he, I suppose, Ananda, would lay down rules about the Community! But this is not my idea, that I lead the Community. or that the Community depends on me: how, then, should I lay down rules about the Community? I am now worn, outgrown, old, aged, far on in years; my age is going on for eighty. Just as a worn-out cart, Ananda, can get along only with all sorts of patching and care, so methinks it is only with patching and care that my body gets along. It is only when by abstraction from all marks of outward objects by the extinction of definite sensations, I maintain that concentration of mind which consists in noting nothing—only then that my body is kept at ease. Therefore I say, Ananda, be yourselves your lamp, yourselves your refuge; have no other refuge: have the doctrine for your light, have the doctrine for your refuge; have no other refuge! How can this be?

"Let us suppose a monk so lives—with so true an estimate of the body, as to be in bodily things austere, attentive, recollected, and to subdue all pain of craving; so true an estimate of sensation, as to be in regard of sensations austere, attentive, recollected, and to subdue all pain of sense; so true an estimate of thought, as to be in regard of thoughts austere, attentive, recollected, and to subdue all pain arising from craving for objects of thought—then a monk is his own lamp, his own refuge, with no other refuge; has the doctrine for his lamp, and for his refuge, and has no other refuge. And whoever, either now or after my departure, shall so live, they will be in the highest place among those who are lovers of the Rule."

After this the Buddha is recorded to have deliberately resolved on dying in three months' time. Mara had tried to persuade him to depart immediately, reminding him of his determination,

[1] A proverbial expression for some point of science or skill kept back, that the teacher might still be superior to his pupil.

at the beginning of his Buddha-hood, not to enter on his final extinction till he had fully preached his doctrine. "Now," cried the enemy, "all that has been done: disciples, monks and nuns, laymen and laywomen have been trained, who can teach and explain the doctrine to others. Let the Blessed One therefore enter on his final extinction." "Be at ease, wicked one," replied the Buddha, "the Tathagata's final extinction is not far distant: at the end of three months he will attain it."

The solemn renunciation of life was marked by a mighty earthquake, such as occurs—we here learn—only on eight occasions; namely, by natural causes; by the supernatural power of meditation in some unusually wise sage, Brahman or Buddhist, or of some deity, higher or lower; and on the occasions of a Buddha's conception, birth, attainment of Buddhahood, setting in motion the royal wheel of the law; of his deliberate renunciation of life; and lastly, of his actual final and utter passing away from existence.

Ananda tried in vain to persuade his master to remain for the rest of the cycle; but he was reminded—and the information must have been as mortifying to Ananda as it is strange to us—that this was by no means the first time that he had had an opportunity of urging such a request. Again and again, in various scenes, the Buddha had given him a very strong hint by saying: "One of my power could easily, if he liked, remain in life all the cycle," and on either of these occasions, if Ananda had taken the hint and begged the Buddha to stay, he would have consented. It was emphatically Ananda's fault, that he failed to make the suggestion till the decision to die had been announced and it was too late. Had Ananda been quicker in taking a hint, the son of Suddhodana would still have been among us![1]

In due time the Buddha arrived with Ananda at the Kūṭāgāra hall, and preparations were immediately made for assembling all the monks of the Vesali circuit. (The technical term is used,

[1] After the publication of the first edition of this book, the writer was charged with a blunder, in having understood "kalpa" here to mean "the cycle," instead of, as Buddhaghosha interpreted it, "the natural term of life." But Buddhaghosha states that some took it as "cycle"; and this is obviously the only rendering that gives any point to the passage. It requires no special powers to live the natural term of life; and in fact Gotama, at eighty, had fairly done this.

equivalent to the Sinhalese, Sīmāwa). Gotama addressed them in an earnest though very technical sermon, insisting on the chief principles of his system as essential to the permanence of religion, and to the good and happiness of gods and men. He ended with the words : " Behold now, monks, I impress it upon you : all (composite) things are subject to the law of dissolution : press on earnestly to perfection : soon the Tathagata's final extinction will take place : at the end of three months the Tathagata will enter on final extinction." Or, as the metrical form of the story expresses it :—

> Full ripe is my age, little of my life remains ;
> I shall leave you and go—I have made myself my own refuge :
> Be untiring, be recollected, and keep to the rules of conduct ;
> Let your resolution be firmly held, guard your thoughts well ;
> Whoso in this doctrine and rule untiringly toils on,
> Shall leave the ocean of repeated births and make an end of sorrow.

In leaving Vesali, Gotama turned, slowly and deliberately as an elephant does, and took a solemn last look at the city ; then he went on from place to place, still giving various instructions to his disciples. One of these is very significant as an indication of the relative date of the Sutta in which it occurs. He addressed the monks on the method of testing or verifying doctrine. Whether a particular doctrine be asserted by a single monk, who professes to be reporting what he actually heard the Buddha say, or whether it be the tradition of a particular monastery or district, or that of one or of many learned elders, there is but one test. The sentences (padāni) and syllables (vyañjanāni) of the dogma under discussion are to be carefully taken and placed beside the sacred text (suttaṃ) and compared with the rule (vinayaṃ). If they do not stand with the text and bear comparison with the rule, then it follows that such a dogma is not the word of the Buddha ; it is that monk's mistake (and so conversely).[1]

[1] Parinibb. S., 39. The words for "text" and "rule" are "Sutta" and "Vinaya," the names of the two (older of the three) collections afterwards called Pitakas. The "learned elders" above are described as "bahussutā," "full of tradition" (smriti) ; as "vinayadhārā," carrying about with them the Rule (or Vinaya), as "mātikadhārā," "knowing by heart the "mātikapadāni" or summaries of contents and lists of abridged rules. All these expressions refer evidently to a fully compiled and classified (if not to a written) text, and mark the late date of the Mahaparinibbana Sutta.

This important passage is succeeded by a more strictly narrative (and, I doubt not, far more ancient) portion of the Sutta, and one in which the composite character of the work is clearly displayed.[1] Gotama and Ananda went on to Pāvā, and were the guests there, with others of the Community, of Cunda the smith. Besides other "hard and soft foods," cakes and curry and rice, Cunda had provided a quantity (pahūtaṃ) of dried pork. The Buddha at once perceived that this pork was not likely to be safely eaten by any one, of all gods and men, except a Buddha. He made his own meal upon it, but ordered what remained to be buried in a hole. The text goes on thus: "So when the Bhagavat [blessed one] had eaten the food of Cunda the smith, there arose in him a fierce disease of the nature of dysentery, violent pains go on, such as lead to death. These pains, however, the Bhagavat, in conscious recollectedness, accepted without complaint. 'Let us go, Ananda, to Kusināra.' The venerable Ananda assented, saying, 'Even so, my lord.'

"Or thus:—

When he had eaten the food of Cunda the smith (so I have heard)
The wise one experienced a disease, violent, such as leads to death.

"Or thus:—

When he had eaten the dried pork
Violent illness arose in the Teacher:
The Bhagavat suffered violent purgings, and said
I will go to the city of Kusinara."

After one or two episodes which may be relegated to a note,[2]

[1] It is founded on the old metrical narrative, which here as elsewhere is free from the interspersion of elaborate doctrinal passages. We have here three versions side by side, (1) the prose of the compiler, (2) a verse (sloka) from which the prose differs but little, and (3) the older and quainter "Trishṭubh" stanza, differing in several points from (1) and (2). In this there is no allusion to the fortitude with which the pain was borne, nor is there in (2), as I understand it. I take the words "dhīro samphusi" to mean "The wise one felt."

[2] The Buddha tells an anecdote of his own calm and concentration, such that a furious storm had raged round him without his noticing it. The next section tells us how Pukkusa, a new adherent, robed him in a set of robes of cloth of gold, but the splendour of these was outshone by the brilliance of the Buddha's skin. For as the day of his decease approaches his complexion becomes pure and lustrous, as at the attainment of Buddha-hood. (What was told simply, in the Maha Vagga, of Gotama, as of Assaji, Sariputta, and others, is here treated as miraculous. It even developed later into a sort of "transfiguration"). See Rhys Davids' note, S.B.E. xi. 82.

the old narrative goes on, in terms which (for the sake of showing the English reader what the metre is like) may be thus roughly translated :—

> On Buddha went, on to Kakuṭṭha river :
> Fair flowed the white water and clear and pleasant ;
> Down thither stept weary and worn the Teacher,
> Great, peerless one, Tathagata, chief of beings !
> The Teacher bath'd, drank, and he cross'd the river,
> He first and chief, follow'd by all the brethren.
> Still setting forth doctrine, the blessed Teacher
> That mighty sage, came to the Mango-Garden.
> Then straight the monk, Cundaka nam'd, he summon'd :
> " Fold now a robe four-fold and spread it 'neath me."
> Straight Cunda heard the voice of the self-controll'd one,
> Fourfold in haste folded a robe and laid it ;
> Down lay the great Teacher, so worn and weary,
> While Cunda sat down on the ground before him.

It may be a mere coincidence that brings the name of this Cunda or Cundaka into close juxtaposition with that of Cunda the smith. For the consolation of Cunda the smith, in case he should feel distress at the thought that the food he had supplied had led to the Buddha's extinction, Ananda was to assure him, as from the Buddha's own lips, that this offering of his, and the first offering of food made when Gotama had just become Buddha, were of all offerings the most meritorious. The result of that action of Cunda's would be long life, beauty, happiness and glory, heaven and sovereign power.

The next stage of the journey was the last.

With a great train of monks the Buddha went to the Sāla Grove ; and there, between a pair of Sal trees in every respect alike, the couch was spread. The Buddha lay down with his head to the north, reclining on his right side, with full consciousness and recollectedness, in a lion-like repose. The Sal trees burst into unexpected bloom, the heavens rained flowers upon the hero's form, and heavenly music was wafted from the skies. But " such signs of honour as these," said the Buddha, " are not the true honours of a Tathagata. Rather," he said, " the monk or nun, layman or laywoman, who lives in the performance of all the duties and ways of religion—such a one pays him the true, the higher honour and service."

Unseen spirits were now crowding the air to get a sight of the

Great Being: not the space of a hair's point for twelve leagues round but was full of deities—some ready to tear their hair in vulgar grief, but some clear-sighted enough to see that "all things are unabiding," and to acquiesce in what was inevitable.

Under the twin Sal trees, before the last moment came, several incidents and discourses, of very unequal interest, are said to have found place. Some are mere heterogeneous notices of rules; some are important summaries of doctrine; but only two classes will be mentioned now—those which are really part of Gotama's biography, and those which in other ways throw light upon the history of the religion.[1]

Ananda is a very well drawn character, and always wins our sympathy. He was slow, as we have seen: during all his master's life he failed to attain rahatship; but his patience and gentleness are very attractive. We are glad to find that he was appreciated. While Gotama reclined between the Sal trees Ananda withdrew, and stood leaning against some doorway, and wept at the thought that his dear master was so soon to pass away, and he still a learner. Gotama sent for him, and comforted him, and uttered (in three parallel sentences) these touching words: "A long time, Ananda, you have followed and served me, with acts of love, with words of love, with thoughts of love, kind, blessed, unvarying, immeasurable." And then he spoke at length to the monks in praise of Ananda, comparing him, for the graciousness of his manners, to a universal monarch. But poor Ananda was immediately to give another proof of the limited range of his powers. He tried to dissuade the Buddha from accomplishing his decease in the insignificant little town of Kusinara. Let him go and end his life rather in some great city, in Rajagaha or Benares. The Buddha rebuked him: "Kusinara must not be called an insignificant town: ages ago it was the royal city of the great Mahā Sudassana [the ideal king], and was adorned with every element of [the conventional description of] wealth and splendour." Ananda was then sent to prepare the nobles of Kusinara for what was to take place; and they came full of grief, and were presented, family by family,

[1] Biographical: Ananda's comfort; the suggestion that Gotama should not die in Kusinara; the Mallians told; conversion of Subhaddha; last warnings and inquiries; the last words; the manner of decease. Historical: Directions about pilgrimages; burial of emperors and Buddhas; erection of dagabas.

to the Buddha. The news of the approaching end decided a certain Subhadda, a religious person of great attainments and importance, who was not yet a Buddhist, to come and inquire of the Buddha. He was converted with curious ease, and became a rahat, the last disciple gained by Gotama himself.

Little more remained to be done. Three times Gotama called on his monks, if there were any point about which any one of them had yet any doubt, now, while he was yet with them, to ask about it. Not one had a point to raise. And the Buddha asserted the conclusion, that there was not one in the whole Community in whose mind one doubt existed in regard to the Buddha, the doctrine, or the Order, the Way or the Path; the most backward of the five hundred had entered indefectibly on the path which must lead him at last to perfect insight.

Then the Blessed One said to the monks: "Behold now, mendicants, I say to you, everything is subject to decay; press forward untiringly to perfection." This was his last word. He then entered into the first stage of meditation, thence into the second, the third, the fourth; from the fourth stage of meditation he proceeded to the realm of the infinity of space, thence to that of the infinity of thought, from that he advanced into the realm of nothingness, thence into that of neither consciousness nor unconsciousness, and from this condition he went on to that in which all action of either thought or perception is at an end.

Ananda, the simple-minded, thought all was over; but Anuruddha, the great metaphysician of the Order, said, "Nay, brother Ananda, this is not final Nirvana: he has entered the state in which all action of either thought or perception is at an end."

Full Nirvana, it appears, is not attained quite unconsciously: the Buddha had to return to consciousness first. He passed back through all the stages which have been enumerated till he reached the first degree of meditation (in which the mind is active). Thence he retraced his course (as if to prove that he had full command of his faculties?) to the second, the third, and the fourth stage of meditation; and out of the fourth stage of meditation he entered on final extinction.

The event was accompanied by a fearful and terrible earthquake; and suitable reflections were uttered by beings of every grade. The supreme Brahma uttered three lines in praise of the Buddha and in concise assertion of his leading principle. But they were far surpassed by the celebrated utterance of Sakka, the chief of the lower gods.

> All things form'd[1] are unabiding:
> Birth, decay—their law is this:
> They come to birth and are dissolvèd:
> Let them cease, and there is bliss!

The utterance of the metaphysician Anuruddha was more definitely an epitaph:—

> There came no strife of gasping breath from that strong heart and steadfast will:
> All longing past, all calm attain'd, did that high sage his date fulfil;
> Accepted that last agony with heart unmov'd and mind at peace:
> As some bright flame extinguish'd fades, so came to him the glad release.

The lines attributed to Ananda almost overdo his character for simplicity:—

> Moment of terror! moment of thrilling awe!
> When glorious Buddha, rich in every grace,
> In final dissolution pass'd away!

Men and deities alike, each according to his degree of detachment from objects of desire, received the news with bitter emotion or with philosophic calm. Anuruddha, as chief of the latter, reminded the brethren how the departed had prepared them to recognize the law of separation and dissolution. And in such converse the night was spent.

For six days the preparations for the burning, which had been entrusted to the Mallian nobles of Kusinara, were carried on, amid acts of homage to the corpse, with dances, music, flowers, and decorations; and on the seventh day, with every sign of honour, borne by eight chieftains of the Mallians, the body was taken—not as had at first been planned, and as would have been usual, around the outside of the city, but, according to a divine intimation, through the very midst of the city—to a spot upon the east of it, where the cremation was to be. No pollution could be caused by such a corpse; on the contrary, all Kusinara

[1] "All things formed," i.e. "owing their existence to the union of elements." The word "sankhārā" is untranslatable. "Things" is inadequate, because "saṇkhārā" implies the argument, that what has been formed by union of elements is liable to be destroyed by their separation. On the other hand, since saṇkhārā includes all objects, no other word than things is large enough.

was knee-deep in flowers, which were showered from heaven to strew the way of the auspicious procession.

In accordance with an idea which we have already met with, the remains of the Buddha were treated, by Ananda's direction, like those of a universal monarch (cakkavatti). The body was wrapped first in a new cloth, then in cotton-wool, then in another new cloth, and so on, till it had been enclosed in five hundred such double wrappings. It was then placed in an iron oil-vessel, and this was enclosed in a second. They then made a mound of all kinds of perfumes, and on this they laid the iron coffin. After a delay, which shall presently be explained, the pile took fire of itself. Every particle of the corpse, except the bones, having been burnt, and not an ash remaining, rain fell from heaven and waters burst up from beneath the earth, and quenched the fire; while the Mallians added perfumed waters.

The Mallians then placed the bones in their own council-hall, and made a lattice-work of spears and a rampart of bows around them; and for seven days, with dance and song, and music and flowers and perfumes, did honour and homage and reverent service.

These proceedings had been delayed for a time for a purpose, which is interesting, from the proof which it affords of the importance attached to the person of the famous monk Mahākassapa. This elder was at a distance when the Buddha died, and the tidings reached him, with his train of five hundred brethren, by their meeting some one who was carrying one of the celestial flowers which had fallen in Kusinara. By the intervention of deities (devatā) the kindling of the pyre was made impossible till Mahakassapa with his following arrived; but as soon as those five hundred monks had come and had walked three times round the mound and done homage at the Buddha's feet, immediately the pile took fire, as has been described.

To obtain a portion of the relics and to erect over it in honour of the Buddha a stūpa (Pali, " thūpo ")—such probably as is now called in Ceylon a " dāgaba," or relic-holder—was now the ambition of all who could claim the privilege.

Gotama had belonged to the royal (or warrior, Kshatriya) caste; so first the king, Ajatasattu, and then the nobles of Vesali, and then the Sakyans of Kapilavastu itself, and three other clans, and with these one Brahman, of Vethadipa—seven claimants in all—asserted their respective claims to a share in the bodily remains and to the right of erecting dagabas. But the Mallians of Kusinara, in whose possession the bones actually were, were unwilling to part with them ; till a Brahman named Doṇa came forward as peacemaker, and divided the relics into eight portions, reserving for himself the vase (doṇi) in which they had been collected. This Brahman by caste was of course a Buddhist by religion ; and the story of his intervention belongs to the older tradition. It is thus recorded in the old verse :—

Hear, rev'rend sirs ! only a word I offer :
Our Buddha dear taught us a law of meekness.
Ill were it if over the distribution
Of *his* remains strife should arise and warfare !
Come, rev'rend sirs, let us in love and concord
Sweetly agreed, make of them eight divisions :
Through many lands thus will the shrines be scatter'd,
And many men won to the faith of Buddha !

NOTE TO CHAPTER III

INDICATIONS OF AN ANCIENT METRICAL LIFE OF GOTAMA

THERE is reason to think that the oldest tradition of the life of Gotama, of which we have any trace, was handed down in a continuous poem, in Trishtubh metre, of the form, "Gantvāna Buddho nadiyam Kakuṭṭhaṃ"; of which poem fragments have come down to us, embedded in the prose narrative. The metre of these fragments is an ancient one, and its use in these books is limited to biographical passages.

I. The antiquity of the metre (though it survived and became a favourite one) is shown by the following considerations :—

(1) It is common in the Vedic hymns.

(2) It is closely allied to the Greek and Latin sapphic and hendecasyllabic.

(3) Passages written in it contain peculiarities of prosody which, from their affinity to Latin prosody, may be thought to be old; e.g. the quantity of *o* common, and the omission and elision of final *m*.

(4) Such passages contain a large proportion of old grammatical forms, such as "have," "brūhi," etc.

II. As to its being limited, in the Piṭakas, to biographical passages :—

(1) Out of about fourteen instances of this metre in the Vinaya Pitaka, seven are in the biographical first four sections of Maha Vagga (i. 1–22); four are in the biographical passage, Culla Vagga, vii. 1–4; and one in a half-biographical passage, M.V. x. 3.

(2) The three which occur in Parinibb. S. are all biographical; referring to Cunda's service, Subhadda's late admission, and Dona's action about the relics.

III. The opinion that they belong to an *early* biography is supported by the observation that none of the additional features of biography or history, which are found in Samantapāsādikā, are supported by verses of this kind.

PART III

THE TEACHING OF BUDDHA

CHAPTER IV

THE BUDDHIST MORAL SYSTEM IN GENERAL

AN author who wishes to describe the Buddhist view of morals in a way intelligible to an English reader, and yet as nearly as possible in the language and spirit of the Buddhist books, is met by considerable difficulties; and it is possible that in stating these difficulties I shall be able to convey some true impressions as to the character and structure of the books from which our materials are to be derived.

Greatly as the metaphysical element in Buddhist teaching has sometimes been exaggerated, it is impossible entirely to separate the discussion of morals from that of the general laws of being. This is true to some extent in regard to any moral system, ancient or modern, Greek or Oriental; for whether we consider that the end of conduct is the attainment of truth, or regard the knowledge of truth as the foundation of conduct, either way the two are intimately associated. But it is conspicuously true in the case of the Buddhist system. Not only did Gotama base his rules on his "Four Truths," but knowledge itself, in the Buddhist view, is almost identified with moral power. The very name, "Buddhism," of a system which is pre-eminently a system of conduct, is derived from "budh," to know. The two are also linked together by another characteristic feature of Buddhism, the emphasis which it lays on meditation. Meditation, by which knowledge is brought to bear on conduct, is in fact a part of conduct. Conversely, meditation, by which truth is arrived at, depends upon the essentially moral conditions of purity and self-control. Of the intermediate position which is thus occupied by meditation, the Buddhist compilers were well aware; and accordingly they described the whole moral course as that of conduct, meditation, and knowledge. We shall see, however, that the knowledge involved is that of a strictly limited group of propositions, and that neither metaphysics nor intellectual subtlety plays any large part in the Buddhist morality as a practical system.

Morals are not clearly separated from metaphysics in the sacred books. It has been usual to say that morality is the theme of the Sutta Pitaka, or collection of discourses, exclusively. This is not the case. That collection is indeed the chief repository of teaching specifically moral; but metaphysical discussion is by no means excluded from it. On the other hand, the Vinaya Pitaka, or collection of Rules of Discipline, is obviously concerned with conduct. It contains a very large element of directly moral precepts and lectures, among which are some of the same discourses that are found in the Sutta Pitaka. The third collection, the Abhidhamma Pitaka, though so often spoken of as deep and subtle, consists in great part of matter similar to that of the Sutta Pitaka: long passages are word for word the same. In fact, parts of the Abhidhamma are summaries of the Sutta Pitaka. If I speak, therefore, in the following pages of "the Suttas," it will not necessarily be implied that my material is taken from the Sutta Pitaka, though that will usually be the case.

But neither in one collection nor in another do we find a continuous and systematic treatment on a large scale, of the whole subject. In very much later days, the Visuddhi Magga, of Buddhaghosha, attempted such a treatment with no small success; but the notion of a volume, setting out the whole of a subject in a continuous treatise, is unknown to the ancient, or "canonical" Buddhist literature.

Nor could such a treatise or course be formed by putting the Suttas together. One is not supplementary to another; one does not take up the subject where the other left off; each purports to be complete in itself. It is true they are extremely systematic in a certain sense of the word, and that many of them cover or summarize a large part of the field[1]—in fact, it is their vice to be each separately exhaustive—but they go over the field in different directions, and divide up the same subject by a great number of independent classifications. For instance, while one leads the disciple to Nirvana by the successive casting

[1] The Sutta translated on pp. 188 sq. is a good instance, and comes as near as any single one could do to giving the reader a notion of the method.

off of a series of "impediments," another takes him to the same end by the rooting up of certain bad habits or states of mind. Under a different name, or even under the same name, the same vice, as, for instance, "hatred," will appear in both series. One Sutta will treat of the three kinds of act—acts of body, of speech, of thought; and the next Sutta will contrast two characters—that of the man who injures both his neighbour and himself, and that of the man who does good to both; and this contrast will consist in the acts, words, and thoughts of the two men. By studying a multitude of such chapters one receives a forcible impression of the teaching as a connected whole; but it is impossible to compile a connected treatise by putting such chapters together. Such an attempt would result in a mass of repetitions and cross divisions.

But it is time to illustrate this more closely. The longest Suttas are hardly longer than a modern essay or sermon; the majority are much shorter; none are so long as the longer dialogues of Plato. I will give an abridgment of the first and second Suttas of the Majjhima Nikāya, or Collection of treatises of middle length.

The first insists on the necessity of an exact knowledge of the true character, as regards impermanence, of the outer world. Such knowledge will free the man from all attachment to the four material elements, earth, water, fire, and air, to animals, to the lower deities, to the various (fully enumerated) higher deities, to the four infinite regions, to the objects of sight, hearing, thought, and consciousness, to unity, multiplicity, and universality, and to Nirvana itself. All this, because delight in things is the root of sorrow. This condition is growing in the growing disciple, and is advanced in the advanced disciple, and is caused by the destruction in him of lust, spite, and stupidity; and this condition is identical with the final perfection of a Buddha.

The second Sutta teaches how to destroy the "āsavas," or "corruptions," of which three are specified—those of desire, of existence, of ignorance. They are got rid of by seven methods, viz. by *thinking* only of such things as tend to eliminate them; by *guarding* the five senses; by recollectedness in the *use* of the conventional list of necessaries; by *resignation* to the conventional list of inconveniences; by *avoidance* of the occasions of evil; by *dispelling* the three wrong reflections—desire, malice, and cruelty; by *practising* the seven elements of supreme wisdom. He who has achieved these has ended sorrow.

From these instances it will be seen in what sense the Suttas are systematic. They are constructed upon numerical systems. There are three wrong reflections; there are eight of this, and four of that: a man may be such and such in ten ways—this numerical method is their system. Analysis, other than numerical division, is very rare. Discussion, in the sense of shaking out a subject and shaking it clear by inquiry, is all but unknown. There is no searching back to the origin of habits; no recognition of the truth that one virtue runs into another, or that a vice may melt into a virtue by imperceptible gradations. All is definite and dogmatic. Hard-and-fast lines are drawn; words are used with unswerving regularity, but little is done to elucidate their meaning. If the meaning of a word is explained, it is by accumulating synonyms, or—what is the best part of the whole method—by similes. But results are given, not inquiries. Nothing is tentative.

Such a method is distasteful to a European reader. We delight in watching the process of inquiry, the balancing of different views. In morals especially, we feel that we have not gone far till we have got behind the *names* of the virtues and the vices. We have been accustomed—the European world has been accustomed since the days of Socrates—to find moral discussion consist largely in such inquiries as, "What is holiness?" "What distinguishes courage from rashness?" And Socrates taught us, once for all, not to expect unqualified answers to these questions. Mixed motives, blended characters—these interest us. But the Buddha knows nothing conditional, and condescends to nothing tentative. There are so many bad ways and so many good: the good are perfectly distinct from the bad: the bad ways all tend to re-birth, and the good ways to deliverance from existence.

Such is a general description of the moral method of the Buddhist books. There are exceptions, and the exceptions are to us the most attractive parts of the Suttas. But they are few. They are oases of genuine human inquiry in a desert of fictitious accuracy.

I have said that we do not find an authorized course of

instruction, or a continuous treatment of the whole subject of morality, but I have also alluded to the outline of such a course —conduct, meditation,[1] knowledge—which presents the received classification of the whole subject. As a guide to a complete arrangement of the whole system of Buddhism it is not at all to be despised. By a persistent regulation of his conduct, a man becomes qualified for the practice of meditation, which carries him, it is pretended, stage by stage to that condition of mind in which he sees into the nature and causes of things, and in attaining this insight or knowledge he has attained the final goal. Such is the received Buddhist view of the moral course; and it is perhaps possible, without much violence, to exhibit all the different parts of the teaching under these three heads.[2] There is a class of Suttas formed on this plan, of which that translated below (p. 188 f.) is a specimen.

But the English reader would not find this an altogether satisfactory order. He holds that insight into the meaning and purpose of life is the origin, at least as truly as it is the result, of intelligent moral conduct. In a treatise, at any rate, he expects to see theory first laid down, and then to see practice directed according to theory. And this order is not unrecognized in the Buddhist writings. It is represented as the historical order in the Buddha's own proceedings. He first arrived at insight, and then, while he went about proclaiming the "Truths" which he had realized, he founded on these "Truths" the specific precepts, and the rule of life, and the methods of meditation. Both points of view are taken; and I suspect that the order—truths, training, conduct—is the older, and that of conduct, meditation, knowledge,[3] the later.

[1] "Samādhi," strictly, the self-concentration by which meditation is possible. The act of meditation in its several stages is "jhāna," but these stages collectively are often called "samādhi."

[2] This is done, not only with great diligence and subtlety, but also with much fertility of illustration and some shrewd observation of life, in the "Visuddhi Magga."

[3] These three, with their result, emancipation, are the four principles from ignorance of which all beings, including him who by discovering them became the Buddha, "ran through the long course of re-birth." Angut. iv. 1, 2. Sometimes the whole is summarized under the two heads "Samatha" and "Vipassanā," tranquillity and clear insight; or these are in the reverse order. Angut. iv. 170. Sometimes, more simply, Vijjācaraṇaṃ, knowledge and conduct.

Whether this conjecture be well founded or not, I think my reader will be most likely to gain a vivid idea and correct notion of the whole teaching, if I first sketch the Buddhist ideal as it appears to me, and then, in the light of the fundamental principles which are implied in that ideal and are formulated in the metaphysical "truths," describe the vices which are chiefly condemned and the virtues chiefly insisted on.

CHAPTER V

THE IDEAL OF BUDDHISM

THE qualities most charming to the Indian mind are gentleness and calm. It is to the exhibition of these qualities in a high degree that we can attribute with the greatest probability the personal influence of Gotama the Sakyan, and his acceptance by his contemporaries as the Buddha; if we assume, and we are not at present justified in doubting it, that his contemporaries did allow him that title. These two qualities, gentleness and calm, are the primary elements in the ideal of the Buddhist moralist. In their degenerate form they both pass into apathy, and there are passages in the Pitakas which recommend what is hardly better than that; but the general tone is nearer to the ideal, and recommends a gentleness that rises into positive love, and a calm which is based upon strength and resolution. The picture which is painted for us of Gotama represents a character not only calm and gentle, but active, genial, not devoid of humour, deeply sympathetic, and intensely human. In the general tenor of the books we miss the humour; we miss much of the sympathy and geniality; but for the most part we are in the presence of an ideal which is human and energetic. There are, it is true, many passages, especially among those that deal with meditation or with supernatural attainments, which entirely leave behind all that is human, natural, probable, all that is genial or attractive, and sail away into a region of empty abstraction, which it would be flattery to call a cloudland. But when these are excepted, we are generally in the region of reality, and are addressed in tones which are earnest even when they are most tedious.

For third, though with an interval, after gentleness and calm. comes *earnestness* as an element in the Buddhist ideal. To be earnest, to be awake, to strive, and not to give up—these are watchwords incessantly repeated. The absoluteness of the repose to which the sage is invited is matched by the intensity of the effort that is required of him in the way.[1]

To these three elements, if a fourth is to be added, it will be that, the name of which we are obliged to represent, for want of a more exact equivalent, by "Purity." This cannot be entirely distinguished from calm; but while that is more philosophical, this is more moral. To be without any flaw of imperfection, passion, or feeling—no ripple ruffling the calm sea, no grain of mud rendering turbid the pure water, no bond or obstacle interfering with independence—this, I think, is the most favourable aspect—the least merely negative aspect—of the quality implied by "Visuddhi." The monk is taught to seek

> the silence of the breast;
> Imaginations calm and fair:
> The memory like a cloudless air:
> The conscience as a sea at rest.[2]

But the idea of conscience has no exact counterpart in the Buddhist system, any more than has the Christian idea of sin, as implying either moral responsibility or the transgression of the commands of a Person.

Gazing out, like the sage of Lucretius, from the serene heights of wisdom, over the varied world of life, but radiating forth, unlike that sage, rays of kind feeling and love in every direction; calm amid storms, because withdrawn into a trance of dreamless unconsciousness; undisturbed, because allowing no external object to gain any hold on sense or emotion, or even on thought; owning nothing and wanting nothing; resolute, fearless, firm as a pillar; in utter isolation from all other beings, except by feeling kindly to them all—such is the ideal "Conqueror" of Buddhism. The last point of vantage by which existence can retain hold on him is gone: he cannot continue to exist!

It is a strange medley of contradictions; of noble ideas pushed to extravagant and impossible degrees.

[1] e.g. in Saṃyut. vii. 22–6, "Seeing that the doctrine has been by me so well spoken, made plain, laid open, proclaimed, all coverings cut, well may any noble youth who has entered the religious life in the faith of that doctrine—well may he exert effort: let skin and muscle and bone alone remain in his body, and flesh and blood dry up, there will be no standing still of his effort till he has reached the utmost point that can be reached by manly strength and manly effort and manly striving."

[2] Tennyson, *In Memoriam*.

This description of the positive element in the moral ideal of Buddhism, though sketched almost entirely in terms taken from the "sacred books," is not, of course, to be found in them in this shape, and claims only to represent the impression which the present writer has derived from those books. It is placed here, not as being in itself an indisputably true impression, but as suggesting a way of arranging the details of which it is a generalization.

In the production of this ideal, the destructive processes are more than the constructive. The removal of bonds and of disturbing influences, of all that causes either attachment or hostility, of all that can load the mind with fear or remorse, of all that can cloud the judgment or the mental vision—this removal of evil will be the principal object of effort. Along with this will go the cultivation of the kindly feelings, as the chief positive aim.

As subsidiary to these comes the choice of a mode of life in which the evil can be best removed, or in which the man can best detach himself from encumbrances. That life is the life of a member of the Sangha or Community. The householder or layman is at a great disadvantage; all the encumbrances have greater hold on him; and so long as he remains in the house-dwelling state, a certain secondary ideal is all he can hope to reach. To this house life a secondary set of aims and duties belongs; to this house life is addressed a special part of the teaching, particularly that which treats of heaven and of hell.

For in the ideal we have described there is no room for aspiration after praise or reward, nor for fear of blame or punishment; neither heaven nor hell has any proper place in the system. If they have any place, it is a secondary one, either as considerations to influence those who have not yet approached the ideal, or as facts which concern those who never approach it. But to the advanced disciple of the Buddha, hell is impossible and heaven indifferent: they are not heard of: the heaven and hell system is the religion of the layman.

Meanwhile, out of this inevitable preference for the ascetic life, and from its wide separation from the house life, there spring two special classes of duties—those of the monks toward their own order and towards householders, and those of the householder towards the monk.

Two important features of the ideal above described may possibly, being negative features, have escaped the reader's notice.

The Buddhist saint stands in no relation of dependence to any being above himself. There is no Creator, no Saviour, no Helper in his purview. Religious duties, properly so called, he has none. He has been his own light, his own refuge. He is what he is by grace of himself alone. Humility would not become him; for gratitude he has no occasion.[1] There is thus excluded, from anything but a temporary or subsidiary position, all that has elsewhere been chiefly meant by "religion," and much of what has elsewhere been known as "virtue."

The ideal we have been considering, although of a human character, is the ideal to which, according to Buddhist principles, not human life only but every form of life may rise. The Buddha has been, in former births, a stag, a dog, a quail; and what is a quail now may hereafter be a Buddha. For there is no impassable barrier between the various grades of life—of deities, men, demons, or brute animals. What is now a demon may, in his demon life, acquire merit which will profit him hereafter as a man. One "karma" or course of consequence may carry him through a succession of lives as an animal, a god, an animal again, a demon, and again as a deity or a man. It is only in the human stage that the highest condition, that of a Buddha, is attainable; but Nirvana is accessible to all: to the superior deities and to men directly, and ultimately to everything that lives. From this ultimate identification of the various forms of life arises a new and distorted branch of morality, giving exaggerated proportions to the duties of men towards the lower animals.

[1] Not a hint is to be met with of anything corresponding to that sense of gratitude to the Divine and Beneficent Power whom all other men and all other religions have recognized as giving "rain and fruitful seasons, filling their hearts with food and gladness."

CHAPTER VI

THE ABOLITION OF IGNORANCE

THE beginning and the end of Buddhism is the abolition of ignorance. Ignorance is not looked at only in the light of a defect, as the mere absence of knowledge: it is thought of as a positive evil. Under its terrible name, Avijjā, it hangs over all living beings like an active plague, ever spreading its effects in misery and death. It plays the part of a cruel giant, hurling poor mortals into hell, or grinding them along in a weary round of slavery. It is the first parent of the whole genealogy of human woe.

This notion of ignorance as a positive malignant power or calamity, is deeply engrained in Indian thought, and is a fundamental element of several of the philosophic systems, especially of that most prevalent of them all—the Vedanta. Ignorance, or nescience, is called "the root of all evil, the seed of the entire course of alternate birth and decay."[1] In the Buddhist mind this has become an instinctive habit of thought. A young man who had been brought up in a Buddhist monastery in Colombo used to express his desire for more education in this way: "I must at any cost get rid of this ignorance."

If ignorance then is so terrible, what is the knowledge that is sought?

It would be an utter mistake to think of Buddhism as addressed chiefly to the intellect, or as concerned with the promotion of learning. Its adherents are not required to furnish themselves with even the rudiments of ordinary culture, or to learn by heart any profession of faith. If Buddhism can be said to rest upon a creed, it is the shortest possible of creeds. There is no course of study prescribed for the ordinary disciple. The highest success is not out of the reach of the simplest. Learning is not highly esteemed.

[1] See Vedanta Sutra. S.B.E. xxxiv. 14, and Monier Williams, *Indian Wisdom*, p. 119.

The ignorance, which has to be abolished, is ignorance of a small body of practical "truths," as they are called.[1] That all which exists is perishable and inevitably subject to sorrow; that sorrow can be destroyed only by destroying desire and all that is associated with existence; and that Buddhism furnishes the way to this result—this conviction is what constitutes knowledge. All beings are by nature plunged in ignorance of these principles (and no wonder, since they are all false !) and an effective conviction of their truth is "knowledge."

All other learning is disparaged. Questions of science, geography, astronomy, or even of metaphysics, are set aside as useless subtleties. Ignorance of these things is not the ignorance that ruins.[2]

Constantly, therefore, as we meet with the terms "ignorance" and "knowledge"; constantly as we find the good Buddhist called the "wise" or the "learned"; characteristically as the Buddha is called "the Omniscient"; yet no emphasis is really laid on any other knowledge than that of the necessary connection of sorrow with desire and with existence. To know this fully is already to have "escaped." The "omniscient" Buddha, the Teacher of the three worlds, is one who has mastered this great principle, and has thereby escaped from further existence, and who teaches this, as the way of escape, to all other beings.

It will be seen now in what sense we say that the abolition of ignorance is the beginning and the end of Buddhism.

It is the beginning, because the whole system is founded on the realization of those "truths" which are the object of "knowledge." These lie at the foundation. The whole religion is said to have started, as far as the present age is concerned, with the discovery of these truths by Gotama, the Sakyan, the son of Suddhodana.

It is the end, because the whole system aims at producing in the disciple a similar conviction. When the disciple has attained that insight, by which the chain of causation is broken and re-birth made impossible—then the whole work has been done. He who sees clearly—no longer believing it on the assurance of others, nor arriving at it merely as a conclusion of reasoning—

[1] Avijjā is expressly defined as not knowing the Four Truths. Sanyut. Nik, xii. 2, 15.

[2] See note at end of this chapter.

that the cause of sorrow is desire, etc., has no longer any duties to perform, has no more virtues to acquire; no more reason to remain in life: his course is ended. This conviction is reached by different disciples at very different speeds. Many, by hearing the preaching of a Buddha, grasp it all at once, and are at once perfect. Others only enter on the course, and have still to run through long ages and many births before they arrive at insight.

It must be repeated, however, that the conviction of these principles is in a sense the starting-point as well as the goal of each disciple's course. Although the "truths" are not apprehended in their formulated shape, and with full personal realization till the end, yet some glimmering of them is necessary to make a man enter on the course at all. He has felt dissatisfied with the world; he is disgusted with the impermanence of things: he cries, "Ah! nothing in the world is eternal!" and so he turns to Buddhism. To arouse this sense of dissatisfaction, to elicit this cry of disgust, is the aim of all the Buddha's sermons and parables to beginners. To deepen this sense of dissatisfaction and to remove all doubt about the impermanence of things, is the purpose to which the training of the Community is directed. And from the detailed or scientific study of any of those things, of whose perishableness he needs to be convinced, the disciple is discouraged: such study does not tend—this is the express ground of the prohibition—to produce dissatisfaction.

Vital knowledge being thus concerned with a narrow range of propositions, deadly error is similarly limited. We read a great deal about the removal of doubt, and about fatal errors or heresies; but these are still concerned with the same point. The great heresies consist in the opinion that things are eternal, or that the self or personality in man has a continuous existence. And in regard to such questions as the ultimate nature of matter, elements, atoms, and such-like, or in regard to the nature of the soul (as we call it), or the existence of the individual, or of the Buddha, after death, whatever may be said is alike a heresy or error.[1]

So far is Buddhism from involving either learning or metaphysical inquiry. The destruction of ignorance is, in fact, a moral rather than an intellectual result.

[1] According to the earlier teaching: in after days the followers of the Buddha indulged freely in these speculations.

If it now be asked, How is this result attained? the answer is in the main such as we have already indicated. The mind of the learner must be awakened to attend to the point on which all turns; the hindrances in the way of his realizing it must be removed, and all the conditions of his life must be so arranged as to lead him to the true conclusion: in particular, and especially if a monk, he must practise the prescribed methods of meditation. Some men are from the outset better prepared than others; the eyes of their mind being purified from the dust of passion, and their hearts being softened by kindly feeling and quickened by enthusiasm or aspiration.

Gotama's own view of this receptivity, which distinguishes the ready hearer, has been shown to us in the tradition of what occurred when he first had become Buddha. He hesitated, the reader will remember, to enter on the task of teaching what he had come to know, because it seemed a hopeless task. "This doctrine," he said, "is not easy to understand for those who are sunk in lust and in hatred; those who are given up to lust and enfolded with thick darkness cannot see it. It is against the stream [of natural inclination], subtle, deep, difficult to see, minute." But the great Brahma urged that it was not hopeless: "There are beings," he said, "who have been born with eyes almost free from dust; they are dying from not hearing the doctrine; they will be understanders of the doctrine."

In many of the narratives of notable conversions, these two stages, the preparation of the hearer and the disclosure of the doctrine, are clearly distinguished. The main portion of the discourse advances the hearer to the highest degree of receptivity, and then the specific fundamental dogmas are stated, and he accepts them at once with personal realization. "When the Blessed One perceived that Yasa's mind was prepared, softened, freed from hindrances, delighted, and believing, then he made known to him that which is the peculiar doctrine of the Buddhas, —suffering, its cause, its destruction, the way."

It is worth while to quote here more fully a beautiful illustration which has been already referred to: "As in a lotus pond some flowers are under water, some reach to its surface, while others emerge and stand up out of the water, and the water does not touch them; so the eyes of some are almost free from dust, those of others covered with dust; some have keen sense, some blunt; some have good characteristics, some bad; some are easy to teach, and some difficult."

The reader must now be invited, if he has been sufficiently prepared, to the rather tedious but necessary effort, of a somewhat closer inquiry into these fundamental dogmas—the "Four Truths" and the "Chain of Causation."

NOTE TO CHAPTER VI

ABSTRUSE QUESTIONS

If the discussion of abstruse questions was discouraged by the Buddha, it is not because they were not—at any rate in the time of the compilers—much on men's lips. We read constantly of such questions as are raised by the antinomian, the fatalist, or the materialist; of theories of the eternity of matter; and even of schools which evaded all by asserting the impossibility of knowing. All such are called "diṭṭhi"—a term which without absolutely calling them false, stigmatizes them as "views." Of these, which are usually expressed in English by "heresies," the Brahmajala Sutta enumerates sixty-two.

What became of the Tathagata after death was a question which the Buddha often declined to answer. (Whether "Tathagata" in that connection means, as usually elsewhere, the Buddha, or—as is commonly said—the "individual," I cannot attempt to decide.) The Buddha met such questions by the counter-question: "Where does the fire go, when it goes out?"

It is worth while here to give an abbreviated translation of a Sutta in which this attitude is adopted; it is called "Vacchagotta's Fire Sutta." (Maj. Nik. 72.)

Gotama was asked: "Do you hold the view that the world is eternal?" He replied, "No." "That the world is not eternal?" "No." "That it has an end?" "No." "That it has not an end?" "No." "That the life and the body are the same?" "No." "That the life is one thing and the body another?" "No." "That the individual exists after death?" "No." "That he does not?" "No." "That he both exists and does not exist after death?" "No." "That he neither exists nor does not exist after death?" "No."

"How is this? You say 'No' to all these questions. What is the evil that you see, that you entirely refuse to adopt any of these views?"

"Every one of these is a mere 'view' (heresy), is holding a view—belongs to the jungle of mere opinion" (the Pali word for "holding" is similar to that for "jungle"), "the vain show of opinion, the writhings of opinion, the bonds of heresy; it involves pain, vexation, despair, and distress: it does not tend to dissatisfaction, or putting away desire, or the destruction or the quieting of it, or to knowledge, or to absolute Buddha-insight, or to Nirvana."

"Have you then any view?"

"This phrase 'view' the Buddha has put away. The Buddha has *seen* this: what form is, and its cause and its end; what sensation is, its cause and its end; what perception, what conformation, what consciousness is, and the cause and the ending of each. Thus by the . . . putting away of all fancied and imaginary notions of self-asserting individualist pride, the Tathagata is set free."

"Whither does the monk, whose mind is thus set free, go to be reborn?" "The phrase 'going to be reborn' does not apply." "Then is he not reborn?" "The phrase 'not being reborn' does not apply." "Then is he both reborn and not reborn?" "No." "Is he neither reborn nor not reborn?" "No."

"To all these questions you answer, 'No!' Here I am utterly at a loss, utterly confounded; and all the satisfaction I had in former conversation with you, Gotama, is gone."

"Be not at a loss, Vaccha, be not confounded! This doctrine is hard . . . and perceived only by the wise: it is hard for you who . . . have been trained and taught in another school. So let me ask you, Vaccha, this question, and answer it as you will. What think you? If fire is burning before you, you know: 'This is a fire burning before me.' If asked what causes that fire to burn, what would you say? 'Its catching hold of grass and sticks (or "the fuel," viz. grass and sticks).' If the fire goes out, you know that it has gone out? 'Yes.' And if asked where it has gone, east, west, north, or south, what would you say?"

"The phrase does not apply, Gotama. When by the exhaustion of the fuel, the grass and sticks, on which it has caught, and by the want of other supply, the fire has nothing to feed upon, it is said to be extinguished."

"Just so, Vaccha, when that form, in virtue of which the individual is so called, is abandoned, rooted out, felled, destroyed, so that it can never come up again, the individual is freed from the appellation of form; is (in a condition) deep, immeasurable, difficult to sound as the great ocean: the phrase 'he is born' does not apply, nor 'he is not born,' or the rest. So when that sensation, and that perception and those elements of being, and that consciousness, in virtue of which he was called an individual, are gone, none of the phrases about being born or not being born are applicable to the case." (It should be remembered that the term which we are obliged to render by "being born" implies strictly no more than "coming" or "going" into a state or condition.)

CHAPTER VII

THE METAPHYSICAL FORMULARIES

THE Founder of Buddhism, if any reliance at all is to be placed on the books which profess to describe his life and his teaching, had he been asked, " What are the fundamental and characteristic elements of your system ? " would certainly have replied, " The Four Noble Truths and the doctrine of the Chain of Causes."

These are not two distinct groups of dogmas; for the Chain of Causes is the fuller statement of that theory of the cause of life with its sorrows, which is embodied in the Four Truths. We might in fact call them one dogma, that of the Causation and Destruction of Sorrow. And this rests on the metaphysical principle, that all things whatever, being formed only by the union of elements, are sooner or later, by the dissolution of those elements, to break up.

It is impossible to exaggerate the importance which is assigned in the sacred books of Buddhism to these two closely-allied formularies. And if the present writer is guilty of repeating himself in regard to them, the excuse must be, that in no other way could any adequate idea be given of the interminable persistence with which his Buddhist authorities recur again and again to these assertions. Though it would be difficult to point to a single passage in which the Four Truths are directly brought to bear on any particular form of conduct, they underlie the whole.

The book of the Rule (Vinaya) opens, as the reader will remember, with the picture of the Buddha in the act of attaining Buddha-hood, or in the immediate enjoyment of Buddhahood attained, sitting under his sacred tree, and revolving in his mind backward and forward the twelve-fold links of the Chain of Causation, through which ignorance leads up to birth and to the sorrows of life. Knowing this, he was a Buddha. His first sermon, which set in motion the triumphant Wheel of his doctrine and system, consisted in the declaration of the "Four Truths." This formulary is constantly spoken of as "the characteristic teaching of the Buddhas;[1] as the "deep knowledge" in comparison with which mere morality is disparaged;[2] as the one incontrovertible, or unambiguous dogma.[3] It is in the search for this that mankind has been so long running through life after life.[4] He who understands them stands at the very door of "immortality";[5] he who sees the Chain of Causes and the nature of things ceases to inquire into past, present, or future.[6] This knowledge is placed above the law of love, and above meditation, as the end for which these are practised.[7] It is the crown of all supernatural powers.[8] A large part of the books is occupied with the statement and restatement of its elements in every conceivable order and combination.[9] The first forty chapters of one Collection (the Sanyutta Nikaya) are almost entirely devoted to the endless turning over of these formularies, and this practice is expressly recommended.[10]

Though I hope I have now sufficiently excited the reader's desire to know exactly what these dogmas are, I must yet, before I present them, remind him what that view of the human soul and of human life is, which they take for granted. For unless we have grasped that view of the human soul and of human life, we shall inevitably misunderstand the "Truths."

Buddhism does not hold that there is any such thing as a permanent independent soul, existing in or with the body, or migrating from one body to another. The Self or personality has no permanent reality: it is but the result of certain elements come together—a combination of faculties and characters. No one of these elements is a person, or soul, or Self, but to their combination the name Self is popularly applied. The death of

[1] e.g. M.V. i. 9.
[2] Brahmajāla S.
[3] Poththapada S. (Digh. Nik. ix. 38).
[4] M.V. vi. 29.
[5] Sanyut. Nik. xii. 28, 37.
[6] *Ib.* 20.
[7] Angut. iv. 190.
[8] Sāmañ. S. 97.
[9] Maj. Nik. ix., for instance, is the multiplication of the Four Truths into the Twelve Causes.
[10] Sanyut. xii. 32. This almost mechanical method is found chiefly in the later parts of the Pitakas, but the estimate of the formularies is the same everywhere.

a man is the breaking up of this combination; not the separation of soul from body, but the dissolution both of the body and of the rest of that aggregate of faculties and characters on which life depended.[1]

Life, then, is a combination; separate those elements and life is at an end. If they never combined, there would be no life, no self, no personality.

But as things are there is at work in the world a force, by which these elements, these faculties, these characters—form, sense, consciousness, mental energy—*tend to recombine.* No sooner has a man died, and his life-elements been scattered, than they enter, under the pressure of this force, into new combinations. A new life is the result. There is a fatal tendency to reproduce life (it arises out of past action, and its name is "karma"), and it takes advantage of a fatal attraction (upādāna), by which the elements of life cling to one another. And so, no sooner is a man dead, by the dissolution of his life-elements, than he is hurried on into some other life by a new combination. For during life he had set in motion that fatal force—all lives set it in motion, and the world is as full of it as matter is of gravity—that aggregate of the results of action, which causes re-combination. It remains, after the man is gone, as a kind of *desire for new life,* and animates, as it were, *with a desire to recombine,* those broken elements of life.

To avoid encumbering the matter with ideas foreign to our European thought, I have spoken so far of *human* life. But in Buddhist thought there is no permanent distinction between human life and other kinds or grades of life. When the life-elements by which a man lived break up, they may reunite to form either a man, or a deity, or a dog. He "goes" according to his "karma." According to the total or resultant force of all the actions of the particular series of lives that is in ques-

[1] Transmigration is not, in Buddhist theory, the evolution of character, nor is "transmigration of souls" a term applicable to what Buddhism teaches. It is not a Buddhist sentiment that finds expression in the lines—

> "The man remains, and whatsoe'er
> He wrought of good or brave
> Will mould him through the cycle year
> That dawns beyond the grave."—TENNYSON.

The man does not remain; though "whatsoe'er he wrought" will "mould" some new combination of elements, not necessarily into a man.

tion, he "goes" to a new condition (gati). In the new condition his life-elements are said (for it is impossible that such a theory should be perfectly consistent) to be new: nothing has passed on from the earlier life to the later except the force which has compelled the new combination. That force is the "action," the moral result of the past combinations in that series.[1] It is this continuity, the continuity of "karma," that enables the Buddhist to say "*he* goes," and to attribute to one being the whole series of lives.[2]

But "karma" itself could do nothing without "upadana." If all tendency to recombine were gone, if the being had been so trained in resisting all kinds of attraction, that there should not remain even that attraction by which life-elements recombine, if "clinging" of every sort had been destroyed in him, then, after his death there would be no recombination, he would be free.

To be thus after death detached, he must be detached here. He must resist all attractions here, that the life-attraction may not reappear after his death. (For there is more in common, than seems to European thought, between the desire of a conscious being for objects which, for instance, he sees, and the "clinging" of the unconscious life-elements to one another. The distinction between the conscious and unconscious is not so essential to the Buddhist mind.) The man who desires to be free must not love life: he must fix his mind on the idea of dissolution, transitoriness: he must convince himself that he need not, and in some sense does not, exist. Then when he breaks up, there will be nothing left: no fuel will remain, not even the least tinder of desire, for the flame of life to catch upon: he will go out altogether.

It is in the light, first, of this view of human and other life (a view not, in its main features, peculiar to Buddhism or newly taught by Gotama) that the Four Truths must be read.

And there is a second feature of the mind of those days which must be recognized, a feature common to all the philosophy of the India of Gotama's time, and present to some degree in the India of all times hitherto—the dreary view of life as a calamity. The fact that man is born to trouble seems to have pressed with

[1] A series is closed by Nirvana, or by the end of the cycle (Kalpa).

[2] See the Sutta on pp. 188 sq.

crushing weight upon the Indians of the sixth century before Christ, and to have led them to formulate for their posterity a philosophy rooted in pessimism, and directed to the one problem, how to escape from the life in which evil is inherent. The same fact exists for all men at all times, and how to escape from evil is a problem which all men at all times have to face. But other nations, whether in hopeless fatalism, or in lightness of heart, or in practical activity, have been able more or less to put the question aside; or when they have dealt with it (apart from the Revelation which teaches that true happiness can live in sorrow and pain) have been content with partial solutions. How shall we be happy after death if not here? How shall we secure as large as possible a share of happiness along with the inevitable trouble? Most men have had enough of hopefulness to address themselves rather to the search for happiness than to the flight from pain. All men, according to Aristotle, seek happiness. But the Indian Aryans, of Gotama's day at least, looked at the dark side; nor did they find in the universality of the fact of pain any reason for feeling it the less. They saw it in the most general and abstract form, and yet felt it most intensely.

The first of the "Four Noble [Aryan] Truths" is the assertion of this: Sorrow is universal. "This, mendicants, is the noble truth of sorrow; birth is sorrow, old age is sorrow, sickness is sorrow, death is sorrow, the presence of the unloved is sorrow, the absence of the loved is sorrow, all that one wishes for and does not get is sorrow; briefly, the five elements by which beings hold to existence are sorrow."

So far as this asserted only the existence of pain, it was no new discovery, but so far as it asserted that pain is the principal fact which ought to be taken account of in determining man's aim and conduct, it was a hideous falsehood. The statement is ambiguous, either obviously true or utterly false. But we must suppose that it was just by reason of its ambiguity that it won acceptance. The whole superstructure of Buddhism was vitiated by the fallacy which underlies this so-called "truth." Appealing to the acknowledged fact that sorrow is inherent in life as it is, men have been persuaded that life cannot be made happy or noble, and that they ought to order their conduct not with a view to ennobling life, but with a view to escaping it. Such, however, is the end which Buddhism professedly aims at.

The second Noble Truth is far more true, and contains, in fact, all that is most valuable in Buddhism. It is thus stated: "This, mendicants, is the noble truth of the cause of sorrow. Desire [literally, "thirst"], that leads from birth to birth and is accompanied by pleasure and pain, seeking its gratification here and there; namely, desire of sensual pleasure, desire of existence, desire of wealth"[1] (or better, perhaps, "of annihilation").

The treatment of sensual desire as the cause of sorrow is the moral, practical, and, from a Buddhist point of view, the superficial part of the system. That the desire of pleasure leads to sorrow is indeed a truth not peculiar to Buddhism; but it is very earnestly insisted on in the Buddhist books. The desire for property is also obviously a cause of sorrow; but that these are the only causes of it is of course untrue: the Buddhist writers saw this clearly, and attribute at least as much evil to hatred. There is something deeper than this intended by the Second Truth.

The characteristic part of the statement is, that the thirst for existence is the cause of sorrow. It "leads from birth to birth." Existence rests on combination: life is nourished only by attachment to objects. Were there no contact with external objects, no contact of touch or thought, there could be no life. All grasping at outward objects is virtually a clinging to existence, it springs from a desire to exist. And it leads to sorrow, because in every part of life, and in the possession or the loss of objects of desire, sorrow is necessarily involved.

Further, and more deeply and universally still, that unconscious but unextinguished craving after existence, perpetuated after death by the act-force of a man or any other living thing—this brings about re-birth, and so sorrow.

[1] *Vibhavatanhá.* There is a curiously wide difference of opinion about the meaning of this word. The European scholars generally understand "desire of wealth or prosperity," taking "Vibhavo" in its sense of "power or prosperity"; while the Pali commentators taking "Vibhavo" as a different word which means "annihilation," render it "that desire which is encouraged by the expectation of annihilation at death—the desire to "eat and drink because to-morrow we die." "Ucchedadiṭṭhi sahagato rāgo vibhavataṇháti vuccati." —*Visuddhi Magg.* "Ucchedadiṭṭhi sahagatassa rāgassa etaṃ adhivacanaṃ.—*Saccavibhang. Atthakathā.* Meanwhile some Sinhalese authorities understand it as desire to escape from Karma, not by Nirvana but by physical annihilation.

The Third Noble Truth is but the necessary sequel of the second. The cessation of sorrow is effected by the eradication of desire. Here again, the words have a more obvious moral meaning and a deeper metaphysical. Obviously—and this forms a large part of the practical system of Buddhism, especially as a monastic rule—by diminution of the list of necessaries, by detachment from objects of desire, by the cultivation of indifference, a large class of pains could be avoided. But this touches only the surface of life. No extension of this principle would lead to Nirvana—though excessive asceticism may lead to death. Gotama asserted a principle which was to go far deeper than the region of pleasures and pains; which was to strike at the very roots of life—the principle that if desire for the fundamental elements of being could be eradicated, if there were no clinging to those elements by whose union existence is rendered possible—then there would be no birth and no sorrow, because there would remain nothing to be born. The living being, he seems to argue, has a hold on life; it has grasped at the conditions of life: if it can loose that grasp, can shake off the longing which has made it cling to those foundations of life, its further existence will be impossible. The sensual desires are but one manifestation of this craving for a hold on things: they are the first to be cast away: but far down below, nearer the central roots of being, are links which must be broken, longings of an unconscious innate thirst for existence which must be extinguished, before a being can escape from the dreary round of birth and death and birth, with its attendant sorrow.

The Chain of Causation carries the inquiry back behind desire, to show how desire itself comes out of ignorance, and having stated the links of cause through which desire comes from ignorance, shows how desire, through existence and birth, leads to sorrow. It is more than an explanation in detail of what the Four Truths state about the relation of pain to desire, because it carries the analysis back to the ignorance, the first root of all evil. It is thus stated: [1] "From ignorance come conformations; from conformations comes consciousness; from consciousness come name and corporeal form; from name and corporeal form come the six fields (of sense); from the six fields comes contact

[1] I have adopted Professor Oldenberg's translation. The word here rendered "conformations" is "Saṇkhārā," on which see above, p. 50 n.

(between the senses and their objects); from contact comes sensation; from sensation comes thirst (or desire); from desire comes clinging (to existence); from clinging (to existence) comes being; from being comes birth; from birth come old age and death, pain and lamentation, suffering, anxiety, and despair. This is the origin of the whole realm of suffering."

"But if ignorance be removed [by the complete removal of desire] this brings about the removal of conformations; by the removal of conformations—and so on. This is the removal of the whole realm of suffering."

"It is utterly impossible," says Professor Oldenberg—and who will attack a metaphysical puzzle which he has declared insoluble?—to trace from beginning to end a connected meaning in the formula." "Even the ancient Buddhists found this a stumbling-block." They make no attempt to elucidate the earlier stages of it. I must be content with a few remarks.

(Around the words "by the complete extinction of desire" I have placed a bracket, because as they stand in the English they might mislead. The "desire" here is not the "desire" or "thirst" which occupies the eighth place in the chain, nor is it the "desire" of the Second Truth. The whole phrase, "by the complete extinction of desire," is one word in the original, and refers to the practical method of extinguishing ignorance, or rather to the character of the man in whom it is extinguished.)

From consciousness to desire the course is not very difficult. Among the root elements of being, or at any rate of life, is consciousness. The conscious being *identifies* outward objects, giving them name and form: thus discriminated they become the *objects of particular senses;* the organs of sense are brought into *contact* with them; thus a keen impression from the object, *sensation,* is conveyed to the mind; the mind, dwelling upon the sensation, *desires* the object.

How desire leads to the *clinging* first to outward objects, and further and deeper down to the elements of life themselves, we have already seen.

Then the whole statement, from the second link to the twelfth, may be read thus: "The conscious being, finding itself in the world of objects, naturally tends to attach itself to them, and to create for itself a continuous series of relations to them, by which its existence is perpetuated in a world of sorrow."

And now perhaps we can read the first link thus: "This is because it knows no better." A being that knows that all existence is sorrow, and knows what causes sorrow, and how it can be destroyed, would allow none of this process to take place. But how ignorance or consciousness or any of those earlier links can exist before existence itself has been produced—this is mystery. And the value which the early Buddhists, and their Founder, attached to all this, remains inexplicable.

In the Pali texts I have never met with any attempt either to explain or to illustrate either particular sequences or the whole Chain. In one or two places a praiseworthy effort is made to explain by illustrations the idea of cause in general. The effect and the cause are like two bundles resting on one another: as the rivers are affected by the sea, as fire arises from sticks, so do pleasure and sorrow arise from contact: as light without something to reflect it falls ineffective, so without pleasure and pain the whole Chain of Causation is null. And so on.[1]

Nor have these dogmas had, for the majority of Buddhist teachers, any bearing on conduct. When the lesson is practical, it is never founded upon those laws which the "Chain of Causes" enumerates; they belong to a region anterior to existence, and therefore, of course, to practice. For instance, there are innumerable passages which urge the destruction of lust or desire; but is there one in which the method recommended is expressly founded on the principle that desire is the immediate effect of sensation? Still less is the relation of consciousness to the "fields of sense" brought to bear on conduct.[2] In fact, the moral system as we find it in the books would lose nothing by the removal of the "Chain of Causation."

And yet it is impossible to doubt—if we have any

[1] Saṃyut, xii. These and other illustrations are drawn out in the *Questions of Milinda*. S.B.E., xxxv., p. 85, etc.

[2] For instance, in Saṃyut, xii. 58 "Name and form" is said to get a hold on the mind, not of the man who indulges "consciousness," but of him who finds pleasure in such things as the heresies, passions, and other "bonds." The origin of "consciousness" is attributed in the same chapter to "bonds," not to "conformations." And in the next, "desire" (which in the Chain is the cause of "clinging") is said to be produced by devotion to "clinging." And all this in a series of passages expressly concerned with the Chain of Causation. So in Maj. Nik. x., pp. 60, 61, "sensation," "clinging," and "the fields of sense" are treated without regard either to their order or to their relation to one another in the series.

history of Gotama's views at all—that this appeared to him in the light of an ultimate and precious truth. He seemed to himself to see clearly all the steps by which ignorance begets birth and pain. The sight of these was his inspiration, his Buddhahood: it sent him forth full of enthusiastic resolve to bring others to the same triumphant vision; full of confidence that it would mean as much to others as it did to him! It is disappointing that we cannot now enter further into his experience.

The isolation of the celebrated dogmas from practical application in the moral teaching is notably illustrated by that to which we have now to return: the Fourth Truth, and the "Eightfold Way" which forms the substance of it.

The Fourth Truth runs thus: "This, O mendicants, is the noble truth of the way of living which leads to the extinction of sorrow: it is this noble Eightfold Way—right faith, right resolve, right speech, right action, right living, right effort, right recollectedness, right meditation.

It may be paraphrased thus: "Desire is eliminated by following the general course of conduct taught by the Buddha." We are obliged to say "the general course," etc., because the Eightfold Way, constantly as it is praised, is never explained. Perhaps the term refers to some system of which all record is lost; perhaps there was an intention to draw up such a system, which was never executed; perhaps the word "Eightfold" had some associations unknown to us; but however that may be, there is no Eightfold Path to be found in the books, no eight branches of study or practice corresponding to the eight names. It is not enough to say that no one, but for this title, would ever have noticed any such divisions or such a method as these eight names imply; the strictest search fails to discover any.[1]

The Eightfold Way is also called, as by Gotama himself,[2] the Middle Way, sometimes as being in the mean between austerity and indulgence, sometimes as a middle between the assertion and the denial of certain metaphysical positions. But neither under this title has the formula any important part in the developed system.

[1] In Saṃyut, xii. 65, The Eightfold Way is compared to an ancient road to an ancient city, made by men of old, which has now been found, repaired, and built. The Buddhas of old trod this way: Gotama, in his wanderings, found it. See Note B at the end of this chapter.

[2] See p. 81 and Maj. Nik. 3, an important Sutta in this connection.

But although these oft-named formulas seem thus to stand apart from the practical moral teaching, the whole of that teaching rests upon a principle which is closely akin to the "Truths" and the "Causes": the principle of impermanence; of the inevitable dissolution of all things, being, as all things are, made up by the union of elements. "Aniccā vata saṅkhārā!"[1] "Ah! composite things are not eternal!" Or, as Rhys Davids renders it, "How transitory are all component things!" This expresses the teaching of Gotama quite as correctly as do the Truths themselves; though the exclamation in this form is not, so far as I have read, ever attributed to Gotama himself, but always to his followers. The sentiment which it expresses is simpler and truer than the "First Truth," and much better calculated to influence conduct. Upon it, rather than on the Truths, Buddhist morality is founded.

On the conviction that all things are transitory depends that feeling of distaste, which drives men, as we have already seen in the history, to lead ascetic lives, and to enter the Community, or, if they remain laymen, to prepare for death by obtaining merit. To awaken and maintain that distaste for the world, are instituted all the processes of meditation, especially the favourite meditation on the foulness of the body; and the rules of the Community are directed (as has been already said) to the same end. Closely connected with the impermanence of outward objects is the unreality of the personal self—a doctrine which has practically influenced the moral system, and which is a special topic of meditation.

To put the practical system shortly, Buddhism teaches: That if men cling to objects, and thence are guilty of lust and hatred and pride, it is because they are ignorant that those objects are not permanent, while by the knowledge of their impermanence men become detached from objects, and their passions are eradicated. This detachment, and the "disgust" which leads to it—though already several times referred to—deserve to be the subject of a separate chapter.

[1] "Aniccā vata mayam!" "Ah! we are all transitory," is the cry of all beings when the lion-like Buddha utters his voice.—Angut, iv. 35. This is "the essential principle."—Maj. Nik., 35.

NOTE TO CHAPTER VII

NOTE ON THE EIGHT-FOLD WAY

THE Eight-fold Way, though constantly alluded to, is seldom treated under its eight heads. It is stated in Maha Vagga, i. 6, 18, 22, named in it, 7, 6; but not, I think, afterwards referred to in the Vinaya.

In other parts of the Pitakas there is no place in which the eight elements of the Way are so treated as to form a complete classification, under eight heads, of the whole Buddhist method. It is generally only named, as in the Dhammapada (i. 20), in Saṃyut, xii. 27, etc., in Maj. Nik., 13. The only attempt I have met with, in the Pitaka books, to exhibit the eight heads as embracing the whole system, is in the Visākha Sutta (Maj. Nik, p. 800, *Trenckner*), where they are grouped in relation to (1) *knowledge*, "right belief" being concerned with the apprehension of knowledge and "right resolution" with its application; (2) *conduct*, "right conduct, speech, livelihood" being connected with moral conduct; and (3) *meditation*, "right effort, recollection, recollectedness" being concerned with meditation. In Saṃyut, 2, 7, 8, the question is asked: "How does good company lead in the eight-fold way?" The answer is: "It promotes right belief, right resolution, right conduct, and right effort."

In other places the eight, or some of them, are applied as categories from the particular point of view the writer is taking. Thus in Maj. Nik., 60, right belief, resolution, speech, are treated as one series opposed to three stages of heresy.

Individual heads, apart from the rest of the series, are sometimes amply treated, e.g. "right belief" by itself is constantly and abundantly enlarged on; so is "right speech" in connection with the prohibition of falsehood. "Sammāsati," in Angut, iv. 30, is opposed to "muṭṭhasati" and "asampajānasati," and "sammāsamādhi" to "asamāhito," or "vibbhantacitto." The only allusion I have noticed to "sammāsaṇkappo" is in Angut, iv. 31, where, however, it is named "sammāpanidhi."

Occasionally individual terms of the Eight-fold Way are used in quite a different connection; as in Angut, iv. 30, where S. sati and S. samādhi form, with "ungreed" and "unhate," four "dhammapadas." So far for the Sutta Pitaka.

In the Suttanta division of Sutta Vibhanga (of the Abhidhamma Pitaka) the eight heads are thus explained: "Right belief" is knowledge or intellectual grasp of the Four Truths; "right resolution" is carrying out this knowledge in a two-fold way, viz. by leaving the world (nekhamma), and by meek and friendly conduct; "right speech" is avoiding falsehood, slander, abuse, and chattering; "right conduct" is avoiding three of the other things forbidden by the Five Precepts, viz. taking life, stealing, and sexual sin; "right livelihood" is the reverse of "wrong livelihood" (micchājīvo), and is elsewhere defined as being distinguished from the livelihood of the poor who take life from poverty and of princes who take life from pride.[1] (The proper livelihood is either that of a monk, or that of a cultivator or of a merchant, as these are supposed not to involve taking life.) "Right effort" is fourfold, as it aims at (1) the destruction of demerit which has been acquired, (2) avoiding the acquirement of new demerit, (3) the acquirement of new merit, (4) the increase of merit by (a) not losing it, (b) increasing it. The terms which describe this effort are such as imply successively the aim, the undertaking, the setting oneself in order for carrying it out (as a man takes up the reins and gets his horses in hand in order to drive), and finally, exertion. "Right recollectedness" is knowing and seeing clearly the true character of (1) the body, (2) the emotions, and (3) the mind. "Right meditation" is the fourfold method of meditation (jhānaṃ), in which the five "coverings" are removed, and five grades of contemplation, ending in "unity" or complete collectedness, are achieved.

Outside the Three Pitakas an elaborate but artificial explanation is given by Buddhaghosha in Sumangala Vilāsini (i. *ad fin.*, p. 314). "Right belief" is fully discussed, and then each of the remaining seven is treated in its effect on the rest of the character (sahajāte dhamme). S. sankappo tests, S. vāco grasps, S. kammanto originates, S. ājīvo purifies, S. vāyāmo exerts, S. sati fixes, S. samādhi unifies. This is not an interpretation of the system, but an ingenious application of the terms from a given point of view. The same author, in Visuddhi Magga, explains particular terms in great detail, e.g. S. ājīvo, under the title of ājīvapparisuddhi-sīlam, in reference to the proper way of monks' begging.

[1] But "micchājīvo" seems to be used in Culla Vagga, i. 14, for all kinds of ill ways of spending time, both by word and deed, especially in games, etc. It is wrongly rendered "lying ways of living"; "micchā" being simply the reverse of "sammā."

CHAPTER VIII

DISGUST AND DETACHMENT

GOTAMA is represented, as we have already seen, as disparaging the studies of physics and even of philosophy, because they do not tend to produce dissatisfaction (nibbidā). This dissatisfaction, or disgust—for so it may properly be rendered—is not only an intellectual conviction that there is no permanent satisfaction to be found in transitory things, but also a positive shrinking from them ; such a strong feeling as sends the man away from his home and his pleasures, crying, " How repulsive these things are, now I see them in their true light ! " When Yasa, the rich young man who had been delicately nurtured, with three several palaces for the three seasons, saw the unseemly appearance of the sleeping women, the " danger " —this is the characteristic word—of it all became clear to him, and his mind was filled with disgust. " Oh ! how distressing ! " he cried ; " Oh ! how dangerous ! "

Gotama himself was led to " go forth " by the same emotion. He used to consider with himself the facts of age, disease, and death, till he determined to escape them by betaking himself to the houseless life. Of this, the well-known story of the three sights—how the prince in driving through the city, saw an old man, a sick man, and a corpse—is a later amplification. It is almost an inevitable embodiment of the recognized law, by which the wish for " pabbajjā," the resolve to become a mendicant, was supposed to be excited by disgust at old age, disease, and death. "Seeing others afflicted, seeing men seized with disease, tormented and overcome by decay, so shalt thou be heedful and leave desire behind, and so never return to existence." [1]

The object most calculated, in Buddhist view, to produce this disgust, is the human body itself, whether living or dead. One

[1] Sutt. Nipat. v. 17. S.B.E., x., b., p. 209.

of the commonplaces, or stock formulas, which constantly recur, is the enumeration of the thirty-two impurities of the living body. Its secretions and excretions are to be separately and minutely contemplated: attention is to be paid to its separate parts and tissues—bone, skin, nerve, and blood, and the internal organs, each in turn, till the man is sickened at himself. He is also recommended to observe a corpse, first newly dead, then cast out on the burial ground, then in each stage of putrescence and all the loathsome accompaniments of decay.

The reader may look for himself at Sutta Nipata, i. 11, in *Sacred Books of the East*, vol. X, b., p. 32, or at the less revolting, but less typical passage in Dhammapada, xi. 2, in the same volume, (a) p. 41. "Look at this dressed-up lump, covered with wounds . . . wasted, full of sickness, and frail. This heap of corruption breaks to pieces . . . these white bones . . . what pleasure is there in looking at them?"

This sort of mental exercise is not only highly commended, but treated as the type of all meditation. It is given in several places as the specimen of right effort of mind or right meditation—not, I suppose, as being the best, but as the commonest and most elementary. "A man should do his best, when a good point of meditation has occurred to him, to keep it before his mind; such as the idea of a skeleton, a corpse eaten by worms, a corpse turning blue, festering, splitting up, blown out by decay."[1]

"All evil passions proceed from the body." "Passion and hatred have their origin thence; dislike and liking and terror are born thence; thence arise doubts, which vex the mind as boys vex a crow."[2] "The dissolution of one's own body is seen by the noble ones to be joy."[3]

Among the few traces of methods of meditation which survive in actual practice in Ceylon, is the recitation, by each young novice, when he is invested with the yellow robe, of the thirty-two impurities of the body.

I cannot but remark upon the degrading effect which must follow on the encouragement of such a view of the body. I know that there have been, in the morbid development of

[1] Angut. iv. 14 *et passim*.
[2] Sutt. Nipat. ii. 5.
[3] *Ib.* iii. 12. Maj. Nik. x. *et passim*.

asceticism among Christians, no small excesses in the same direction; but they have been morbid and exceptional; they have never been supported by doctrine. Christianity has never ceased to assert the glorious and eternal destiny of the body. There is room for a true disgust, which may ennoble a man. It was the sight, momentary and unsought, of the pitiable decay of a human body which had been clothed a little while before in beauty and pride, that aroused the " nibbidā " that sent Ignatius Loyola to a life of self-sacrifice. But to dwell long and frequently on the ignoble aspects of our bodily nature is base, and a treason to humanity. One's manhood resents it. It is refreshing to contrast the healthy and manly tone in which Shakespeare can both acknowledge all the weakness of our poor bodies, and stand in awestruck admiration too at their nobleness. Science has taught us indeed to see, even in the several organs and in the processes of flesh and blood, nothing but what is wonderful and admirable; but the Jewish Psalmist—before the days of the microscope—had struck the highest note of all, when he thought how his body from the first had been fashioned by its Maker, fearfully and wonderfully made.

And if a Christian ever is led to speak, as Barrow somewhere does (comparing it with the reasonable soul) of " this feculent lump of organized clay, our body " ; yet he will not hesitate to think with admiration, both of the bodily members and of the senses ; as when he teaches us to thank God for " a comely body framed by His curious artifice, various organs fitly proportioned, situated, and tempered, for strength, ornament, and motion," by Him Who " by His kind disposal furnishes our palates with variety of delicious fare, entertains our eyes with pleasant spectacles, ravishes our ears with harmonious sounds, perfumes our nostrils with fragrant odours, cheers our spirits with comfortable gales, etc." [1]

In Buddhism the way of treating the body never varies, I believe, from the base point of view which I have described. But apart from the consideration of the body, there are other considerations, more philosophical and less sensuous, by which " nibbidā " is excited ; and the disgust with the impermanence of things sometimes rises, as in the case of Gotama himself, to a noble discontent.

[1] Barrow, *Sermons*, i. 200.

Indeed we meet here with a patient and well-directed effort to grapple with the practical problem, and to trace the evil of lust to its earliest manifestations; to cut up, as the books say, the root of it. The Buddhist disciple will carefully avoid giving any external object a hold upon him, or allowing himself to take hold of, or to rest upon any external thing. To this end he will guard his senses with the utmost care. The sphere of each sense will be regarded by him as a region of danger, and he will be constantly on the watch lest either sense should form a link between him and its object; lest any pleasure or pain should establish itself in his consciousness in consequence of the contact of eye, ear, tongue, nose, touch, or thought (the simpler motions of thought are reckoned with the senses, which are counted as six) with anything seen, heard, tasted, smelt, touched, or perceived in the mind. He guards these senses (the phrase is incessantly repeated), covers them up, and shuts out impressions. If any assail him he says to himself, "This is a vain impression, the effect of an unreal appearance of things, which have no permanent being," and so he throws it off.

He is recommended, in order to avoid impressions, not to observe—the rules generally take their form from the sense of sight—any detail or characteristic of any object. He should not know, for instance, when he sees a figure, whether it is a man or a woman; whether the object before him is a stone or a mango, a good mango or a bad one; lest, observing details, he should linger on them, and attachment be produced. A curious play on words gives point to this advice. A mark, or characteristic detail, is called in Pali "nimittaṃ," and in regard to this, its strict logical meaning, the disciple should not "apprehend details"—not be "nimittagāhī." But the same word had a popular use in reference to the marks of female beauty, and "nimittagāhī" then stands for "falling in love." The disciple must avoid being captivated by any object.

This analysis, which deserves, I think, serious admiration, is sometimes pushed beyond the region of sense into that of logic. He should cultivate abstraction, lest attention to details should give room for desire.

Another phase of the same treatment of this matter, though more abstruse still, is important, because it has determined many forms of expression which are common in the books, and explains the position of "Name and Form" in the Chain of Causation.

What assails the sense is an individual object. It owes its capacity for assailing the sense to its being particular and definite, and to its being recognized as such. When therefore the mind has identified any object, realized its form and given it a name, the mind has submitted itself to the influence of that object, and the next step will be to attach itself to it. In order then to be free from the dominion of outward things, we must refuse to identify, or to compare, or to let the mind pass from one to the other or dwell on each in turn. We must withdraw attention more and more from particular objects of sense or thought, till there is no perception of differences, till we are conscious only of a formless universe, of a colourless infinite, till even the distinction between finite and infinite has vanished; till no idea whatever remains. The conclusion is unpractical, and indeed absurd; it is an instance of what I have called "noble ideas pushed to extravagant and absurd degrees."

While the disciple practises in himself these methods of detachment, there is a good deal of an obviously practical kind that can be done to make his course easier, by actual removal of the objects which men desire, or of the habit of depending on them. To be without possessions, and to care for none; to have few necessaries: this is the favourable condition. To secure this wise men find home life cramped and full of disturbances; they "go away" into the free open-air life of him who has nothing to lose. They wish to be like the solitary rhinoceros, to sail away like the swan and be at peace; to be like a bird, which carries no weight but its wings! The monk, in particular, has no belongings except the "four requisites"—clothing, food, bedding, and medicine, and these are of the simplest kind. With these he is to be content. While he uses each, he makes a special effort of recollectedness, reminding himself that he takes them only as necessaries, and does not cling to them. When he takes up his robe, he is to say to himself, "I take this merely to protect my body from heat and cold and other inconveniences." This exercise is very highly commended, and its practical value is entirely lost sight of in view of the merit which it is supposed to secure. "If a monk in the use of his robe, his alms-food, his dwelling, his medicines and condiments, exercises unlimited recollectedness of mind, unlimited in each of these cases will be his accumulation of good deeds and merits, and reward of joy, bliss-producing, heaven-ensuring, leading to all delight and joy and happiness and pleasure and bliss." It is as impossible to calculate the merit in each of these acts as to calculate the waters in the sea.[1]

The preciousness of seclusion, and its necessity to the attainment of insight, form the subject of innumerable sermons, and many Jataka stories (stories of what the Buddha did in former births) are devoted to this theme.

Innumerable too are the similes by which detachment is illustrated. The monk who has overcome desire has cut the strap, the thong, the chain, the bar: he has dammed up the waters, cut down the forest, crushed the snake; the arrow is drawn out of his wound; the streams are dried; he is like a well-thatched house which no rain can enter. No fuel is added to the fire, or oil to the lamp of lust; the hot vessel is cooled; the tree is rooted up. Dearest image of all, he is like the pure lotus leaf, to which no water can cling.

Such is a sketch, in the language as exclusively as possible of the Pitaka books, of the aim and method of the Buddhist ascetic, in his search for "detachment."

It is natural at first sight to compare the Buddhist's seclusion with that of the Christian monk, and even to compare the detachment of the Buddhist with that of the Christian. No doubt there have been Christian monks whose solitude was retirement and no more. But if the two *ideals* are to be compared—and this is what is to our present purpose—it will at once appear that the contrast is more important than the resemblance; for the Buddhist's solitude is a withdrawal from all things to nothing; the Christian's, from other things to God.

In seeking for freedom by diminishing the number of necessaries, and for opportunity by seclusion and leisure, the Christian ascetic agrees with the Buddhist. But they differ *toto cœlo* in their views both of what they leave and of what they seek. The Buddhist leaves the world and mortifies the body because he thinks them worthless or even evil in themselves: the Christian leaves the world because he himself is sinful, and liable through his own fault to make a bad use of God's good

[1] Angut. iv. 51.

creatures; and in leaving them he feels that he sacrifices them to God. Even more complete is the contrast in regard to what each seeks. The Christian would "go away," if he could, from every created thing, that he might go to God, the One and infinite Good. He strives to shut the senses, to shut out the world, to forget self, because he has in view an infinite field for the exercise of all his faculties upon a perfect object. The Buddhist would, in theory, withdraw his faculties from all exercise whatever.[1]

It is impossible to imagine a greater interval between two ideals, for the interval is strictly infinite; between that which contains only the negative, and that which adds to it the infinite positive.

Here is the climax of Buddhist attainment:—

"Then the Blessed One entered into the first stage of deep meditation. And rising out of the first stage he passed into the second. And rising out of the second stage he passed into the third. And rising out of the third stage he passed into the fourth. And rising out of the fourth stage of deep meditation he entered into the state of mind to which the infinity of space is alone present. And passing out of the mere consciousness of the infinity of space he entered into the state of mind to which the infinity of thought is alone present. And passing out of the mere consciousness of the infinity of thought he entered into the state of mind to which nothing at all was specially present. And passing out of the consciousness of no special object he fell into a state between consciousness and unconsciousness. And passing out of the state between consciousness and unconsciousness he fell into a state in which the consciousness both of sensations and of ideas had wholly passed away."[2]

Contrast with this the Christian aspiration:—

"If to any the tumult of the flesh were hushed, hushed the images of earth, and waters, and air, hushed also the poles of heaven, yea the very soul be hushed to herself, and by not thinking on self surmount self, hushed all dreams and imaginary revelations, every tongue and every sign, and whatsoever exists

[1] Happily the theory is not fully carried into practice, though it affects practice injuriously. The next chapter will show a better aspect of its application.

[2] Above, p. 49.

only in transition, since if any could hear, all these say, 'We made not ourselves, but He made us Who abideth for ever.' If then having uttered this, they too should be hushed, having roused only our ears to Him Who made them, and He alone speak, not by them, but by Himself, that we may hear His Word, not through any tongue of flesh, nor angel's voice, nor sound of thunder, nor in the dark riddle of a similitude, but might hear Whom in these things we love, might hear His very Self without these (as we too now strained ourselves, and in swift thought touched on that Eternal Wisdom, which abideth over all)—could this be continued on, and other visions of kind far unlike be withdrawn, and this one ravish, and absorb, and wrap up its beholder amid these inward joys, so that life might be for ever like that one moment of understanding which now we sighed after; were not this, Enter into thy Master's joy?"[1]

NOTE TO CHAPTER VIII

THE SUCCESSION OF BIRTHS

THE idea of an endless succession of lives, through which every being is passing, occupies a prominent place in Buddhist thought. The disciple is encouraged to dwell upon this idea until the mere sense of weariness from contemplating so interminable a series arouses his disgust. Sickening at the sight, he resolves to have nothing to do with external objects, or even with those internal acts of consciousness, with which the tedious rotation of birth and death is associated.

It is not the idea of retribution, by the transmigration of a greedy man into a hog, and so on, nor even that of variety, in one being's passing through so many forms (though both these ideas are admitted), but it is the idea of weary interminableness that is the ruling aspect, in Buddhist thought, of what is popularly called "transmigration." The books labour to excite this idea by a multitude of illustrations, of which many are collected in the fifteenth book of Saṃyutta Nikaya.

If a piece of clay the size of a jujube seed were taken to represent your father, another similar piece of clay to represent your grandfather, a third his father, and so on, the whole earth would be used up before the series of your ancestors was exhausted. The tears each man has shed over his fathers amount to more water than all the oceans. Every one has been every one's father, mother, son, and so on. Certain ascetics were told that the blood they had shed when slaughtered as oxen, goats, birds,

[1] St. Augustine. *Confessions*, Bk. iv. (Oxford translation).

dogs, etc., or the blood they had shed in having their hands cut off as thieves, exceeded all the waters of all the seas. The bones of one individual in the course of an age ("Kalpa") make a great mountain. A Kalpa is so long, that if a solid mountain were lightly brushed with a cloth once in a hundred years it would be worn away long before a single Kalpa was exhausted.[1] Yet we are told that few beings in proportion are born again as men; they are but as a nailful of dust is to the whole earth. Man is hurried through this series of lives by a mechanical necessity. He "falls" out of one life into another, according to his deeds, as a stick thrown into the air falls inevitably, whether it falls on this end or on that or on the middle.[2]

Is there not good reason then to be disgusted with the round of lives in which beings run their weary and endless course? And is it not worth while to strive to get free from it?

As soon as one sees the cause of it all—that death is due to birth and birth to being—sees in fact that suffering is inevitably associated with existence—then one is free. The mass of past sorrow is incalculable; but to one who has taken the first step in the Buddhist course, what remains is insignificant.[3]

With these ideas is connected one of the most celebrated and most striking of the Buddhist utterances; that said (in later Pitaka books) to have been uttered by Gotama at the moment of his attaining "knowledge": Anekajātisaṃsāraṃ, etc. About the construction of a leading word in this passage, European scholars differ. The following is a literal version of the interpretation given by the Buddhists themselves:—

Through the long series of many births I ran without attaining,[4]
Seeking the house-builder. Birth again and again is sorrow.
House-builder! thou art found out; thou wilt build no house again:
All thy beams are broken, the ridge-pole of the house is shattered.
My mind has reached where elements unite no more; I have attained the extinction of desires.—(Dhammapada, 153, 154).

In spite of the poetical grandeur of these verses, and in spite of some old grammatical forms in them, they belong to a comparatively late stage of the Pitaka literature. They consist of an elaborate collection of stereotyped metaphors. The identification of the "housemaker" (taṇhā or karma) with Mara (for to Mara the phrase, "diṭṭho si," "thou art seen through," is regularly applied) is alien to the earlier ideas of the Maha Vagga. And the metaphor of the house and rafters, though often found in later Suttas, is not in the Vinaya.

[1] For the length of a Kalpa, its beginning and ending, see Angut, iv. 156. For the size of the world, *ib.* iv. 45.

[2] Saṃyut, xv. 9, *et passim.*

[3] *Ib.* xiii. 1, 2.

[4] Modern scholars would render "anibbisaṃ" by "incessantly."

CHAPTER IX

THE VICES

THE cultivation of solitude is habitually recommended by the Buddhist writers, as has been shown in the last chapter, with a view to unmeaning, and indeed impossible, states of abstraction. And this is always treated as the higher way. To this the advanced disciple aspires, leaving behind him, as if it were merely a preliminary achievement, the rooting out of passion. But it is the preliminary achievement which is really practical, and it is the teaching of this part of the course which is of real value. It has not, indeed, the chief place in the great Suttas, but it is not overlooked; and the passages which keep upon this lower but truer level, and deal with the struggle against the ordinary passions, place the principle of "detachment" in a more favourable light.

He who keeps in view the impermanence of things, and so cares nothing for them, will neither desire nor resent. He wants nothing, and nothing hurts him. Lust, therefore, and hatred and anger are got rid of.

These are two of the Evil Ways, or Evil Conditions, a classification of moral evil familiar to all Indian systems, and probably far more ancient than Buddhism; but one of which the Buddhist moralists make constant use. The two principal Evil Conditions are lust or passion, and spite or hatred, but to these stupidity and fear are generally added. The usual formula is represented by the lines—

> Whoso transgresses right, by lust, by hatred, by stupidity, or by fear,
> His reputation wanes away like the moon in the dark half of the month.[1]

Sometimes a more general word, "Passion" (Rāgo), is substituted for "lust," and sometimes for "fear" we find "pride." "Stupidity" (moho) here means originally "confusion of mind" and has a wide range of meaning. It often signifies the want of

[1] Angut, iv. 17, *et passim*.

self-respect and self-command which goes with a bad conscience and with loss of reputation ; occasionally, denseness and inability to see into the profounder truths. Definitions and illustrations of the four ill conditions abound especially in the later books, and the efforts made to help the disciple to avoid them are sincere and earnest.

Another classification of faults, more technical and more characteristically Buddhist, is that of the Five Hindrances (Nīvaraṇa)—greed, malice, sloth, pride, and doubt. Another grouping is that of the four Yogas or " attachments," which are also, from a different point of view, classed as the Four Corruptions (āsava) : these are love of pleasure, love of existence, false doctrine, and ignorance. It cannot be said that much light is thrown on the origin of the faults or the nature of the temptations which lead to them, by these classifications ; but at any rate occasion is given for insisting upon the evil of each vice. The following passage, which is a little abbreviated, is, I think, a fair specimen of the method : " There are four Attachments, mendicants : what are the four ? The attachment of the love of sensual pleasure, that of the love of existence, that of heresy, that of ignorance. What, mendicants, is the attachment of the love of pleasure ? When a person does not recognize in their true nature the up-coming and the down-going of sensual pleasures, the enjoyment of them, the danger of them, and the way out of them—in him who knows not all these, in regard to the objects of sensual pleasures, there is a sickness for pleasure, a delight in pleasure, a love of pleasure, a fainting for pleasure, a thirst for pleasure, a fever for pleasure, which is sunk in pleasure, and goes along with the desire for pleasure—that is called, mendicants, 'the attachment of the love of sensual pleasure.' "

The same sentence is then repeated with " existence," and again with " heresy " in the place of " pleasure." In the fourth sentence, the " six regions of contact," that is, the objects of sense and imagination, are substituted for " ignorance." What was a forcible and appropriate sentence in its original application becomes unmeaning in these mechanical repetitions.

The groups which have so far been mentioned place the faults which they enumerate in no scientific order ; unless, indeed, the four attachments or corruptions may be regarded as following the order (reversed) of the Chain of Causation. But the classification of faults under the Ten Bonds does purport definitely to assign the order in which each vice successively is to be rooted out.

The first three Bonds are of the nature of heresies; belief in one's own personal existence and claims, doubts, and misuse of low kinds of religious rites; these are the first faults to be got rid of. The two next are love of pleasure and hatred; while the other five, in overcoming which the highest moral success consists, are passion for what has form, passion for what has not form, pride of honour, pride of attainment, and ignorance. The reader will see in this a certain advance in analysis. The disciple must first desire to shake off personal existence, and must be a convinced follower of the Buddha, rejecting all Brahmanical and superstitious rites; he will then grapple with the more obvious and grosser vices, lust and hatred; but the eradication of spiritual faults will come later, and the destruction of ignorance, by direct insight, will come last of all.

In the Mahali Sutta[1] these ten bonds are treated of in their relation to those four progressive stages of spiritual attainment, which are often called the Four Paths; though they are really four stages in one path.

"Is it for the sake of realizing these exercises of meditation that mendicants lead the religious life under the Buddha?" "No, Mahali, it is not for the sake," etc. "There are other principles higher and more advanced than these, for the sake of realizing which mendicants lead the religious life under me."

"What are these other principles?" etc.

"By destruction of the three (first) bonds a mendicant becomes 'entered into the stream,' and can never fall to a lower condition, is fixed (in the right way), is certainly destined to the attainment of perfect knowledge. This, Mahali, is one of the higher and more advanced principles," etc.

"Again, further, Mahali: a mendicant, by the destruction of the three bonds and by reduction to a minimum of passion, hate, and stupidity,[2] becomes a 'once-comer,'—after one return to this world he will make an end of sorrow. This, Mahali," etc.

[1] Digh. Nik. vi.

[2] Stupidity, not being a "bond," is out of place here. Passion and hate are the fourth and fifth bonds.

" Again, further, Mahali : a mendicant, by destruction of the five (remaining) bonds of this lower world, becomes 'supernatural'; he enters into Nirvana from an upper world; he cannot return to this world. This," etc.

" Further, again, Mahali : by destruction of the corruptions, a mendicant attains even in this world by his own knowledge and direct insight the emancipation of the mind, the corruptionless emancipation of pure knowledge. This, Mahali, is," etc.

" These, Mahali, are the higher and more advanced principles, for the sake of realizing which mendicants lead the religious life under me."

" Is there, sir, a way—is there a course, for the realization of these principles (or conditions) ? "

" There is, Mahali, a way," etc.

" What, sir, is the way ? "

" It is the sacred Eightfold Way, namely, right belief," etc. " This, Mahali, is the way, this is the course, for the realization of these conditions."

A division still more plain and untechnical is that of Act, Word, and Thought. This is often repeated, but little use is made of it. I have seen no passage which touched on the relation of thought to word and to action. As a rule, the distinction is used only to subdivide, without illustrating, the other groups. For instance, in the treatment of anger, we read :—[1]

" Beware of bodily anger and control thy body : leave the sins of the body : with thy body practise virtue."

" Beware of the anger of the tongue, and control thy tongue," etc.

" Beware of the anger of the mind, and control thy mind," etc.

A much better use of the distinction is found[2] where unchastity is reckoned as the defilement of the body; lying, slander, and abuse as the defilement of the tongue; and lust, malice, sloth, pride, and doubt as the defilement of the mind.

But it is time to have done with these lists and enumerations. They cannot be omitted, for they form a very large part of the whole. But I will try to show what flesh is upon these bones.

It is by their condemnation of *hatred* and ill-will that the

[1] Dhammapada, 231. *S.B.E.* x., a., p. 59.

[2] Angut. iii. 119, 1.

Buddhist moral writings are most popularly and favourably known. It is a pleasure to quote such passages as these:—

"He who holds back anger like a rolling chariot, him I call a real driver: other people are but holding the reins."

"Let a man overcome anger by love, let him overcome evil by good; let him overcome the greedy by liberality, the liar by truth."[1]

"Him I call a Brahmana who is tolerant with the intolerant, mild with fault-finders, and free from passion among the passionate."[2]

"Him I call a Brahmana from whom anger and hatred, pride and envy, have dropped like a mustard seed from the point of a needle."[3]

But we shall see more of this, when we come to treat of "kindness."

Greediness and avarice are often vigorously condemned: they are especially temptations of the householder.

"The greedy in their selfishness do not leave sorrow, lamentation, and avarice; therefore the wise recluses leave greediness, to wander in sight of the security (of Nirvana)"[4] The connection is the same in other places, where the good householder is described[5] as "free in giving away, with hands accustomed to make offerings, fond of giving, fond of the distribution of gifts." Avarice is regarded as a "dirty" vice.

Sloth, which is not exactly the same as want of religious effort, is not tolerated (in the books). It is said to be produced and increased by dissatisfied, drowsy, yawning stupidity, caused by eating and by attachment of mind; it is overcome by energy, activity, and effort. It is associated with sensual pleasure, malice, pride, and doubt.[7]

In the treatment of *pride* these writings appear to great advantage, because they introduce not only the synonyms, which are the weakest part of their method, not only the similes, which are, for the most part, their nearest approximate to analysis, but really give a variety of instances of the vice and of its different causes and occasions.

"Let him not be proud, for that is not called bliss by the

[1] Dhammapada, 222, 3. S.B.E. x. a., 58. [2] *Ib.* 406, 407.
[3] *Ib.* 406, 407. [4] Sutta Nipata, iv. 6. See S.B.E. x., a, 155.
[5] Angut. iii. 42. [6] *Ib.* i. 2, 3, 8. [7] *Ib.* iii. 57, 1, etc.

good. Let him not, therefore, think himself better (than others, or) low, or equal to others; questioned by different people, let him not adorn himself."[1]

"The person who, without being asked, praises his own virtue and (holy) works to others, him the good call ignoble, one who praises himself."[2]

The wise man is indifferent to both praise and blame. When praised he is not elated. He knows, but is not proud of his knowledge.[3] He is readier to take note of his own faults than of those of others.[4] As it is very beautifully said: "One should be ready to tell one's faults, for the sense of shame swiftly fades. The conscience of a monk should be as tender, his sense of shame as keen, as that of a virgin bride."[5]

False pretension to supernatural attainments is among the unpardonable sins (see p. 119 f.), and all false professions and pretensions are condemned.[6] Especially the monks are warned against being elated by honours, entertainments, reputation, and the like. The writers are never tired of repeating a proverb to this effect: The fruit of the plantain is its bane, so is honour the bane of the monk. This was especially illustrated by the fall of Devadatta.[7]

This danger from the gain, entertainment, and reputation which virtue itself secures, is associated not only with pride but also with lying. It is dreadful; a bait by which men are caught; men are entangled by it as a long-wooled goat is by thorns, many go to hell through it: it eats into the skin, the flesh, etc.:[8] it is like a hair rope on the leg.[9]

[1] i.e. boast of his family. Sut. Nip. iv. 14. S.B.E. x., b, 175.

[2] S.B.E. iv. 3, p. 149. [3] S.N. ii. 13. [4] Dh. 50, S.B.E. x., c, 50.

[5] Angut. iv. 74 (paraphrased). I have given the sense of the passage, but have expressed it more delicately.

[6] Tevijj. S. Cetoh. S., etc. S.B.E. xi. 195, etc.

[7] Angut. iv. 68, etc. [8] *Vide supra*, p. 97.

[9] Saṃyut. xvii. xviii., where there are over forty Sutras upon it.

CHAPTER X

THE VIRTUES

IT is a curious thing, considering how fond the Buddhist books are of lists of vices and of mental attainments, that they have no corresponding list of virtues. There are the four ill-conditions, the ten bonds, the three corruptions, and a multitude more of lists of faults. There are the four meditations, the four supernatural powers, the ten forms of intellectual strength, and so on. But I know of no numerical list of virtues.

Virtues are not valued, theoretically at least, for themselves: they are not positively good, only relatively, as means of escape from existence. For, according to the theory of "karma," good actions are no less fatal than bad ones in keeping the doer in existence. He must be reborn and reborn, to enjoy the fruit of what he has done; and good conduct as well as bad conduct must be overpassed and done with, before he can get free. The perfected Buddhist "has nothing more to do."

Whether this is or not the true explanation of the absence from the Pitakas of a classification of virtues,[1] the fact is convenient for our present purpose: we can follow an arrangement of our own without doing any violence to the Buddhist method.

First let us take, what is the glory of Buddhism, the doctrine of lovingkindness (mettaṃ). The word meant originally friendship, and it is mainly, I believe, by Buddhism that its meaning has been enlarged. The next Buddha, as later Bud-

[1] The ten Perfections (pāramitā) are no exception to this, for they concern only Buddhas; but they form the nearest approach to a list of virtues, and are by no means a scientific arrangement: the place occupied by knowledge (paññā) is alone enough to show this. The ten Perfections are those of giving, conduct (or obedience to the precepts), leaving the world, knowledge, energy, patience, truth, firmness, lovingkindness, resignation. They are valued, not for their own sakes, but as accumulating capacity for Buddha-hood. "The attainment of Buddhahood with all its superhuman attributes (e.g. omniscience) is the result or consequence of the vast accumulation of merit during the exercise of the pāramitās in anterior births."—Childers, *Dictionary of the Pali Language*, s.v.

dhist belief holds, is to be named Maitri, "the loving one." Whether this expectation is regarded as having been moulded by the worship of Mitra or Mithras, or as an unconscious prophecy of the coming of Him who is Love, it is at any rate a proof of the place which this virtue once occupied in Buddhist thought.

I propose to discuss it under four heads—in its widest sense as lovingkindness and sympathy, and in three special senses, as the spirit of unity, as meekness, as unwillingness to hurt.

Gotama the Buddha is represented as having devoted himself to preaching his doctrine out of kindness to gods and men, out of compassion. He is often described as looking abroad with supernatural sight on the worlds of gods and men, and sending out his compassion towards all. But while this is the governing principle of his life he is not often presented to us as an example of this virtue in particular acts. With the exception of that which is narrated above (p. 36) no signal act of kindness is recorded of him as an historical person.

In manner, he is represented as extremely courteous and winning; in his method of teaching, considerate and patient. To opponents he was generous. Several times, when a rich convert proposed at once to transfer to Gotama and his monks all the liberality which he had been bestowing on members of rival religious orders, Gotama dissuaded him. When insulted, as the later books make him often to have been, by rival teachers, he was a pattern of patience. For the jealous Fire-worshipper, who feared Gotama's reputation would outshine his own on his own festival, Gotama showed consideration by withdrawing from the scene. Even towards his bitter and murderous enemy, Devadatta, he maintained an attitude of perfect patience and dignity. For the feelings of Cunda, who gave him the pork which brought on his final illness, he showed a touching tenderness. Towards his affectionate but rather slow-witted friend, Ananda, he was at once severe and considerate.

How is it, that while the legends have lavished every extravagance, in their reports of Gotama's supposed conduct in earlier "births," in attributing heroic action to stags and hares and elephants, we meet with so little to illustrate the lovingkindness of the actual Gotama?

As regards the older portions of the record, I cannot doubt that the reason is that they tell the simple truth. Gotama, like his followers, was more a receiver than a giver; and those who recorded what was remembered of him found no acts of kindness on a large scale, and were not much interested in acts of kindness on a small scale. Such things were not expected of an ascetic any more than they are expected now in Ceylon from a monk. As regards the later narratives, Professor Oldenberg's explanation is probably correct. The Buddha had attained that to which (as I have noticed at the beginning of this chapter) moral achievements are only a means. He "had done all that had to be done." After he had become a Buddha, any action but that of teaching would have been out of place. So the exercise on a vast scale of the various virtues was relegated to the region of former births, in former ages, and under former Buddhas, in whose time he, who was to be the Buddha of this age, was a Bodhisat—a being destined to be a Buddha.

But there is a further reason. The lovingkindness of Buddhism is rather a temper than a motive of action. It may have existed to the full in Gotama, without manifesting itself in act. As a temper, it is the characteristic aim of his teaching.

"A little love," he says, "is better than vast gifts."[1] It leads to high conditions in future births."[2] In the Kassapa Sīhanāda Sutta the Buddha discusses the common saying, "It is hard to be a Brahman or a Samana" (ascetic, particularly Buddhist). In contrast to the labours and austerities to which this saying refers, the Buddha says: "The mendicant who cultivates lovingkindness in his heart, without enmity and without malice, and by destruction of the corruptions attains even in this life by his own insight the realization of the corruptionless emancipation of the mind, the emancipation of knowledge—he, Kassapa, is rightly called a Brahman and a Samana."[3] Of such a monk it is said in another Sutta:—[4]

"He lets his mind pervade one quarter of the world with thoughts of love, and so the second, and so the third, and so the fourth. And thus the whole wide world—above, below, around, and everywhere, does he continue to pervade with heart of love, far-reaching, grown great and beyond measure.

"Just, Vāseṭṭha, as a mighty trumpeter makes himself heard, and that without difficulty, in the four directions; even so of

[1] Saṃyut. xx. 4. [2] Angut. iv. 190.
[3] Digh. Nik. viii. 16. [4] Tevijja S. iii. 1. S.B.E. xi., p. 201.

all things that have shape or life, there is not one that he passes by or leaves aside, but he regards them all with mind set free and deep-felt love."

The following is from the Sutta Nipata :—[1]

"As a mother at the risk of her life watches over her own child, her only child, so let every one cultivate a boundless (friendly) mind towards all beings; and let him cultivate good-will towards all the world . . . standing, walking, or sitting, or lying, as long as he be awake, let him devote himself to this mind: this (way of) living, they say, is the best in the world."

The spirit of *unity* and concord is a matter to which a very important place is given. In the biography of Gotama we have seen (p. 101) how he is said to have taken occasion, at the end of his career, from the case of the Vajjians, to urge unity upon his followers. But out of many passages that might be cited, the most charming is one which recurs several times, but which I may abridge from the translation of the tenth book of the Maha Vagga. Anurādha, Nanduja, and Kimbila, were three monks who lived together in the Eastern Bamboo Park. The Buddha visited them, and after asking, as was his custom, how they fared, he said: "And do you live in unity and concord, without quarrels, like milk and water (mixed together), and looking at each other with friendly eyes?" "Certainly, Lord, we do so live," etc. "And in what way do you so live?" etc. Then each in turn replied for himself, and all used the same words: "I say to myself, Lord, it is all gain to me, indeed it is high bliss to me to live in the company of brethren like these. Then do I exercise towards these venerable brethren friendliness[2] in my actions both openly and in secret. I exercise towards them friendliness in my words, and friendliness in my thoughts, both openly and in secret. And I say to myself, 'What if I were to give up my own will and live only according to the will of these venerable brethren?' Thus, Lord, I give up my own will and live only according to the will of these venerable brethren. Our bodies, Lord, are different, but our minds, I think, have become one."

In treating of the use of speech we shall see with what fullness

[1] S.B.E. x., ii. 25.

[2] *Mettaṃ.* The same word which I have rendered, in its widest sense, loving-kindness.

and earnestness the duty of saying what will promote unity is insisted on.[1]

The temper of *meekness* may be called perhaps the favourite theme of Buddhist writers, whether in discourse or in birth-story or fairy-tale. Its motto is the couplet : " Hatred is not appeased by hatred at any time; but it is appeased by unhatred: this law is eternal." And the verse that precedes this is excellent: " He abused me, he beat me, he defeated me, he took what was mine; in those who do not cherish that, hatred is appeased."

Instead of quoting more of such sentiments I must give in illustration of them a sketch of the story of Dīghāvu. It was told to some monks among whom quarrels had arisen.

The great king Brahmadatta of Benares set out to war against Dīghīti, the poor king of the comparatively insignificant realm of Kosala. Dighiti offered no resistance, but fled in disguise with his queen to the neighbourhood of Benares; and Brahmadatta took possession of his kingdom and all that he had. When it came to Brahmadatta's knowledge that the fugitive king and his wife were living in disguise close to his city, he sent for them and had them both put to death with the utmost cruelty. Their only child, Dighavu, whom for safety's sake they had caused to live apart from them, happened to be coming to pay his parents a visit, when he saw them being led out to execution. As soon as his father, Dighiti, saw his boy, he said to him these enigmatic words: " Do not look long, my dear Dighavu, and do not look short; for not by hatred, my dear Dighavu, is hatred appeased, but by not-hatred, my dear Dighavu, hatred is appeased."

Having done what he could for the funeral of his parents, Dighavu went into the forest. There he cried and wept to his heart's content. Then he wiped away his tears, entered the city of Benares, and persuaded the king's elephant trainer to accept him as an apprentice. " And young Dighavu," said Gotama to the monks, " arose in the night at time of dawn, and sang in the elephant stables in a beautiful voice, and played upon the lute. And King Brahmadatta heard his singing and playing on the lute, and asked who it was who sang and played so well. They told him it was the elephant trainer's boy, and brought Dighavu to the king. He played and sang before the

[1] See the Sutta translated on p. 191.

king, and charmed him, and became his favourite attendant; and ere long, O monks, King Brahmadatta of Kasi (Benares) gave to young Dighavu a position of trust."

One day when the king went hunting Dighavu was acting as charioteer. He contrived to get separated from the rest of the chariots, and after a long drive the king grew tired, and lay down to rest with his head in Dighavu's lap. Now, thought the lad, is the time to satisfy my hatred against the murderer of my parents and the despoiler of my realm; and he drew his sword. But the dying words of his father came into his mind, and he put up his sword. A second time and a third time he drew it, and returned it to its sheath.

At that moment the king awoke, having had, as he said, a frightful dream. The son of Dighiti, he dreamt, had come upon him with his sword. "I, O king," said the lad, "am Dighavu, Dighiti's son. You have murdered my parents and robbed us of our realm: now is the time for me to satisfy my hatred." "Grant me my life, dear Dighavu!" cried the great king, falling at his feet. The young man spared him, returned to his post of charioteer, and drove the king home.

Brahmadatta asked Dighavu the meaning of those last words of his father, King Dighiti—"Do not look long, and do not look short," and the rest. "'Not long,'" he replied, "means, let not your hatred last long; and 'not short' means, do not be hasty to fall out with your friends." The other words his conduct had already illustrated. Then Brahmadatta restored to Dighavu his father's realm and goods, and gave him his own daughter to be his wife.[1]

Consideration for animals must have mention here, for the books in many places teach it, not merely in connection with the rule against taking life, but as a form of kindness. Would that it were a rule for the practical conduct of Buddhists now! Unhappily, it is a matter of universal observation in Ceylon, that the very rule against destroying life appears to be taken as the sanction for any extent of cruelty which does not involve

[1] Maha Vagga, x. 2. See S.B.E. x. 298. This story is interesting in many ways. It is a tale of old mythical times, and yet is not a "birth story," i.e. the hero is not identified with a previous life of the Buddha. Further, in its close resemblance in several points to the history of David in his relations with Saul, it is one of several indications that the Old Testament narratives, as well as the Greek myths, had reached the India of Buddhism.

killing. But it was not so, in theory at least, with the authors of the Pitakas, nor with the compilers of those "Jātakas" (birth-stories) of which the people are still so fond. In the Jatakas a genuine sympathy for animal life, with that racy rustic humour which accompanies it, is often made the means of giving point to the moral, that the dumb animals claim of us, not merely the cold technical avoidance of killing, but friendliness that will neither hurt them nor cause them fear.

It is carried to a fantastic length in the tenderness for vegetable life, which is required at any rate of monks, under the larger rules of conduct. This belongs, I fancy, to the later and "Rabbinical" stage—so to compare it—of the system. In one of the oldest books we find Gotama inclined to treat as a vulgar error, or at least as a thing unproved, the notion of vegetable "life."[1]

We shall have occasion to touch on this matter again. Here I will notice, though it may be scarcely relevant, a curious passage about love or kindness to the whole race of snakes, which occurs in more than one place. In it the sacred word "mettaṃ" is bestowed abundantly on every sort and tribe of serpent, with the addition of a wish that none of them may hurt the speaker. It is in fact a charm, or "pirit," against snakes, which has been boldly dragged into the company of Buddhist moral maxims.

"At one time the Buddha was dwelling at Savatthi, in the Jetavana, Anathapindika's park, and at that time a certain monk had been bitten by a serpent in Savatthi, and had died. A number of monks came where the Buddha was and saluted him, and took their seats respectfully beside him; and as they sat respectfully beside him, those monks said to the Buddha:—

"Here, Lord, in Savatthi, a monk has been bitten by a serpent and has died."

"That monk, probably, O monks, had not radiated forth lovingkindness on the four royal families of snakes. If that monk, O monks, had radiated forth lovingkindness on the four royal families of snakes, that monk, O monks, would not have been bitten by a snake and have died. And what are the four royal families of snakes?

"The Virūpakka royal snake family, the Erāpatha, the Chabyāputta, and the Kaṇhāgotamaka royal snake family.

[1] M.V. v. 7, 1.

Now probably, monks, that monk had not," etc. " I command you, monks, to radiate lovingkindness on the four royal families of snakes, for the protection of yourselves, for the guarding of yourselves, for a charm to keep yourselves safe."

Then follow the verses :—

My love is on the Virupakkas, on the Erapathas is my love ;
My love is on the Chabyaputtas, and on the Kanhagotamakas ;
My love is on the footless ones, on the two-footed is my love ;
My love is on the four-footed, on the many-footed is my love.
May no footless one hurt me, may there hurt me no two-footed,
May no four-footed one hurt me, may there hurt me no many-footed one !
May all beings, all that live and all that are, universally
See all happiness ; and may no sort of ill befall !

And then in prose :—

" Infinite is the Buddha, infinite is the Doctrine, infinite is the Community ; finite are the creeping things—the snakes and scorpions, the centipedes, the woolly-bellies (spiders) and lizards, and the mice. My protection is made, my charm is made ! let the creatures depart ! Glory to the Buddha, glory to the seven perfect Buddhas, say I."

Such is the sixty-seventh Sutta of the fourth division of the Anguttara Nikaya. But nowadays the number of the creeping things, in Ceylon at least, is no longer finite.

Would that the Buddhists of the present day would more frequently charm their animals with love ! The bare rule against killing commands little of our admiration ; but the kind-heartedness which finds in the dumb creatures something to love and sympathize with—fellow-feeling for all that can feel—this has a wonderful attraction. There is something in it that wins the love of men, so that those who are kind to animals are called humane.

The sentiment of pity for animal life is found not only in the Pitakas and Jatakas. It pervades, as we shall see, the inscriptions of Asoka, who seems, if we may judge from the chronological order of his edicts, to have grasped this first among Buddhist principles. He not only professed and enjoined regard for animal life, but instituted hospitals, as he says, throughout India for brutes as well as for men, and planted herbs which would be useful for their treatment. His kindly action found imitation among the Buddhist kings of Ceylon, notably in

Buddhadāsa, whose provision for the medical treatment of animals, as well as his own extraordinary skill and benevolence in personally attending them, forms an amusing episode in the Mahavansa (chap. xxxvii).

Here it may be noted that the credit of having first founded hospitals belongs undoubtedly to Buddhism. Nor can any reader, who has before him the passages which we have been considering in this chapter, under this head of "mettaṃ," claim for either Old or New Testament the exclusive communication to man of the theory of disinterested kindness and the law of love. The same Holy Spirit Who wrote our Scriptures gave to some of the Buddhist teachers no despicable insight into these truths.

But it was not until that Holy Spirit animated the Christian Church, that a Community was formed, in which these truths became a powerful—I might almost say an appreciable—factor in human life.

Filial piety and reverence for old age are taught by the Buddhists with much emphasis. They were genuine Brahman virtues, as is acknowledged in the following passage:—

"These families have a place with Brahma in which the sons offer religious honours to their parents in the sacred chamber; these families have a place with the teachers of old, with those who are worthy of sacrifice. ("Worthy to offer," or "worthy of their share in" sacrifice.)

"For 'Brahmas' is a title of fathers and mothers, 'teachers of old' is a title of fathers and mothers, 'worthy of sacrifice' is a title of fathers and mothers.

"Why? Because fathers and mothers are great benefactors to their sons, their introducers, feeders, and guides in this world. . . . Therefore let the good man honour and succour them with food and drink, with clothing and lodging, with rubbing, with bathing, with washing of the feet: for waiting thus on father and mother good men praise him here, and after death he rejoices in heaven."[1]

"The gift of the whole world with all its wealth would be no adequate return to parents for all that they have done."[2]

The teaching is touchingly illustrated in the following story:—

A certain monk had a quantity of robes in his possession.

[1] Angut. iii. 31. [2] *Ib.* ii. 4.

They ought, of course, to have been placed at the disposal of the Community, but he proposed to give them to his father and mother. The other monks told this to the Buddha, and he replied, "Since they are his father and mother, what can we say, O Bhikkhus, though he give them to them? I allow you, O Bhikkhus, to give (robes in such a case) to your parents."[1]

Among those who lose in life is the rich man who fails to support his aged parent. He is reckoned as an outcast.[2] There are said to be four ways in which a man goes altogether wrong, and is foolish and unwise and bad, and destroys and ruins himself, and is guilty and regarded as guilty by the wise, and produces great demerit: these four are—misconduct towards mother, misconduct towards father, misconduct towards a Buddha, misconduct towards the disciples of a Buddha. He is blamed by the wise here, and after death he goes to hell.[3]

Akin to filial piety is *reverence for age*. This duty is frequently impressed upon members of the Community, and constantly provided for in the Vinaya rules. The hatred of "old age,"[4] as a form of misery always coupled with death, did not prevent the early Buddhists from being faithful to the Brahman tradition of respect for the old, any more than the theory that birth is misery was held to justify ingratitude to parents. "He who always greets and constantly reveres the aged, four things will increase to him, viz. life, beauty, happiness, power.[5]

"Do they reverence the old?" was one of the questions asked by Gotama about the Vajjians: if they did, they might be expected to prosper.

Under the head of *giving* we now come to what corresponds in the Buddhist system to what we understand by liberality, generosity, and self-sacrifice. I am afraid it cannot be said that either of those terms has an equivalent in Pali. The second certainly has none; and the idea is foreign, as far as I can judge, to Buddhist thought. Liberality and self-sacrifice are the nobler aspects of what, in their commoner aspects, must be rendered "giving" (dānaṃ) and "giving up" (cāgo). I will discuss

[1] M.V. viii. 22, S.B.E.

[2] Sut. Nipat. i. 6, 7.

[3] Angut. iv. 4. Cf. *ib.*, ii. 12, 7, and see Sigālovāda Sutta translated in Rhys Davids' *Buddhism*, p. 144.

[4] The word "jarā," the decay of strength, though generally rendered "old age," is quite distinct from the words for old age in its honourable sense.

[5] Dh. 109. S.B.E. x., a, 33.

these terms as impartially as possible, and with ample illustration, though I confine myself entirely to the Pitakas.

Giving is seldom spoken of simply, apart from mention of the recipient. As a rule, when used simply, the term means giving to monks. Indeed, I have not noticed one exception to this rule. Nor is there much, if anything, about giving to the poor as such. We do indeed read occasionally of great distributions by kings and rich men, but they are almost always to religious mendicants. It is possible that the idea of a class of needy poor was not familiar to the India of those times. But in the immense majority of instances, the idea of "giving" is qualified by the character of the recipient. To give to "the wise" is so much better and more profitable, that all other idea of giving is utterly overshadowed by this. It is no doubt a deep-seated Indian notion that a gift is from the inferior to the superior. The higher the recipient, then, the more precious and meritorious the gift. That to a Buddha is greatest, then (in later books) that to a "self-Buddha,"[1] then that to a disciple, in the order of attainments. The smallest gift or service done to one of these exalted beings may lead to an immense reward.

Vacchagotta asked the Buddha whether it was true that he taught that gifts ought to be given to himself alone and not to others. The Buddha repudiated the charge, and said it was very wrong to prevent a gift being given to others. "Is it likely that I," he said, "who teach consideration for the smallest worm, should have no consideration for men? But I do teach, Vacchagotta, that what is given to the good has great reward, and not what is given to the bad."[2]

Again: "There are two kinds of persons to whom gifts should be given in this world—the learner and the advanced saint:—

> The learner and the saint in this world
> Are worthy of offerings from those who bring gifts:
> They are upright in deed, word, and thought;
> That is the field for those who bring gifts;
> Then what is given has great reward.[3]

The fourth Sutta of the third book of Sutta Nipata is occupied with answering the question put by a Brahman: "I delight

[1] Pacceka Buddha, i.e. one who has attained Buddha-knowledge, but keeps it to himself; see p. 43.

[2] Angut. iii. 57, paraphrased.

[3] S.B.E. x., b, 76.

in offering, O Gotama, I desire to make an offering, but I do not understand it; do thou instruct me; tell me in what case the offering succeeds." The answer is prolonged through some twenty stanzas, but comes, in short, to this: "The good," that is, the Buddha and his followers, "these deserve the offering." These you should worship and honour with food and drink; so the gifts will prosper." In the next Sutta the same instruction is given to a Buddhist householder, and he is told also in what temper of mind he is to be himself, while he gives—calm, purged from hatred, and full of lovingkindness.

It follows of course from this theory, as it was necessary for practical maintenance, that the Community is the great field for "giving." Gifts are the seed, whose crop is "merit," and the best "merit-field" is the Sangha. And it is in this character that the Sangha is oftenest commended to the reverence and confidence of the layman; it is not so much a teaching body as a receiving body. All other giving is lost sight of in comparison with this, and the word comes almost exclusively to mean giving either to individual monks or to the Community. It is the essential part of the layman's duty, the necessary correlative of the mendicant's rule. Its commonest form is the offering of food, the special function of women.

The Buddha was once visiting a faithful woman who provided him with every kind of food, offering it with her own hands. After the meal he said to her: "A good religious woman who gives food gives four things to the recipients. What four? She gives vital force, she gives beauty, she gives happiness, she gives strength. By giving vital force, she becomes partaker of vital force, human or divine; by giving beauty, she becomes partaker of beauty; by giving happiness, of happiness; by giving strength, of strength, human or divine." Then follow the verses:—

The woman who gives well-made food, clean, nice, and full of flavour,
That gift given to the upright, the virtuous and exalted,
Accumulates merit upon merit, and has great reward, and is praised by
him who saw all the worlds.
Thinking then of such an offering, let those in this world who are wise
Purge out entirely the mud of stinginess; so will they be unblamed, and
go to heaven.[1]

Of Suttas to this effect there is a large collection. The group

[1] Angut. iv. 57.

ends with one which insists on the blessedness of those householders who give to monks the "four requisites"—robes, food, lodging, and medicines.

By day and by night, for ever their merit increases;
And heaven is the place he goes to, having wrought a favourable "karma."[1]

There is no hint that in this matter "virtue is its own reward," still less that such conduct pleases a Divine Ruler, or is like a Father in Heaven. The inevitable mechanical result of giving to monks is merit and future prosperity. It is entirely for one's own good that one gives. The first offering made to Gotama himself, that of the two merchants, was made, it is expressly said, for their own good. And it is chiefly as giving opportunity for acquiring this merit that the Community is valued by those outside it. The laity are injured when good monks leave a place and bad ones succeed them, because "the opportunities of almsgiving are spoilt."[2]

So far we do Buddhism no injustice when we say that the idea of giving falls very far short of that which is represented by the word "charity," even in its modern degraded use. The giver sows with a view to a crop, which is to be his own; and the course of his liberality is strictly determined by the calculation of the return in merit to be expected. There is in this a portion of the truth; for "whatsoever a man soweth that shall he also reap"; but it is only a fraction of the truth which was taught by Him Who said, "Your Father shall reward you," and, "That ye may be the children of your Father which is in heaven. In the absence of any knowledge of a Father in heaven, to be imitated and to reward, it was scarcely possible that the Christian ideal should be conceived.

There is a nobler aspect of "dānaṃ," or "giving," when it is used in composition with "dhamma" or "doctrine." The phrase means giving the doctrine, a gift which consists in the communication of the truth.[3] "There are two kinds of gifts, the gift of food and the gift of doctrine; and of these two, the gift of doctrine is the better."[4] The substance of this teaching

[1] Angut. 60.

[2] Culla Vagga, i. 13, 4.

[3] Vidyādānaṃ mahādanaṃ. Mahabhārata, quoted by Padfield, *The Hindu at Home*, p. 203.

[4] Angut. ii. 13, 1, a little abridged.

is expressed, though the phrase "dhammadānaṃ" is not used, in the following :—

"Three persons are great benefactors of another person. What three? The person through whom another has gone for refuge to the Buddha, the Law, and the Community; the person through whom another obtains knowledge of the Four Truths; the person through whom another obtains final insight and emancipation. There is no benefactor greater than these; and it is no easy thing for that man to requite those benefactors—not by all the respect and homage or all the gifts and service he can offer."[1] In another place, this spiritual benefit is beautifully indicated as the best return a son can make to his parents.[2]

This is the only gift that the monk can give. Silver and gold he has not (or ought not to have); his dānaṃ is dhammadānaṃ. And one who has fulfilled this part is called a liberal monk, and his merit is greater than that of the monk who has only known and attained for himself. He is to the latter what the Sambuddha is to the Pacceka Buddha. In the Sumana Sutta a princess asks Gotama what difference there is, supposing both to be reborn in the god-world, between the condition of a monk who has been a "giver" (dāyako) and that of one who has kept his attainments to himself (adāyako). The answer is, the former enjoys greater long-life, strength, and wisdom. "And what if each be reborn as a man and become a monk?" "He will obtain the 'four requisites' with ease or in abundance." "And what if both be 'rahats'?" "There is then no difference; Nirvana-bliss is but one and unqualified."

Such are the main features of the treatment of the virtue of "giving."

"Giving up" (cāgo) is an idea developed from a rather different point of view. In this the ruling thought is not of the recipient, but of the act of surrender. It is a nearer approach to an entirely unselfish act. In Angut. iii. 70, 8, the disciple is taught to consider to what bliss those who are now deities in the various heavens have attained, by their faith, their conduct, their *giving up*, and their knowledge, and to say, "If I imitate them in these, I shall be born there too." But in that passage, as certainly in many others, it is the giving up of vices that is meant.

[1] Angut. iii. 24. [2] *Ib.* ii. 4, 2.

But we must not altogether omit—for they have their value as parables—the famous illustrations of self-sacrifice attributed, in supposed former births, to him who was afterwards to be Buddha. The perfection of "giving" (dānapāramitā) was fulfilled by the Bodhisat, when, as King Vessantara, he gave his wife and children to Indra disguised as a Brahman; when, in the Sivi birth, he gave his two eyes to a blind Brahman; and —most famous of all—when, as a hare, he leapt into the fire to be roasted for a Brahman's dinner. In each of these tales the compiler[1] (one of the latest, I think, admitted within the Pitakas) represents the act as the issue, not of any sense of pity or enthusiasm or self-sacrifice, but of the coldest calculation of results: "If I do not make this surrender I shall not attain Buddha-hood."

There is a nobility still about this; but it is the nobility of a strong desire to attain Buddha-hood, and of readiness to pay a high price for knowledge: it is not the temper of unselfish self-sacrifice. The original idea has been degraded by the insensibility of the versifier. It must have been on the lips of very different preachers that these parts of Buddhist teaching—mettaṃ, dānaṃ, cāgo—won the hearts of men. But no mere teaching on such topics is worth much—whether it be in Buddhist books or in Christian—unless it is embodied in real human deeds.

[1] Of the Cariya Pitaka.

CHAPTER XI

THE PRECEPTS

IN the popular conception of Buddhism by Buddhists now, the most prominent place is occupied, not by the Four Noble Truths, or the Twelve Nidānas (Links of Causation), or the Eightfold Way, but by the five precepts of conduct, the five rules, in Sinhalese, "pansil." These are the prohibitions of (1) destroying life, (2) taking what is not given, (3) sexual offences, (4) lying, (5) drinking intoxicating liquors.[1]

But it is an interesting fact that these do not hold any such place in the original system. They are not found, as five, in the most ancient manual of discipline. They are not among the discoveries made on the night of Buddha-hood, nor are they mentioned in the first sermons. They do not occur in those earliest chapters of the Maha Vagga, which we regard as containing in a nutshell the authentic kernel of Buddhism. They never occur in any discourse which bears marks of being more than conventionally an utterance of the Buddha himself.

In the Vinaya Pitaka they are found among other rules for monks—among the ten—but never stand by themselves, with one exception. In the fable of the elephant, the monkey, and the partridge, which is introduced into the later part of the Vinaya, it is stated that the partridge and his friends lived happily, keeping the five precepts.[2]

Nor is the number five constantly adhered to, for in many cases, perhaps in a majority, the fifth prohibition is omitted.

They are found in a statement of the duties of laymen, with special reference to the conduct of man and wife.[3] They are quoted roughly in a passage of the Sutta Nipata, which teaches that what really defiles a man is not ceremonial impurity but sin,[4] and in another part of the same book more elaborately.[5]

[1] This is the usual order, but it varies occasionally, e.g. in Sutt. Nipat. ii. 14.

[2] Culla Vagga, vi. 6, 3.

[3] Angut. iv. 53, 5.

[4] Sut. Nipat. ii. 2.

[5] *Ib.* ii. 14.

In the more exhaustive Suttas, such as the Tevijja Sutta,[1] they are stated under the heading (of more modern date) of "Little Rules of Conduct," but even in these the fifth prohibition is sometimes omitted.

From the position which they hold in the books—one of a definiteness gradually increasing from the earlier passages to the later—and also from their nature, we may confidently infer that the Five Precepts did not, as such, form part of Gotama's original proclamation. We may reasonably doubt whether they had assumed, even by Asoka's time, anything like the prominence which they have since acquired; for it is unlikely that in that case they would have found no place in his edicts.

Their history is probably this. They were originally formulated, with the other five of the group called the Ten Rules (sikkhāpadāni), for the guidance of the monks. As lay disciples increased around the Community, these were selected from among the ten rules as those to be enforced on the laity. The laity were not, it must be remembered, originally under rule at all. And afterwards they were (in the language of Christian religious communities) "associated" with the monks to a certain degree only. On occasions, or for a limited time, the associated laity might take on themselves eight of the rules, or even the ten; but only the five were ordinarily laid upon them. (And the same is still the case in Ceylon.) These five are those considered most essential to moral character, and are specified, from among the ten, as those for the breach of which a novice was to be expelled.[2] But one of the five, having been originally intended rather as a ceremonial than as a moral rule, occupied an uncertain position.

However this may be, the Precepts represent a later and a popular form of the moral system. It is on a lower level altogether (from a Buddhist point of view) than the Truths and the Causes, and has a humbler aim. It is adapted not to the early enthusiasm but to later days. But since it is now the best known and most practical part of Buddhism, its five Prohibitions must be separately discussed.

§ 1. The first Precept, against destroying life, has both a ceremonial and a moral side. I have already spoken of its

[1] S.B.E. xi., p. 190. See Maj. Nik. 41, *et passim*.
[2] M.V. i. 60. See i. 56.

moral aspect—that in which it would be chiefly urged upon the laity. In its ceremonial aspect it is often exaggerated. The use of a filter, lest small creatures should be destroyed in drinking; the injunction to be careful in throwing away a liquid, that it should fall either on water which had no worms in it or on ground on which there was no grass; the condemnation (in a late book[1]) of the killing of a dangerous snake; these are exceptions to the common sense which guided most of the early Buddhist regulations. But this exaggeration does not seem ever to have been carried to such lengths as by the Jains.

The monk eats meat. Gotama himself habitually did so, and died, as we know, from the consequence of a meal of pork.[2] And the offering of that flesh is commended as one of the two most meritorious offerings ever made. The monk may not encourage an animal's being killed for him; but seeing that he is invited to a meal on the morrow, and that on his accepting the invitation the host goes away to prepare the feast—nothing occurs oftener than this, and it was the case with Cunda's pork —there is no real scrupulousness about the killing of animals for food.

There are indications of a Brahmanical aspect of this precept, in which it is applied particularly to killing cows and oxen,[3] and, on the other hand, of an anti-Brahman aspect of it in which it is a direct attack on Brahman sacrifice. This is a very common moral in the "birth-stories," but it occurs also in the Sutta Pitaka.[4] Among the evils involved in Brahman sacrifices, besides the slaughter of animals, the destruction of grass and wood for fuel is condemned.

But the most interesting fact connected with the ancient insistence on this rule is the virtual promulgation of it by Asoka in his earlier edicts. In the earliest group, he says that he not only has withdrawn his patronage from sacrifices, but has reduced to a minimum the supplies for the royal table. At a later date he had given up eating meat altogether.

That Asoka, as soon as he fell under Buddhist influence, in-

[1] Udāna, 13.

[2] No other meaning can be reasonably assigned to "sūkaramaddavaṃ."

[3] A horrible torture is assigned to the murderer of an ox. Saṃyut. xix. 2.

[4] Sutta Nipat. ii. 7; Saṃyut. xv. 13; Angut. iv. 39. Digh. Nik. v., etc. The use of "samārabhataro" in this Sutta is to be compared with the use of "ārambhati" in the edicts.

sisted so strongly on the avoidance of taking life, proves—if proof were wanted—how prominent this element of Buddhist teaching already was; but that the Five Precepts, as such, did not hold, in his day, any such position as they do in later Buddhism, is shown by the facts that he not only does not refer to the Five Precepts, but does not use for "taking life" the term (pāṇātipāto) by which it is always known in them.

The public announcement of this maxim by royal authority, as a counsel if not as a law, for a vast continent, is surely one of the most curious events in the history of the human conscience. It cannot be too clearly or too confidently stated that the Buddhist conscience was misinformed. Taking the life of animals for suitable purposes is not wrong. The judgment of the best men in the wisest races of mankind accords with the teaching of Revelation upon this point. The conscience of Gotama (if he really held this), of Asoka, and of the Buddhist world, was at fault; yet this erroneous piece of moral law has been promulgated with such a publicity and earnestness, and imperial authority, as probably was never placed at the service of any other single precept. The very characters in which it was recommended are marked at this day upon the face of India.

§ 2. The prohibition of stealing, or "taking what has not been given," is not much enlarged upon. In the later books, as might be expected, it is exaggerated; as where one is condemned for smelling a flower, as having taken a scent which did not belong to him. Of the elaborate enumeration of all imaginable instances of this and other offences, which is found in the Vinaya Pitaka, I propose to speak later.

§ 3. Prohibition of false speaking. This is often qualified by the words "conscious and deliberate." Deliberate lying is frequently and vigorously condemned, and many illustrations are given of the evil of it. The rules against sins of speech occupy as large a space as all the other four rules together. He who lies is guilty of all sin.[1] It is mentioned as chief among the evils to which men are led by gain, honour, and fame.[2] The liar goes to hell.[3] A hint is given of the late date at which part of the Vinaya was compiled when it is said, of some monks of Gotama's day: "At that time men were speakers of truth, and

[1] Maj. Nik. 61. [2] Saṃyut. xvii, 11.
[3] Dh. 22, etc. etc.

keepers of their word."[1] But the most remarkable thing about this rule is the way in which it is expanded. Under this head is condemned every kind of unkind speaking, whether as abuse or violent speaking to a man's face, or as slander behind his back. The passages are many, and some of them are excellent.[2] Not only must what is bad be avoided, but such language is to be cultivated as will give pleasure and promote unity.

The pupil of a monk is to warn his tutor if he sees him on the verge of offending with his tongue.[3] A man should speak well of his neighbour even if unasked.[4] Some slanders, however, are worse than others. Speaking against a Buddha is a terrible sin, and we read of the awful consequence of a slander against the two chief disciples, Sariputta and Mogallana.[5]

Further, under the same head, chattering and talking nonsense are forbidden. Probably this has in view the dignity of members of the Community, and their keeping distinct—which is much insisted on—from those outside. Too much fondness for talking to householders is often condemned.

On the whole the moral teaching of the Buddhist books about the use of speech is practical, full, and high-toned.

§ 4. The third precept, which forbids impurity, is generally briefly stated, and so left. I should prefer so to leave it now; but if a just estimate of the Buddhist teaching is to be formed, two points in regard to this subject must be noted. In the first place, offences against this rule, though classed among the gravest possible offences, are usually treated as breaches of a ceremonial rule, and not as sins; and accordingly that which in itself is really no sin at all—for instance, the return of a monk to his own wife—ranks with the grossest sins. Secondly, the rule is qualified, where it occurs in that code which most scholars consider the very oldest part of the Buddhist literature, by the addition of words which it is impossible to quote, but which show a depravity of the moral standard, a misconception of the moral proportion of things, which is perfectly appalling.

§ 5. In comparison with the real importance of the second, fourth, and third, and the immense fictitious importance of the

[1] Culla Vagga, vii. 1, 3. S.B.E. xx., 228.
[2] As in Tevijja Sutta and in Digh. Nik. everywhere.
[3] M.V., i. 25, 10. [4] Angut. iv. 73. See *ib.* 100.
[5] S.N. iii. pp. 73, 119; and iv., p. 117, S.B.E.

first rule of conduct, the emphasis laid on the fifth, which forbids strong drink, is trifling. As I have already said, it is frequently absent from the list, even in the most exhaustive and systematic Suttas.[1] The use of strong drink is conspicuously absent from a list of the things which certainly bring a monk to hell.[2] It is condemned in a monk, whose bright light it obscures,[3] and to refrain from it is excellent for any one.[4]

"Let the householder who approves of (adopts) this dharma not give himself to intoxicating drinks; let him not cause others to drink, nor approve of those that drink, knowing it is madness.

"For through intoxication the stupid commit sin, and make other people intoxicated: let him avoid this seat of sin, this madness, this folly, delightful to the stupid."[5]

This is the strongest passage on this subject that I have noticed. I have met with no instance of any history of the evil consequences of it; no births in hell of drunkards, or the like.

When it is mentioned (in its place in the list) it is usually associated in terms of equal importance with warnings against frequenting theatres and dancing and music halls, as one of the forms of idleness, rather than as a degrading habit, or as leading to mischief. One can only wonder how a rule so little insisted on, and so little observed by the laity except in fulfilment of special vows, can have kept its place in the Five-fold Code at all.

[1] e.g. Tevij. S., Brahmaj. Sutt., Saman. S.; but see Kutādanta S. 26.
[2] Angut. iv. 64.
[3] Culla. V. xii. 1, 3. Angut. iv. 50.
[4] S.N. ii. 4.
[5] Dhammika S. 22. S.B.E. x., b, 66.

CHAPTER XII

SPECIAL MORAL RULES OF THE COMMUNITY. THE PATIṂOKKHA

THE principal Rules of Conduct in the case of monks—or rather, the principal prohibitions—are embodied in a list or manual, known as the Pātiṃokkha. This word means a "method for clearing oneself of guilt by confession." The list is divided into several groups, each of which follows more or less closely the classification implied in the "Five Rules," which were considered in the last chapter.

First come the four "conditions of defeat," or irremediable faults, fatal to the status of a regular disciple of the Buddha. The first of these is any act of sexual intercourse.[1] The second, in a curious form, forbids stealing. The form of the third, which corresponds to the prohibition of taking life, is interesting because it seems to show a recognition of the special value of human life. It runs: "Whatsoever Bhikkhu shall knowingly deprive of life a human being, or shall seek out an assassin against a human being, or shall utter the praises of death, or incite another to self-destruction, saying, "Ho, my friend, what good do you get by this sinful, wretched life? Death is better to thee than life!" If so thinking, and with such an aim, he by various argument utter the praises of death, or incite another to self-destruction, he, too, is fallen into defeat, he is no longer in communion."[2]

The fourth fatal offence is a form of lying, such as might be the fault of persons in an advanced moral condition; a form of it which would be specially destructive to the spiritual progress of the individual and injurious to the Community. The description of it will interest the reader. "Whatsoever Bhik-

[1] It is here that the words occur, "antamaso," etc., to which I have referred as showing so shocking a depravation of the moral sense.

[2] S.B.E. xiii. 4.

khu, without being conscious of extraordinary qualities, shall give out regarding himself that insight into the knowledge of the noble ones has been accomplished, saying, 'Thus do I know, thus do I perceive,' etc., and at some subsequent time, whether on being pressed, or without being pressed, he, feeling guilty, shall be desirous of being cleansed from his fault, and shall say: 'When I saw not, I said that I saw, telling a fruitless falsehood'; then, unless he so spake through undue confidence, he too has fallen into defeat, he is no longer in communion."

These four great crimes are recited in the formula of warning addressed to monks at their first admission.[1]

After these four irremediable faults come the thirteen called (from the nature of the formalities by which they can be atoned for) "Sanghādisesa." Of these, five are connected with uncleanness; two, with taking life; providing for care, in erecting a hut for the monk's use, that danger to animal life is avoided; while the remaining six are faults of the tongue—lying, slander, obstinate false teaching, causing division, and so on.

We may pass by the two rules called "Aniyata"; the "Nissaggiya Pācittiya," offences against the special rules of the Community as to use of bowls, robes, medicines, etc., and the rule which forbids the possession of gold and silver; and we need only glance briefly at the ninety-two Pacittiya rules. Some of these are curious. Out of about five which are directed against taking life, one forbids digging, lest worms should be killed. Though agriculture is popularly held to be one of the harmless livelihoods, it is entirely forbidden, on account of this scruple, to the monk. Under the head of theft there is only one rule among the ninety-two, and this forbids picking up and keeping a jewel which may have been dropped. Twenty are intended to prevent occasions of sexual offence, ten against slander or false pretensions. Some are against indecorous conduct, including drinking; and several, whether on the ground of indecorum or because war is associated with killing, forbid attendance at military parades and the like.

The collection of prohibitions, thus grouped and distinguished, has been called a Manual for Confession, being recited by the monks at their fortnightly meetings. But it does not occur as a manual in the canonical books. In one of the oldest canonical

[1] M.V., v. 78.

books, called the Sutta Vibhanga, every rule in it is to be found; but they do not follow one another continuously: each is embedded in a great quantity of explanatory matter. First comes the Rule, with the circumstances under which it was enacted; then comes—in many instances—a word-for-word commentary or glossary; this is followed by a number of cases and illustrations. Only after these we come to the next Rule, and so on. The Patimokkha, or bare Collection of Rules, might fill, as a manual, fifteen pages; the Sutta Vibhanga fills, as abbreviated in the printed edition, two hundred and sixty-six. Obviously in such a case, the manual might be a summary of a previously existing treatise, or it might be the nucleus out of which the larger work has grown. In this case, the belief of Buddhists is that the Sutta Vibhanga is the utterance of the Buddha, and the Patimokkha a summary of its contents. European scholars, arguing especially on the existence of the ancient Glossary between the Rule and the Illustrations, are convinced that the opposite is the true order of events. They are probably right.

But since the Sutta Vibhanga—that is, the amplified work—is a part of the canon, believed by Buddhists to be the Buddha's own words, and apparently part of the canon from the earliest days of its compilation,[1] we cannot leave it out of reckoning or discuss the morality of the Buddhist books as if they contained only the Patimokkha.

It is worth while, therefore, at the expense of some tediousness, to give the reader some idea of the way in which a moral principle is discussed in the work I am describing. I take a few samples out of the twenty-seven closely-printed pages which contain, with many abbreviations, the chapter on theft.[2]

First, a very long story—over four octavo pages—is told about a monk named Dhaniyo. The other monks, at the end of the three months of retirement in the wet season, broke up the grass huts in which they had lived, and carried away the grass and sticks. Dhaniyo did not leave like the rest, but they, while he

[1] This is implied in M.V. i. 36, 14, where probably "Suttaṃ" is the Patimokkha and "Vyañjanaṃ" the Sutta Vibhanga. But I have far too high an opinion of Gotama to believe for a moment that he had anything to do with the Sutta Vibhanga as it now stands.

[2] Oldenberg, *Vinaya Pitaka*, 1.

was on his begging-rounds, broke up his hut and carried away the grass and sticks. This occurred three times. Now Dhaniyo was a potter's son; so he made himself a nice little hut of clay; but this, because it implied some danger to animal life, the Buddha condemned, and ordered it to be destroyed. Dhaniyo then went to the forester, and begged some wood of him; and the forester gave him some cartloads of the king's deodar timber. The prime minister inquired for the timber, and was surprised to learn from the forester that the king had given it to Dhaniyo. He found on inquiry that this was not true, and the forester was brought bound before the king. But as he was being dragged along, Dhaniyo saw him, learnt the cause, and went with him to the king. The king treated the monk with great respect, but asked whether it was true that he (the king) had given him the timber. Dhaniyo prevaricated about it, and was dismissed by the king with a severe rebuke. People were scandalized at this misconduct and untruth in one of the monks who made such high professions, and the matter was brought to the Buddha. The Community were called together, and Dhaniyo was publicly rebuked for taking timber when it had not been given. The Buddha then asked a monk who had formerly been a nobleman what was the minimum value of theft for which the king would execute, imprison, or banish a thief; and on learning that the amount was so and so (one " pāda) he promulgated the rule:—

" Whatsoever monk, with intent to steal, takes anything ungiven, being such that kings, catching a thief taking it, would execute, imprison, or banish him, as a robber, a fool, a madman, or a thief, that monk so taking ungiven is 'defeated' and expelled."

Then follows a story—nearly a page—of how some bad monks robbed the king's stores of a quantity of material for robes, and disregarded the Buddha's rule, on the pretext that it applied to a forest only and not to a town. This led to the promulgation of the rule in a new form, with the words, " whether in forest or town."

Next come seven pages of explanations of the terms used in this rule, and in a curious gloss upon it, of which explanations the following may serve as specimens :—

" Punish " means " punish with hand, or foot, or rod, or stick, or half-rod, or by cutting"; "bind" means "bind with ropes, chains, fetters, or in house prison, or city prison, or village prison, or town prison, or putting under restraint"; "banish" means "banish from village, or town, or city, or district, or province"; "in the earth" means "goods placed in the earth, dug in, or covered," and so on. Then we have such refinements as these: If a monk looks a second time with thievish mind at goods placed in the earth, or looks for a spade or a basket, or goes near, he is guilty of a fault. If he breaks the sticks or creepers at the place, he is guilty of a fault. If he moves the earth, or lifts it, or takes it away, he is guilty of a fault. If he handles the pot, it is a fault; if he shakes it, it is a great offence; if he moves it, an unpardonable offence.

In the same sentence follow about twenty more possible cases, each with its gravity assigned. Of sentences like this, each with its ten or twenty possible cases, there follow between twenty and thirty.

Then comes a sentence to this effect. A monk tells another monk to take away such and such an article; it is a fault. That monk, meaning to take it, takes it; both are guilty of an unpardonable offence. A monk tells another to take away such and such an article: he, meaning to take it, takes away something else: the mistaken one is not guilty; the one who would take away is guilty of an unpardonable offence. A monk tells another to take something: he, meaning to take another thing, takes it: both are guilty of an unpardonable offence. About seventeen more cases follow.

About fifty cases are then briefly enumerated. This ends the first section on Theft.

The next section consists of about one hundred and fifty cases of the following form: "At that time some mango stealers dropped a mango and ran away: the monks, thinking, 'Make haste before the owners see us,' with thievish mind ate it: the owners blamed them as no true monks. They felt remorse, and went and confessed it to the Buddha, who decreed that they had been guilty of an unpardonable sin." The same with a jambu fruit (told in full), the same with a tamarind, and so on. One knows not whether to be more annoyed at the silly accumulation of cases, or at the utterly technical and uninstructive character of the decisions.

The explanation, which is given even now by Buddhist authorities, of this tedious accumulation, is that it was necessary to mention every form of theft, lest any form, not being specially forbidden, should be thought lawful. Such a notion was no doubt in the minds of those who were capable of covering leaf after leaf with these pretended instances. But it is not the notion of any one to whom moral principles are a living reality. It betrays a marvellous deadness of the moral sense, an utter ignorance of what constitutes the meaning and value of moral action or restraint. It is the work of men to whom conduct had become a matter not of principle, or motive, or character, but of mechanical conformity to rule. Convinced as I am that these "instances" were drawn up, not indeed after the Pitakas, for they are often alluded to in Pitaka books, and the knowledge of them commended, but long after the death of Gotama and his early disciples, I see in them a proof how the moral sense was benumbed by Buddhist views of life and by the manner in which the monks even then lived.

Let those who talk of comparing the Buddhist morality with the Christian, compare this method of illustrating a commandment with that by which Our Lord Jesus Christ, in the Sermon on the Mount, let in by a word a flash of light on the inner meaning and life of each precept as He touched it; or with the way in which His Apostle showed up the root and value of outward morality when he said: "Lie not one to another, brethren, for ye are members one of another." The two moralities have no more in common than a list of bones on paper has with a living body.

A worse thing has to be said. This method of innumerable illustrations, by pretended cases in which monks so acted, of every way in which a command can be broken, is applied to sexual offences with still greater fullness. The pages devoted in the Pārājika book to the other three great faults together are about seventy; those devoted to offences against purity are forty. In the Sanghādisesa, the proportion is even larger. It is impossible to do more than glance at the pages, as one turns them over in disgust; but it is right to say deliberately, that they go far beyond specifying all possible forms of licentiousness, to expatiate in regions of impossible and unimaginable obscenity.

I do not wish to put on this a worse construction than is absolutely necessary, but the least that can be said is this: the deadness of moral feeling, which can allow the moralist to compile such lists on any topic, is immensely more signal when he applies the method to this.

CHAPTER XIII

MONASTIC RULES OF THE COMMUNITY

THE disciplinary rules of the Community, as distinguished from the moral rules, need not detain us very long. They have in great part already come before us.

The "Foundation," as it is often said, of the monastic life consists in the four "Resources," the minimum of dwelling, dress, food, and condiments. These and their qualifications are dwelt upon in the Vinaya Pitaka, in the minutest detail; for instance, all the possible materials of which slippers may or may not be made are enumerated; but the important features of the Rule are but few. They may be grouped under three heads: the conditions and ceremonies of admission into the Community; the method of conducting its business; the seasons for assembly and for retirement.

Admission, etc. Boys were to be admitted to the condition of novices—having renounced the world but not having entered into the full profession of the Community—from the age of fifteen; in exceptional cases, as soon as they were old enough to scare crows.[1] The candidate had his head shaved, put on the yellow robes, and declared his trust by a threefold repetition of the formula: "I take refuge in the Buddha: I take refuge in the Doctrine: I take refuge in the Community."

Each younger monk was to be under a tutor, and his relation to him was to be like that of son to father, every possible respect, attendance, and consideration being due on the part of the pupil, and all possible help and guidance being given by the tutor. A very similar relation was that between scholar and instructor; the difference probably is, that while any monk could be instructor (ācāriyo), only he who presented the lad for admission could be tutor (upajjhāyo).

[1] M.V., i. 51. The rules for admission, novitiate, etc., are gathered from different chapters of the first book of Maha Vagga.

Cripples and deformed persons, slaves, debtors and criminals, persons in the king's service, and animals,[1] were expressly disqualified for admission; nor could any one be admitted without the permission of his parents.

The novitiate continued at least until the age of twenty, and then full admission might be conferred. This important ceremony could not take place except in a chapter of at least ten, and the monk who, as tutor, presented the candidate must have been himself at least ten years in full profession. The candidate was to be warned, lest he should afterwards find the life harder than he expected, that he could not look for more than the minimum of necessary things, etc.; viz. for food, morsels given in alms; for clothing, rags from a dust-heap; for dwelling, the foot of a tree; for medicine or condiment, a filthy liquid.[2] All beyond these, he was to be warned, was indulgence—not necessarily forbidden, but not to be claimed.

Having been carefully instructed as to his part in the ceremony, the candidate was asked whether he was in any way disqualified; for instance, by leprosy or certain other diseases, or by debt; whether he was twenty years old, and had his parents' consent; and who was his tutor. He then made his humble request three times to the Community to "draw him out" (of the world) and to receive him. A resolution to that effect having been duly proposed and carried, he repeated the "refuges," was warned of the four great faults that involve expulsion, and so was received into full standing in the Community.

Assemblies, Chapters, etc. The institution of the Uposatha,[3] or day of strictness ("abstinence" in a general sense, rather than "fasting"[4]) is said to have been adopted from Brahman ascetics, who used to recite their doctrine on the four quarter-days of the moon—the eighth and the fourteenth or fifteenth of each half month. The Vinaya does not prescribe for these days any other recitation of doctrine than that of the Patimokkha,

[1] It is amusing to read, "Let the animal, O monks, that has not received the 'Upasampadā' ordination not receive it; if it has received it, let it be expelled from the fraternity." S.B.E. xiii., p. 219. The second question asked of the candidate for full admission was: "Are you a human being?"

[2] See above ch. iii. p. 30.

[3] Sinhalese, "pohoya," popularly, "poya."

[4] In fact, special "uposatha" meals are mentioned as an indulgence M.V., i. 30, 4.

or manual for self-examination, of which the contents have already been described. The monks were to come together—all who dwelt within a certain defined area—the smallest number being four; and any one who was absolutely prevented from coming was to send, by a proxy, the assurance of his having kept the rule. The lists of offences were recited from memory[1] by some chosen monk, audibly and carefully, the rest solemnly promising attention, and undertaking to disclose any breach of any rule of which they might have been guilty. As rule after rule was recited, if no fault was disclosed, the officiant was to say, "I take it from your silence that you are clear," and so to proceed. How confession was to be made, if there was any fault to be disclosed, the original rules do not say.[2] It must have been intended that confession should be made to the whole chapter. But it is elsewhere provided that no one conscious of a fault should come at all; that one should confess his fault privately to a brother monk before coming into the assembly;[3] and that if a fault occurred to the memory of any one who had come, he should privately consult his neighbour about it. Out of this probably grew the later form of the procedure, according to which confession is made secretly by each to his neighbour in the chapter.

Here may be mentioned a somewhat similar ceremony called Pavārana,[4] which was appointed to take place at the end of the annual retirement, or "was." The monks were to assemble, and each in turn, from the eldest down, was to invite the rest to tell him of any fault which had been seen or heard or suspected in him. With the principle of such a proceeding, the detailed rules, as in the case of the Patimokkha, are inconsistent; for they assume that the course will be, if any fault is alleged, not to tell it in answer to the above invitation, but, by alleging it beforehand, to exclude the delinquent from the ceremony altogether. The theory of mutual candour, on which the institution was based, was too high for practice. The detailed rules are concerned with preventing false accusations.

Although it is not originally prescribed that any other business than the Patimokkha should be transacted on Uposatha days, yet it seems clear that at the same chapters other matters were dealt with; such as the admission of a novice or a monk, the

[1] Emphasis is laid on the importance of knowing it by heart. M. V. i. 26, 14.
[2] M.V. ii. 3.
[3] *Ib.* 27.
[4] *Ib.* iv. 13.

appointment of a reader, a manager of the dining-hall, or other officer, the delimitation of boundaries, the decision of a disputed question about a rule or a text. Whatever the question, the chapter proceeded by a fixed method of resolution. A leading or senior monk proposed the resolution : " Let the Community of monks hear me! Such and such a thing is proposed. Let any one who is in favour of it be silent, and any one against it speak. I put it to you the second time (in the same form), and a third time." He then announces the result : " The Community is in favour of it, therefore it is silent. This I take to be the decision." In some cases the proposals were announced only once before the question was put, but the procedure was always substantially the same. In such chapters members guilty of the great offences were to be expelled ; others were to be censured, suspended, or restored. The Uposatha Hall would thus grow to be, what it is now in Ceylon, the chapter-house of the local branch of the Community.

Seasons, etc.: " *Was.*"—The rule that a portion of the year should be spent, not in travelling about, as the Buddha and his followers at first travelled, but in retirement, is said to have been suggested to Gotama by the complaints of people who were scandalized at seeing his monks walking about in the wet season. " In the rains," they said, " the earth is covered with young plants and multitudinous germs of life ; and even the heretical ascetics are careful to avoid injuring these, and make themselves retreats, as the birds make themselves nests at that season of the year.

There was a choice of two periods for beginning the retreat—the full moon of June–July and that of July–August ; in either case it was to last three months. For an urgent reason, connected with religion, the monk might leave the place in which he had resolved to keep his retreat (" vasso," the " rains " ; Sinhalese, " was "), but on no account for more than seven days. Care was to be taken in the choice of a place, that the retreat might not be interrupted; and several unsuitable places, such as the branch of a tree, or under an earthenware vessel, were forbidden. To spend the time in a caravan on a journey, or on board ship—strange to say—was allowed.[2]

As a rule the place chosen seems to have been a regular Vihara

[1] M.V. iii. 1. [2] *Ib.* iii. 12.

(monk's "dwelling"), often apparently that in which the monk always lived (by Buddhaghosha's time this seems to have been usual[1]); but already in Gotama's lifetime the custom began, which now gives its character to the "was" in Ceylon, of great people inviting monks to spend the retreat with them.[2]

There is no prescribed way of passing the time, nor are any special duties assigned in the Vinaya to this season of retirement.

Whether in the rainy season or at other times, it was of course intended that a considerable part of a monk's time should be spent in meditation, and the advanced disciples are often represented as so engaged; but it is an instance of the practical character of the early Rule, that no attempt was made to enforce upon all so difficult a practice. The elaborate systems of what may be called mechanical meditation or self-mesmerism by mechanical processes (kammaṭṭhānaṃ) belong to a later phase. In these, the monk was recommended to induce peculiar conditions, first of sight and then of mind, by gazing intently at some bright or coloured object—a small circle, water in a bowl, a point of light, and so on; and for certain special meditations, to practise efforts of attention to the actions of breathing. We do not read of these in the earliest books.

The theory of the meditative state ("samādhi," or "concentration") and of the several processes or stages of meditation (jhāna) is set forth, in its ordinary form, in the Sutta on page 89. The four stages are briefly these. In the first, the mind is at work, and both active pleasure and passive happiness are felt; in the second, the mind has ceased to act, but there are still the feelings of pleasure and happiness; in the third stage, active pleasure has ceased, and a calm happiness alone remains; in the fourth, nothing remains but indifference to all sensations and emotions, whether of pain or pleasure.

The attainment of the fourth stage is the starting-point of the various kinds of supernatural powers. The monk who is in the fourth stage of meditation can pass thence into the formless worlds; which are spoken of sometimes as conditions—for instance, in the account of the Buddha's last meditation—sometimes as if they were actual places. This is often extended to actual journeys to the different heavens—those of Brahma, of the thirty-three gods, and so on; and when monks are sent on

[1] See the passage quoted, S.B.E. xiii., p. 299 n. [2] M.V. iii. 14, 1.

errands of this kind it is sometimes noted, at any rate in the Commentaries, that they entered first into the fourth stage of meditation. It was from that stage that the Buddha performed the supernatural act of deliberately entering on Nirvana.

As the Sutta above referred to shows, among the supernatural capacities (iddhi) to which meditation leads are those of remembering one's own former existences, and of seeing the passage of all beings from life to life. Elsewhere is added to these the power of reading the thoughts of others.

All who have reached the Fourth Jhana possess, it is pretended, the power of working miracles, especially of flying through the air, water, or earth; of causing startling displays, especially of flames and smoke; of creating for the occasion bodies, or the likeness of bodies; and so on.

Miracles, being thus of universal attainment by "rahats," are not treated as of much importance. Gotama himself despised them. He generally told one of his monks to make the display, if it was necessary in any case to gain the attention of an individual or of a multitude by such means. He is represented as disparaging miracles as credentials, because any one may say they were done by magic, or by virtue of ordinary austerities.[1]

On the whole the life of a member of the Buddha's Community was encumbered by very few rules. Of rules to prevent indulgence there is an immense accumulation, but very little demand was made on the monk's time. The aim in view was to secure him freedom, and to leave him time and room to train himself. Against idleness and all the other ills which too much leisure and too much solitude bring, the precautions were few and ineffective. In contrast with the endless interference with individual freedom which marked the Brahman system, the liberty which Gotama offered must have been charming indeed. But a life almost without social duties and entirely with necessity for exertion, physical or mental, is not a life which the average man can lead with safety. As Aristotle said of solitude, it is fit only for either a god or a beast. There is too much propriety in the favourite similes in which it was compared, by the Buddhists themselves, to the life of an elephant or a rhinoceros.

[1] Digh. Nik. xi., *ab init.* The miracles exhibited to the Jatilas by Gotama are an exception, and are not the only reason for ascribing to that narrative a later date than that of the chapters which precede it.

CHAPTER XIV

THE FEMALE COMMUNITY

THE Community of Nuns was never in practice a very important part of Buddhism, either in the primitive Indian system or in Ceylon; though it may have been specially fostered for a while in Asoka's day, and seems to have been recently revived to some extent in Siam and in Burma. It is represented in the Vinaya Pitaka as an afterthought, and as one reluctantly admitted by the Buddha.[1] He is said to have been persuaded to form a Community of Nuns on the pressing and repeated application of his aunt, Mahāpajāpati, who had nursed him after his mother's death. Three times the application was refused. Mahapajapati cut off her hair and put on yellow robes, and appeared travel-worn and tearful before Ananda, who was moved to plead her cause. Even to Ananda the request was granted only with great reluctance. Eight rules were laid down, which appear mainly intended to regulate the relation of dependence in which the female community was to stand towards the male; and Pajapati was admitted. Nothing is said of the admission of others with her, though it is constantly taken for granted that there were many. Thus, although the application of Pajapati is recorded in detail, the account of the formation of the Female Community is very meagre indeed in comparison with that of the Community of men.

But what is most curious is the prophecy attributed to the Buddha in reference to this institution. He had no sooner instituted it than he announced, as we read, that it would be the ruin of his work! "If," Ananda, "women had not received permission to go out from the household life and enter the homeless state under the doctrine and discipline proclaimed by the Tathagata, then would the pure religion, Ananda, have lasted long;

[1] Culla Vagga, x., a late book; confessedly later, and probably very much later than 381 B.C.

the good law would have stood fast for a thousand years. But since, Ananda, women have now received that permission, the pure religion, Ananda, will not now last so long; the good law will now stand fast for five hundred years. Just, Ananda, as houses in which there are many women and but few men, are easily violated by robber burglars, so, Ananda, under whatever doctrine and discipline women are allowed to go forth from the household life into the homeless state, that religion will not last long."[1] The entrance of women will be like that of mildew in a field of rice; like blight upon sugar-cane. But the eight rules which had been laid down would be an embankment to prevent overflow and loss. The Nuns were to follow the rules prescribed for monks as far as these were applicable, and in other matters to be guided by their own sense of what was best. Their acts were not valid without confirmation by the monks, and they had to repair to the monks for instruction.

In other parts of the Vinaya the existence of nuns is constantly taken for granted, but there are scarcely any direct accounts of them or of any institutions connected with them. The pious women who are prominent, and many women are in the Vinaya Pitaka, are not nuns; and it is the same, with at least one exception, in other Pitaka books. What is said of monks is constantly repeated of nuns, but the existence of the latter is still chiefly a theoretical existence.

Professor Oldenberg (*Buddha*, p. 381) says: "It is to be doubted whether at any time there was in the spiritual sisterhood a degree of influence which could be felt bearing on the Buddhist Community as a whole." This is a very cautious way of stating it. The Professor remarks in a note that the numbers given in the Dipavansa of monks and nuns in Asoka's day, exaggerated as they are, throw a certain light on the relative importance of the two orders. "The Chronicle speaks of eight hundred million monks, and of only ninety-six thousand nuns"; more than ten thousand monks to one nun.

There is one book which is treated as belonging to the Pitaka collection, called Therigāthā, or "Stanzas spoken by Female Elders." It contains some ancient verses, but for the most part it belongs to the latest stage of the canonical literature, as is evident from its being crowded with technical terms and lists,

[1] Culla Vagga, x., 1, 6. S.B.E. xx., p. 325.

and even summaries of the allusions, metaphors, and striking expressions which the older books contain. In most cases these verses have no historical setting, and even when they are attributed to persons whose names occur in the Vinaya, in connection with Gotama's life, such as Pajāpati, Nandā, or Ambapāli, they are merely verses which any one might have written, and to which those names are affixed. It cannot be said, therefore, that the Therigatha add anything to our knowledge of the nuns.

Most of them narrate, briefly or at some length, the religious "experiences" of the supposed authors. They generally end by saying: "I have attained Nirvana"; or, "This is my last body"; or, "Mara [or death], thou hast no more power over me." Some say: "It is now just a week since I attained emancipation." They say how long they had gone on—sometimes many years—without making any progress, and on what occasion they were converted. Several claim to have been converted by the Buddha himself, and at such and such a place. A great many owe their conversion to a very earnest nun called Paṭācāra. And they tell us of their former life. "I was rich and lived in luxury"; "I was high-born and courted by many"; another had been a fire-worshipper, or a heretic, or a very bad woman. Some comment on their own loss of beauty, and draw a moral from the ravages old age has made on them.

Several of the longer passages describe nuns resisting the entreaties of lovers who say:—

An' ye sall walk in silk attire
And siller hae to spare;

or of parents who urge that the suitor

is chief of Erringtown
And lord of Langly Dale.

The last of all is an elaborate and almost romantic account of the Princess Sumedha, whom the beautiful Prince Anikaratta, with all that her parents could do to aid him, tried in vain to divert from her resolution to renounce the world.

As regards later history, Asoka speaks, in one of his later edicts, of the "many female mendicants." This is indisputable evidence of the existence of the institution in his day.

In the account of Mahinda, the converter of Ceylon, and his sister Sanghamitta, the bearer of the Bo-branch, we shall see great importance given to the female community, as founded in Ceylon. The Mahavansa tells us what multitudes of women then entered it. But the position of the institution in the Mahavansa is very similar to its position in the Vinaya Pitaka. After its foundation it hardly appears again, except in allusions. A king sends his daughter to the convent, or he builds a hall for the nuns; but except in this incidental way they make no figure in the chronicle.

The traditions of Ceylon are in keeping with this. There are, so far as I know, no places named after nuns, no stories about famous nuns, none of their dwellings or halls, so far as we know, remain. In the later century, when the Sinhalese kings brought monks to revive the institution, from Burma or Siam, we never read of their bringing nuns or noticing the want of them.

There are none, or very few, in Ceylon now; and the received opinion, I believe, agrees with the conclusion to which I have been led, that the institution of female mendicants was never much developed either in Magadha or in Ceylon.[1]

[1] See a little more of the history in Chap. XXIV, p. 230.

CHAPTER XV

RELIGION OF THE LAITY

IN the last chapter but one I showed what form the fundamental principles of right and wrong, as Buddhism teaches them, take in their application to monastic life. We have now to look at these principles of conduct in the form in which they concern the laity, as we may call those who, while accepting the Buddha's teaching, have not bound themselves to the discipline of the Community, but continue in home life. The teaching was for all living beings in "the three worlds"—for deities of every grade, for human beings, for demons, and even for brutes; but the discipline was primarily for the members, male and female, of the Community, and only secondarily for the householder. For him one at least of the Five Rules of Conduct takes a different form. He is not called to celibacy, but is required to be faithful to his wife. In regard to this duty the teaching of our books is excellent. The ideal Brahmans, or the Brahmans of old, are commended because they did not buy their wives, but married for love.[1] And the husband and wife who have lived together here in equal faith, conduct, renunciation, and knowledge, may hope to be together in the next world.[2] The strong things that are said against women and against all intercourse with them, are intended for monks: about women, as members of the household, the tone of the Pitaka books is respectful and generous.

Nor can the layman be expected altogether to avoid taking life; it is no blame to him if he kills animals for the table. He incurs, however, the demerit of such actions, and their evil consequences in future births: this is his misfortune, and a good reason for abandoning, as an act of prudence, a mode of living which involves it. But neither by taking life, nor by drinking alcohol—except after a special vow—is the layman guilty of any rebellion against Buddhism.

[1] S.N. ii. 7. [2] Aṅgut. iv. 55. See S.N. i. 6, 18. Sigālovāda S., etc.

While his life is full of "danger" and almost inevitably involves demerit, he has the opportunity of accumulating on the other side a balance of merit, by well-placed gifts, seed sown in the right field, that is, given to the Community. He may secure many births in heavens and few in hells. But he is never any nearer to ultimate escape from existence or secure of not going down into the three low states—as brute, or goblin, or in hell, until he has entered the paths of Buddhist training; while direct entrance on Nirvana, from the lay-life, is beyond his hopes.

"Two whose mode of life and occupation are quite different are not equal; a householder maintaining a wife, and an unselfish virtuous man. A householder is intent upon the destruction of other living creatures, being unrestrained, but a Muni always protects living creatures, being restrained.

"As the crested bird with the blue neck (the peacock) never attains the swiftness of the swan, even so a householder does not equal a Bhikkhu, a secluded Muni meditating in the wood."[1]

But there is no reason altogether to exclude the householder from the benefits of piety, as described in such sentences as the following:—

"He who has done meritorious acts is happy here, is happy after death, is happy in both worlds; he is happy and delighted when he sees the purity of his own course of action (kamma). . . . He is glad when he thinks, 'I have wrought merit'; still more glad when he has entered on some happy condition (in the next life)."[2]

The Buddha was asked whether any householder, who had not abandoned the bond of household life, did, after the dissolution of the body, reach the end of sorrow (Nirvana). "No," he replied. He was then asked, "Has any such householder gone to a heaven after death?" "Not one hundred," he replied, "nor two hundred, nor three, nor four, nor five hundred, but many more householders than that, without leaving the bonds of household life, have gone to heaven after death."

The case of the orthodox layman is thus much better than that of the heretical ascetic. For the next question was, "Has any naked ascetic (ājīvako) made an end of sorrow?" "None." "Has any gone to heaven?" "In ninety-one cycles, I can

[1] S.N. i. 12. S.B.E. x., b, p. 35; and see *ib.* ii. 6, *ib.* p. 46.
[2] Dh., 18.

remember only one naked ascetic gone to heaven; and he held the doctrine of the fruit of actions and the necessity of action."[1]

In another Sutta Gotama is said to have revealed that multitudes of his lay followers, of pure and chaste lives, had got rid of the first five attachments,[2] and were sure of entering Nirvana from the next world, without returning here; that multitudes, even of householders, who lived in the enjoyment of worldly goods but were religious and attentive to teaching, were past all doubt and secure of their ultimate future.[3]

Although, therefore, it is impossible to go straight from household life into Nirvana, that end may be secured in the nearer or further future, and in any case a birth in some heaven may be expected by the good layman.[4]

The regular course of instruction for laymen is as follows: The preacher speaks first of giving, then of conduct (the five prohibitions, etc.), then of heaven; then he speaks of the dangers of pleasure and the profit of retirement from the world. Only after these have been grasped will he speak of the characteristic teachings of the Buddhas, the Four Truths, and the like. The type of all such instructions is to be found in the following account, which I quote from Professor Rhys Davids' translation, of the conversion of a vast number of King Bimbisara's subjects, when the king himself had embraced the Buddha's teaching.[5]

" Then the Blessed One perceived by his mind the thoughts of the minds of those eighty thousand overseers over the townships, and held to them a discourse in due order; that is to say, he spake to them of giving, of righteousness, of heaven, of the danger, the worthlessness, the depravity of lusts, and of the advantages of renunciation. And when the Blessed One perceived that they had become pliant, softened, unprejudiced, upraised, and believing in heart, he proclaimed that which is the special doctrine of the Buddhas, that is to say, suffering, its origin, its cessation, and the path.

" Just as a clean cloth, from which all stain has been washed away, would readily take the dye, just even so did those eighty thousand overseers over the townships obtain, even while sitting

[1] Maj. Nik., 71.
[2] See p. 93.
[3] Maj. Nik., 73.
[4] Udana. v. 3, *et passim.*
[5] M.V. v. 1, 9. S.B.E., xvii., pp. 4, 5.

there, the pure and spotless eye of the truth; that is to say, the knowledge that whatever has a beginning, in that is inherent also the necessity of its dissolution.

"And having seen the truth, having mastered the truth, having understood the truth, having penetrated the truth, having overcome uncertainty, having dispelled all doubts, having gained full knowledge, dependent on nobody else for the knowledge of the doctrine of the teacher, they said to the Blessed One: 'Glorious Lord! glorious Lord! just as if one should set up, Lord, what had been overturned, or should reveal what had been hidden, or should point out the way to one who had lost his way, or should bring a lamp into the darkness, in order that those who had eyes might see visible things, thus has the Blessed One preached the doctrine in many ways. We take our refuge, Lord, in the Blessed One, and in the Dhamma, and in the fraternity of Bhikkhus. May the Blessed One receive us from this day forth while our life lasts as his disciples who have taken their refuge in him!'"

To such disciples later in their course such a sermon as the following is constantly addressed:—

"Then the Buddha addressed the Pataligama disciples. 'There are five losses, householders, incurred by him who does not obey the rules of conduct. What five? By neglect he incurs great loss of property, a bad report of him goes about; if he goes into any company, whether of warriors or of Brahmans or of householders or of ascetics, he enters it without confidence and in confusion; in the moment of death he is bewildered; and after death and the dissolution of the body he goes to some evil condition or place of torment or hell. These are the five losses incurred by the man who does not obey the rules of conduct. Exactly the reverse is the case of the good man, and after death he goes to some happy condition or to heaven.[1]

For a monk, indeed, the desire to be born, for instance, as one of the thirty-three deities, is a "low motive"; it comes of desire; and good conduct produced thereby is imperfect. But for laymen and for women it is the recognized incentive. Those monks who attain supernatural vision and can see the re-births of other beings, see many entering on life in the various heavens through good conduct in act, word, and thought.[2] Such rewards

[1] M.V. vi. 28, 4, abridged. [2] Maj. Nik. iv., *et passim*.

are promised to a continued course of good conduct; but the layman is encouraged also by the prodigious fruit which he is told may spring from single acts of merit. For a single offering of food a person is often born in heaven, and that not once but for a long succession of lives. In fact, the heavens are peopled, and even ruled, by deities who have earned their place by such offerings.

On the other hand, there are innumerable places of torment,[1] to which those go whose conduct has been bad in act, word, or thought, or who have been guilty of some one atrocious crime, such as that of the slanderer of Sariputta, or that of Devadatta, when he drew blood from the foot of the Buddha. Such and such a character, or the doer of such and such a deed, is frequently said to be "as good as cast already into hell," just as the virtuous are said to be "as good as gone to heaven already."

The doctrine of heaven and hell is thus especially the layman's religion. The higher attainments and the final goal of Nirvana are left out of sight, and a simple religion is provided for simple folk. It is in fact much more of a religion than the philosophical training of the monks.

The Sutta called the Discourse of Happiness (or, possibly, "of auspicious rites")—the Mahāmangala Sutta—is especially intended for the laity. The favourite use of the word which forms its title is in reference to domestic festivals and home happiness.[2] It commends especially, as among the greatest of blessings, "Waiting on father and mother, protecting wife and child . . . giving alms, taking care of relatives, ceasing from sin, and from intoxicating drink, reverence and humility, contentment and gratitude, patience and pleasant speech," together with opportunities of intercourse with the wise and good, and of hearing the law and religious conversation.[3] The Sutta goes on to extol Nirvana, but this picture of a quiet and religious domestic life is its characteristic part. It is constantly repeated now by the monks in Ceylon, and it is a great pity that nobody understands it.

[1] See, for instance, the series of tortures described in Sanyut. xix. 1 *seq.*

[2] As in the Sinhalese, "magul gedara."

[3] S.N. ii. 4. See the whole in S.B.E., vol. x., p. 44. The next Sutta in importance as regards lay conduct is the Sigalovada Sutta, of which Professor Rhys Davids has given the substance in *Buddhism*, p. 143.

CHAPTER XVI

CASTE

THE statement that Gotama set himself to oppose the system of caste, or that he announced, as a prominent feature of his teaching, the equal admission of all men into his Community, would not be justified by the Pali books. He recognized the fact of caste, but treated its distinctions as insignificant as compared with those of character.

He is represented as often speaking of the miseries of low caste,[1] and as acknowledging the advantages of high caste, *ceteris paribus*.[2] The pride of his own Sakyan birth is owned, even in putting it aside;[3] and the observance of caste rules by Brahmans is commended.

As a matter of fact, he found, according to the records,[4] most of his early followers in the two highest castes; though it is believed by modern Buddhists that he preferred middle rank and held the cultivator's life the most favourable for his religion.

Some have thought that Gotama announced at least a protest of the royal (or Khattiya) caste against the exclusive assumptions of the Brahmans. But the fact that the Buddhavaṃsa (or history of Buddhas) represents a majority of previous Buddhas as Brahmans shows that this was not the Buddhist tradition. Indeed it does not appear from the Pitakas that the Brahmans held an acknowledged position as superior to the Khattiyas: it is sometimes implied that the Khattiyas were superior.[5]

And if it had been the intention of Gotama, as understood by his followers, to announce a revolt against the caste system, it is not likely that the Buddhavansa would have taught that all Buddhas had been either Brahmans or Khattiyas.

It is an exaggeration, therefore, to describe Gotama as a champion of equality against caste tyranny.

[1] Saṃyut. iii. 4. [2] Angut. iv. 85. [3] Culla Vagga, vii. 1, 4.
[4] Sutt. Nipat. ii. 7. [5] Saṃyut. iii. 3, 6. Angut. iii. 13, 1.

On the other hand, both the rules of his Order and his general teaching were practically opposed to the caste principle. All well-born men were equally admissible to the Community ;[1] the idea of caste conferring any claim to status in it is repudiated :[2] all such distinctions are merged in the Community as the rivers in the sea.[3] And as regards the dominion of caste outside the Community, his teaching was calculated to undermine it : it was noble and just.

The passage in which Gotama is represented as refuting the notion that there is a difference of *species* between the castes, often as it has been quoted, cannot be omitted here. (The English reader may need to be reminded that the essence of " caste " as distinguished from " rank " is, that " caste " is a *birth* distinction, and supposed to be indelible. The word " jāti," which we render by " caste," means also " birth.") This celebrated passage is the Vāseṭṭha Sutta of the Sutta Nipata, and is translated by Professor Fausböll in *Sacred Books of the East*, x. 109 *seq.*

Vasettha and Bhāradvāja refer to Gotama the controversy about birth, whether one is a Brahman by birth or by deeds. " I will explain to you, O Vasettha," said the Buddha, " in due order the distinction of living beings according to species, for their species are manifold. Know ye the grass and the trees, although they do not exhibit (it), the marks that constitute species are (for them), and their species are manifold. Then (know ye) the worms and the moths and the different sorts of ants, the marks that constitute species are for them, and their species are manifold."

The same is said of the four-footed animals, small and great ; of the serpents, and the long-backed snakes ; of the fish which range in the water, and of the birds that are borne on wings and move through the air. As in these species the marks that constitute species are abundant, so in men the marks that constitute species are not abundant. Not as regards their hair, head, ears, eyes, nose, lips, or brows ; not as regards their neck, shoulders, belly, back, etc. ; nor as regards their hands, feet, etc., or voice, are the marks that constitute species, as in other species. Difference there is in beings endowed with bodies, but amongst men this is not the case ; the difference among men is nominal. For

[1] Maj. Nik. xi., *et passim*. [2] Culla Vagga, vi. 6, 2. [3] *Ib.*, ix. 1, 4.

whoever among men lives by cow-keeping—know this, O Vasettha, he is a husbandman, not a Brahmana. And whoever among men lives by trade, he is a merchant, not a Brahmana." So with the artisan, the thief, the soldier, the king. "And whoever among men lives by performing household ceremonies—know this, O Vasettha—he is a sacrificer, not a Brahmana. And I do not call one a Brahmana on account of his birth or of his origin from (a particular) mother; he may be called 'bhovādi,'[1] and he may be wealthy, (but) the one who is possessed of nothing and seizes upon nothing, him I call a Brahmana." Then in twenty-seven stanzas the qualities of a good Buddhist disciple are enumerated as constituting the Brahmana: "The man who knows his former dwellings, who sees both heaven and hell, and has reached the destruction of births, him I call a Brahmana." For what has been designated as "name" and "family" in the world is only a term; what has been designated here and there is understood by common consent. Adhered to for a long time are the views of the ignorant; the ignorant tell us, one is a Brahmana by birth. Not by birth is one a Brahmana; nor is one by birth no Brahmana; by work one is a Brahmana, by work one is no Brahmana, just as the husbandman, the artisan, the merchant, etc., are such by *what they do*. The discourse ends by insisting on "karma" (what is *done*), the product of action, as the one great ruling force.

In Assalāyana Sutta[2] we read:—

Assalayana says: "The Brahmans, O Gotama, say thus: the Brahmans are the best caste (literally, the best colour); every other caste is inferior. The Brahmans are the white caste; every other caste is black. The Brahmans alone are pure; those who are not Brahmans are not pure. The Brahmans are the (only) real sons of Brahma, born from his mouth, sprung from Brahma, created by Brahma, heirs of Brahma. But what do you say, sir, about this?"

Then the Buddha asks him whether the wives of the Brahmans are not subject to all those ills and disabilities connected with child-birth to which other women are subject. Assalayana is obliged to confess that this is so, and that the Brahmans put forward their claims in spite of this.

[1] That is virtually "arrogant." See Childers, s.v.

[2] Translated by Prof. Rhys Davids, *Hibbert Lectures*, p. 52.

The Buddha then, applying a comparative method of inquiry, such as we sometimes claim to be modern, asks whether in adjacent countries, such as Bactria and Afghanistan, there are not differences of colour similar to those between the Brahmans and other castes, and yet in these countries whether slaves cannot become masters and masters slaves ? Again Assalayana confesses the fact, and that the Brahmans put forward their claims in spite of it.

Gotama goes on to ask : " How think you, Assalayana ? Is a man who is a murderer, a thief, a libertine, a liar, a slanderer, violent or frivolous in speech, covetous, malevolent, given to false doctrine—will such a one, if he be a Khattiya, or a Vessa, or a Sudda, be born after death, when the body is dissolved, into some unhappy state of misery and woe, but not if he be a Brahman ? " Assalayana replies that the Brahman is in this respect exactly on a par with the others. Gotama then proceeds to put the contrary case ; and Assalayana declares that those who do the contrary to all these evil things are equally reborn into some happy state in heaven, whether they are Brahmans or whether they are not. Gotama asks what force or what comfort there can then be in the claim to especial purity which the Brahmans make.

But he carries the argument still further. " What think you, Assalayana ? Is it the Brahman alone who is able, in this land of ours, to cultivate friendliness, kindliness, charitable feelings ; or can the Khattiya, the Vessa, and the Sudda do so too ? "

And when Assalayana acknowledges that they are all equal in this respect, Gotama compels him to grant that they are equally pure in their bodies, and that the flame kindled by an outcast, by means of two pieces of wood taken from a dog's drinking vessel or from a pigsty, will light a sacred fire as shining and beaming and bright, and as good for sacrificial purposes, as a flame kindled by a Brahman or a Khattiya by means of sweet-smelling sandalwood.

Then, still questioning, Gotama points out that, whereas when a mare is united with an ass the offspring is a mule, different from both father and mother, the union of a Khattiya and a Brahman, or *vice versa*, results in offspring which resembles both the parents ; so that it is clear there is no such difference of species between the castes as there is between a donkey and a horse.

Finally, he asks the young Brahman scholar, "To which of two brothers, one an initiated student and the other not, would the Brahmans themselves, on sacred and solemn occasions, give the precedence ?"

"To the initiated student," replies the Brahman ; "for what thing given to an uninitiated person, not a student, will bear with it great advantage ?"

"But if the initiated student be of bad character and evil habits," rejoins Gotama, "and the other be of good character and virtuous habits, to whom then will the Brahmans themselves give the precedence ?"

"To the uninitiated," is the reply ; "for what thing given to a man of bad character and of evil habits will bring with it great advantage ?"

"But in the former answer you yourself, Assalayana," says the master, "have given up the pre-eminence of birth, and in the latter the pre-eminence of acquaintance with the sacred words. And in so doing you yourself have acknowledged that purity of all castes which I proclaim !"

"When he had thus spoken," says the Sutta, "the young Brahman Assalayana sat there silent, awkward, distressed. looking downwards, reflecting, not able to answer."

Then Gotama tells an appropriate story, winding up with a kind word to the young scholar. And the Sutta concludes with Assalayana's confession : "Most excellent, Gotama, are the words of thy mouth ; most excellent ! May the venerable Gotama receive me as a disciple and as a true believer, from this day forth as long as life endures !"

I add an abridged translation of Ambaṭṭha Sutta.[1]

Ambattha, a young Brahman, is sent by his tutor, Pokkharasādi, to visit Gotama, and to find out whether the reports of his excellence are true ; in particular, whether he has the thirty-two marks, which distinguish one, who, if a layman, will be a universal emperor, or if a mendicant, a Buddha. The monks welcomed Ambattha as a very well-born and distinguished person whom the Buddha would be glad to talk to.

Ambattha began by showing some discourtesy. Instead of sitting down respectfully, as was usual, he walked up and down while he saluted Gotama. Gotama asked him whether it was

[1] Digh. Nik. iii.

his custom to salute elderly Brahmans in that way. "No," said Ambattha; "a Brahman before entering into conversation with another Brahman would adopt the same attitude as the person addressed. But to shavelings, monklings, mere owners of property,[1] black men, men sprung from the foot of Brahma, we use the same manner of address as I have used to you." Gotama asked him to remember his business, adding that he assumed the airs of a person of culture only because he was really uncultivated. This expression, "uncultivated," made Ambattha very angry, and he became openly insulting. "The Sakya race is haughty, abusive, hasty, and overbearing." Such mere owners of property, he said, ought to pay reverence to Brahmans. He proceeded to give an instance of the rudeness of the Sakyans. When he once went on some business to one of their gatherings, they poked and nudged one another and made fun, but took no notice of him. Gotama replies that even sparrows chatter and amuse themselves in their own nest, and Kapilavastu is the Sakyans' home. Then Ambattha plainly states his claim. There are four castes, Gotama—Khattiya, Brahman, Vessa, Sudda; of these four, the three (Khattiya, Vessa, Sudda) are attendants to wait on the Brahmans; so it is not right that mere owners of property like the Sakyans should not reverence the Brahmans." This was the third time the young man had applied the expression "mere owners of property" to the Sakyans.

Then the Buddha thought: This is too bad, the way this young Ambattha is disparaging the Sakyans as mere owners of property! Suppose I ask him about his own clan? So Gotama asked him, "Of what clan are you, Ambattha?" "I am a Krishnayan." "The Sakyans, then, if you go back in the genealogy, are descended from your masters, and you are descended from a slave of the Sakyans." And this he explains by a curious genealogical legend, according to which the Sakyans were derived from some banished princes of the family of the great Okkāka, while the Krishnayans descended from a slave woman of the same king.

Hereupon the young men who had come with Ambattha

[1] *Ibbhā.* Of this and of the following word curious and inconsistent explanations are given. The above is the best I can arrive at, as being nearest to the literal meaning, but it is hardly satisfactory.

struck into the conversation. "Do not so severely disparage Ambattha as slave-born. Ambattha is a noble and learned youth, and well able to hold his own with you."

To which Gotama replies: "If you hold that Ambattha is ill-born, and ignorant, and unable to maintain the discussion, then let him stand aside and you carry on the discussion with me; but if you hold Ambattha well-born, and learned, and competent, then you please stand aside, and let Ambattha and me talk."

To this they agreed. Gotama then proposed a question to Ambattha. The form in which it is proposed is very curious, and singularly un-Socratic, but frequently occurs in the Buddhist dialogue.

"Here, Ambattha, is a reasonable question which comes to you: against your will you must answer it. If you do not answer, or go from one thing to another, or are silent, or go away, then and there your head will split in seven. What think you, Ambattha? What have you heard from the tradition of aged Brahmans as to the origin of the Krishnayans?"

Ambattha was silent. Gotama repeated the question. He was still silent. Then Gotama said: "Answer now, Ambattha; this is no time for you to be silent. Whoever fails to answer when asked a reasonable question by the Tathagata for the third time, his head will split in seven."

At the same time a demon with a blazing iron sledge-hammer stood in the air over Ambattha, ready to carry out the threat. Ambattha saw him and his hair stood on end; he ran for protection to Gotama and begged him to ask his question again.

And when the question had been repeated, Ambattha acknowledged that the received tradition of the Krishnayans' origin was exactly as the Buddha had stated it. Ambattha's friends were then as strong in disparaging his birth as they had before been in maintaining it; and Gotama begged them not to speak so severely of him as slave-born, for the slave-girl's son had become a great Rishi, and had returned to King Okkaka, and compelled him, by a threatening series of miraculous plagues, to give him his daughter.

Gotama then asked Ambattha, "If a man is the son of a Khattiya by a Brahman woman, will he get seat and water among Brahmans?" "He will." "And be admitted to share their dish and bowl?" "Yes." "Will they admit him as a student of the mantras?" "Yes." "Will they give him their daughters?" "Yes." "Will Khattiyas anoint him to Khattiya rank?" "No." "Why?" "Because he is not born (of their caste) on the mother's side." "Will the son of a Brahman by a Khattiya woman be received to seat and water, bowl and dish among Brahmans?" "Yes." "Will they admit him as a student?" "Yes." "Give him their women?" "Yes." "Will Khattiyas anoint him?" "No." "Why?" "Because he is not born (of their caste) on the father's side."

"Then, Ambattha," says Gotama, "whether you look at it from the woman's side or from the man's,[1] the Khattiyas are higher and the Brahmans lower. Take the case of a Brahman who is expelled in disgrace by his fellow-Brahmans, will Brahmans receive him, or eat with him, or teach him?" "No." "Will they give him their women?" "No." "But if a Khattiya is expelled by Khattiyas, will Brahmans receive him, feed him, and teach him?" "Yes." "Give him their daughters?" "Yes."

"Then even when a Khattiya is in the utmost disgrace, the Khattiyas are the superiors and the Brahmans the inferiors?"

This has all been an *argumentum ad hominem*; the true moral is attached at the end.

"It was a Brahman, Ambattha, who uttered the verse:—

> The Khattiya is best among those who reckon family[2]
> But the man of perfect conduct and knowledge is best among gods and men.

and this, I think, Ambattha, is very well said."

The following, though adopted by the compiler of the Sanyutta Nikaya, is evidently of Brahmanical origin:—

> Ask not of race, but ask of conduct:
> From the stick is born the sacred fire:
> The wise ascetic, though lowly born,
> Is noble in his modest self-control.

[1] This rendering is hardly borne out by the commentary, but I can find no other intelligible.

[2] So the Buddhist authorities, ancient and modern, understand the words, "ye gottapaṭisārino." Prof. Rhys Davids, in a note to his *Questions of Milinda*, S.B.E. xxxv., p. 229, renders: "those who observe the rules of exogamous marriage," as if "going from family to family."

Subdued by truth, subject to discipline,
Perfect in sacred love, trained in holy conduct,
The truly invested sacrificer—him call to your rites;
He offers seasonably, and is worthy of the gift.[1]

Teaching of this sort is a commonplace of the later Brahmanism, as well as of Buddhism. In the Mahābhārata—where indeed there is a great deal that is thoroughly Buddhist in substance if not in origin—we read, for instance: "The Brahmana who is vain and haughty, who is addicted to vices and wedded to evil and degrading practices, is like a Sudra. On the other hand, I consider a Sudra who is always advanced with these virtues—righteousness, self-restraint, and truthfulness—as a Brahmana. A man becomes a Brahmana by his character."

[1] "Sacrificer's fee." Saṃyut. vii. 1, 9.

CHAPTER XVII

GENERAL ESTIMATE OF THE MORAL SYSTEM

IN looking back at the moral system which we have sketched, the reader will no doubt be impressed by the vividness with which, from amid the dull enumerations, the merely imaginary stages of attainment, and the irrelevant metaphysical speculations, there stand out certain noble features, exhibiting a high ideal of purity, kindness, and moral earnestness. I do not wish to detract from that impression. I share it, and continued study of the books does not weaken it. But I should not be putting the whole case before my reader unless I pointed out to him, not only, as I have done, the qualifications which apply to those points in which the Buddhist theory of morality excels, but also those regions of feeling and action in which it is almost entirely defective.

The emotions are as nearly as possible discarded. Their exercise is as far as possible restrained. The temper of kindness is not an exception to this, for it is only an attitude, not an active emotion. Thus a large part of the sphere of duty is unprovided for. One is in danger of forgetting, in admiring the theory of self-restraint, that the emotions are in fact a region in which human excellence is very greatly exercised and developed; and that a system which sets them aside, as if they tended only to evil, which knows nothing of good desires, righteous anger, holy sorrow, reasonable fear, or just hatred, so far libels human nature, and is doomed to be so far ineffective.

The motive which Buddhist morality recognizes, if it can be said to recognize any, is wholly selfish and individual. It is not for the love of truth or goodness, nor for the benefit of others —to instance the two principal motives recognized by other merely human systems—it is solely for the individual's own advantage that he is incited to cultivate virtue. Nor is it a very brave or noble selfishness. It seeks, not to make the best of self, like the Greek selfishness, but to escape from pain and from the burdens of life. It is not ennobling.

And the idea of duty is utterly absent. From first to last, the sacred books are terribly consistent in failing to recognize any sort of "obligation." An indignant expostulation with some monk whose conduct is unworthy of the principles and the rule which he professes hardly amounts to an assertion that he *owes* anything even to the Community. Much as we read of effort, it is always effort for self, effort to attain independence and quiet; never work for the sake of work, or work for the sake of others, or work for the sake of duty. Such a system is unsocial. If it recognizes the propriety of mutual kindness, it recognizes—except in certain family relationships—no duty of mutual service or action.

For, in fact, it is in the main theoretic and artificial. It invites a man to turn his back on life as it is. In the contemplation of an endless series of lives, the paramount importance of this present life is overlooked by the theorist, and to some extent is concealed from all who are taught to believe in that series of lives. To make the most of one's opportunity while one lives; to have done something before one dies, whether for oneself or for others—no such ambition is set before the Buddhist. He has no aim in life except to escape from it.

This defect spoils even the theory itself, and the statement of it. They want enthusiasm. They want aspiration. Compared with the dead levels of the lists of vices and of the supernatural attainments, an expression here and there, in some isolated sentence, or some ecstatic outburst of the Buddha himself, or of one of his disciples in the delight of conversion, may have almost the ring of enthusiasm; but on the whole the Buddhist view of human hopes and possibilities is pale and cold. I will not contrast it with Christian hope: it is enough to turn from the Pitakas to a dialogue of Plato. There is much in Buddhist moral theory which may be contrasted favourably with part of the Greek standard; but when one turns from the Suttas to an utterance of Socrates, one feels as if one had escaped from some of those gloomy passages, which Plato describes, within the earth, to drive among the chariots of the gods along the open crest of heaven, catching sight, if only for a moment, of the eternal truths, and feeling the capacities of immortality.

For with all its proud claims and assertions of attainment, Buddhism does in effect deny the high capacities of man. The Brahman ideal of absorption into the One Supreme Being was nobler and nearer truth. That Buddhism knows nothing of such absorption,[1] if only because it admits no Supreme Being, is now at last beginning to be understood. The Buddhist theory makes the fatal mistake of supposing that it is grand to have nothing and no one to look up to. The monk, if he has attained the further stages of his course, can look down, it is pretended, on deities and all that is divine. Sakra, prince of the gods, and the great Brahma himself, are supposed to pay homage to a monk. But this does not exalt the monk: it takes away from him the opportunity of being great. There is no reality about it: if it is a kind of greatness, it is one not compatible with humanity. Buddhism degrades man by denying that there is any being above him.

A similar complaint may justly be made against that which Buddhism does propose as man's final goal and aim, extinction or Nirvana. No language could be too strong to express the indignation with which a true sense of human dignity rouses us to protest against this dreary calumny. But although the strict theory is, that the goal of the saintly life is the extinction of existence, this plays but a small part among the considerations which the "sacred books" enforce. To the ordinary layman the prospect is held out of an indefinite continuance of life in happy places; and for the monk, if such there be, who aims at Nirvana, it is chiefly in this life, in a passionless calm beyond the reach of temptation, doubt, or effort, that he is taught to seek it. Here, as in many other points, the necessity of meeting to some extent the demand for reality has made the Buddhist system better than it logically ought to be.

But in view of such defects as I have been indicating, I cannot, for my part, rank this system, regarded as a theory of human life and action, with the best of those which, apart from divine revelation, men have formed.

[1] See note at the end of this chapter.

NOTE TO CHAPTER XVII

NOTE ON THE ERRONEOUS NOTION OF "ABSORPTION," ETC.

THERE is a popular notion that "union with deity" is set forth in the Buddhist sacred books as an aim or prospect. This is, I believe, a complete mistake. Such a doctrine would obviously be inconsistent with other principles of Buddhism; and although even primitive Buddhism is not perfectly consistent with itself, it was hardly possible that it, or any system, should find room for so glaring an inconsistency as this would be. I have seen no passage which gives colour to the notion.

It is chiefly, if not entirely, founded on the language of the Tevijja Sutta (translated in *Sacred Books of the East*, vol. xi.) and parallel passages about (what is there rendered) "union with Brahma." Professor Rhys Davids, in his very able preface to the Sutta (p. 164), shows that "union with Brahma" cannot, in this Sutta, mean adoption into God as the final goal of Buddhism; since, first, the idea of Brahma is not at all the same as the idea of God; and secondly, the union supposed could be only temporary—a "temporary life as an angel in the Brahma heaven."

I would go further, and say that the word "union" in this connection is incorrect and misleading.

There are three phrases in the Sutta, "Brahmasahavyatā" (§ 41), "Brahmuno sahavyupago" (§§ 34, 81), and "Brahmānaṃ sahavyatā" (§ 37), which mean respectively, "Brahma-companionship," "gone to the company of Brahma," and "Companionship of *Brahmas*" (plural). The phrase, "go to be born in the companionship of that being" ("upapajjanti tassa sattassa sahavyataṃ"), is used in Brahmajāla Sutta (§ 4), where there is obviously no idea of absorption or identification, or even of union, but only of *living under the same conditions*. Further, in the Tevijjā Sutta itself, the aim or hope in question is illustrated, not by any simile which implies absorption or union, but by the supposed aim at getting to the sun or moon (16), the desire to climb up into a dwelling (21), to cross a river (23), to cross to a "happier" land (36). Finally, Gotama says that he is like one whose native country the *Brahma world* is, so that he can be in no difficulty about the way to *that world*.

Life in the Brahma world is no such uncommon thing; the present Mahabrahma was once a man: after a Brahma-god life, ordinary people either come back to human life or descend even to infra-human conditions; but a fairly advanced monk, if re-born in the Brahma world, will pass thence to Nirvana (Angut. iv. 123). Tissa-Mogallana, who presided at the "Third Council," was "a Mahābrahmā" when he was invited to return to this world for that purpose.

Whatever then be the meaning of Brahma sahavyatā in Brahmanical doctrine, in the canonical books of Buddhism it implies only "life in the Brahma-world"—what is more often expressed by "Brahmalokupago."

PART IV

THE ERA OF ASOKA

CHAPTER XVIII

ASOKA

BETWEEN the time when Gotama died and the middle of the third century B.C., the system which we have been considering took shape, and the "canonical" literature—or far the greater part of it—was compiled. Thus much we can affirm with safety. But the earliest date, and indeed very much the earliest, at which we meet with indisputable historical evidence in regard to Buddhism is that of the Edicts of Asoka.

Asoka was King of Magadha—or, as we may fairly say, Emperor of India—from about 270 B.C. to about 232 B.C. The "Edicts," or public notifications of the King's opinions and commands, are documents, varying in length from two to perhaps thirty sentences, which were published at different dates during his reign, by being very legibly engraved on rocks or on pillars. They were thus inscribed in a great number of places,[1] and of many of them a considerable number of copies have been found and read. Of others there are but two copies,

[1] In the Fourteenth Rock Edict, the king writes: "My realm is vast . . . many inscriptions have been already cut, and I shall have many more cut." And in the Seventh Pillar Edict: "Wherever stone pillars or stone tablets exist, there let this edict be inscribed."

The places, in which survivors out of this great number of inscriptions have been found, are distributed over the length and breadth of India. Two, written from left to right, in an alphabet of Semitic origin, are in the far north-west; one is close to Mussoorie; some are near Bombay, others in Orissa; others in Rajputana and in Central India, and even in Mysore.

As regards the scale and shape of the inscriptions: On the rocks, the engraved surface, artificially smoothed, varies very widely in size and in shape; in several instances it extends to 16 or 17 feet by 8 or 10; the letters ranging from 1 inch to 2½ inches, and being very deeply cut. On the pillars, the writing is engraved either in vertical columns (the round pillar being treated as if it were square) or in continuous lines round and round the pillar; the letters are usually about 1 inch high. In most cases the words are separated, a practice not observed in palm-leaf books.

and of some only one; but all suspicion that any of them may be a later forgery is excluded by the nature of the material, by the form of the writing, and by the contents. Of one the date is proved beyond dispute, by the mention in it of certain Greek kings whom the writer claims as his contemporaries, and whose dates are known from western sources.

To go a little further into detail. The number of distinct documents is reckoned as thirty-four.[1] But in this are included two pillars which record visits of King Asoka to what he believed to be Gotama's birthplace, and to another sacred place; and three inscriptions which merely record the donation of certain cave-dwellings. They are found in over twenty different places; in some cases carved on the living rock, and in some on pillars, magnificent monoliths of finished workmanship erected for the purpose; while a few, as has been intimated, are in caves. The Edicts, which are the important documents for our purpose, number twenty-eight,[2] and are engraved, not each on a separate rock or pillar, but in groups or series. A series of fourteen Edicts, which had been probably issued at different times between the King's eleventh and his fourteenth year, were engraved together in his fourteenth year on rocks; the series being more or less complete in each of the seven places where these rocks have been discovered. Similarly in the twenty-seventh year of his reign, he had a series of seven Edicts published together, which are found more or less completely on each of the surviving pillars (which, as it happens, are seven in number). To each of these series one or two documents were added afterwards on the same rock or pillar; and a few Edicts stand alone. The most important of these—and in some respects the most important of all—is that which is known as the Bairāt or Bhabra Edict. This is beautifully written on a granite boulder, small enough to have been removed to the rooms of the Asiatic Society in Calcutta.

The reader will see that we have here guaranteed contemporary evidence for the facts, whatever they are, which the inscriptions disclose as to the events and the state of things in the reign of their author. Who, then, was their author? The name of Asoka is not to be found in them. The author is Piyadasi, or

[1] See Vincent Smith, *Asoka*, p. 106 ("Rulers of India" series).

[2] Or twenty-nine, if the Kausambi variants are counted as two.

in full, Devānampiya Piyadasi Rājā (King Piyadasi, delight of the gods), as he styles himself in most of them. Most of them begin: "King Piyadasi, the delight of the gods, says." Why, then, are these still popularly called "the Edicts of Asoka"? Because Asoka and Piyadasi are two names of the same person, and Asoka is the name by which he is best known to the Sinhalese Chronicles, and from them was first known to the European world.

The history of the identification of Piyadasi with Asoka is one of the romantic chapters in the history of knowledge. George Turnour, a high official in the Ceylon Civil Service, made acquaintance, by the help of Sinhalese scholars, with the Pali chronicles—the Mahavansa, or Great History, and the Dīpavansa, or History of the Island—which had been preserved in Ceylon; and he published[1] a description of the former with a translation of it, which laid the foundation of all subsequent study, both of the Pali language and of Buddhist history. The portion to which his attention and that of his readers was specially directed was that earlier part of the chronicle which includes the record of the conversion of the island to Buddhism. It was there described how the great Asoka, king of Magadha, had been a famous promoter of Buddhism. Having been originally a patron of the Brahman religion, he was converted, said the historian, to Buddhism, and set himself to propagate it throughout his vast kingdom, which extended over the whole of India, and even to recommend it to potentates beyond his own borders. He erected innumerable "dāgabas," or relic-shrines, and maintained innumerable monks; he sent out missionaries to preach the doctrine of the Buddha everywhere; and in particular, his son, Mahinda, introduced it into Ceylon.

Such was the statement of these old Pali writers, which Mr. Turnour brought to light. But this was not all. The Sinhalese Chronicles were not indefinite, but dealt with dates. They contained a complete list of kings, not only from the regions of mythology to the days of Gotama Buddha, but from those days onwards without intermission to dates at which they could be adjusted, in the sixteenth and following centuries, with European history. Turnour then gave to the world a chronological history of Buddhism, which included, of course, a definite date assigned to Asoka. It was true that, side by side with the list of kings

[1] 1837 A.D. and onwards.

with the length of each king's reign, ran another list, that of the succession of presiding monks, and that the two lists did not exactly tally; but the discrepancy was only of some sixty years, and Mr. Turnour suggested a very probable way of accounting for it. Thus, to those who were acquainted with Mr. Turnour's work, Asoka was a known personage with a definite character, and a definite place in history.

This was known, however, to comparatively few, when, from the other end of the vast region which Asoka had claimed as his dominion, the other side of his history—the other half of the token—was brought to light. Asoka began to speak for himself; or rather, Piyadasi spoke, and his tones and language revealed his identity with Asoka.

In the years 1837 and 1838 the indefatigable genius of James Prinsep, by comparison of many scattered inscriptions and coins, discovered the key to the long-lost alphabet, or alphabets, in which these Edicts, and many other monuments only less ancient, are engraved. The deciphering of unknown alphabets (though by the aid of a bilingual text Champollion had accomplished it for the hieroglyphics) was then a less common achievement than it has since become; and in this case there were but few hints from outside the inscriptions themselves. But Prinsep noticed while copying a certain group of short inscriptions, each of which stood by itself on one of the pillars of the stone railing round the dagaba of Sanchi, in Central India, that two characters occurred invariably at the end of each. The pillars seemed likely to bear the record of some pious offering, and the inspiration came to him that these characters might be the word for "gift." He applied this key, tested the two letters in one connection after another under that supposition, and found that it solved the problem: the two letters, with the point which followed them, did represent Dā-Na-ṃ, "donation." In a marvellously short time (for the characters are large and the inscriptions are in the main extremely distinct) several inscriptions—those on the Pillar of Feroz Shah, at Delhi, and others—had been provisionally deciphered, and an attempt at a translation was published. They contain such passages as the following:—[1]

"Thus saith King Piyadasi, beloved of the gods, I have caused

[1] Not taken exactly from any one edict; but see Second Pillar Edict.

this edict to be engraved in the twenty-seventh year of my consecration.

"What is this religion? It is to avoid evil and to do good, to practise kindness, truth, and liberality, and purity of life.

"I have given alms to men and animals, supplied them with water, etc. I have instituted officers to promote religion in all the countries," etc.

George Turnour no sooner saw the *Proceedings* of the Asiatic Society of Bengal than he sprang, with a confidence which further inquiry justified, to the conclusion that these were inscriptions of the Asoka of the Mahavansa. The evidently vast extent of his rule, the name of Magadha itself,[1] the humane tone of his proclamations, were enough to invite the identification: the statements, that he had not always held the same views but had formerly been regardless of the life of animals, that his conversion occurred some years after his enthronement, and other such coincidences, made it almost a certainty. But when it was further disclosed that in one of the edicts were mentioned certain Greek kings—Ptolemy, Magas, and others—whose date approximately coincided with that which the Mahavansa ascribed to Asoka; and further still, when it was noticed that Asoka was said in the chronicle to have been the grandson of Chandragupta, while Greek history had in the same place and date a Sandrakottos (an almost exact transliteration of the same name), the fact that one was Asoka and the other Piyadasi could not stand in the way of the identification. For, indeed, what does Asoka mean but "sorrowless," or Piyadasi but "beholder of delight"? They were both rather epithets than names, and of kindred meaning.

But whatever doubt might remain in the most sceptical mind was soon to be removed. It was observed that, although the Mahavansa knew this monarch only as Asoka, its sister chronicle—its elder sister if not its parent chronicle—the Dipavansa (history of Ceylon) knew him as Piyadasi. When the lines were quoted, "Asoka was anointed king in Mahinda's fourteenth year. Asokadhamma, after his coronation, obtained the miraculous faculties; exceedingly splendid and rich in meritorious works (he was) universal monarch of Jambudīpa. They

[1] It is found only in the inscription of Bairat. In the fifth Girnar Edict the king writes "at Pātaliputta," where the corresponding copies have "here."

crowned Piyadassi," etc.,[1] the question was at an end. The veracity of Turnour's Ceylon historians was established to an unexpected extent, and the edicts could be studied with the certainty that they were contemporary evidence of a known date. Further discoveries and decipherment added further confirmation to this conclusion.

The chronological position of Piyadasi is established, as has been said, by the mention of five Greek kings in one (the XIIIth) of the Rock Edicts. Of this particular edict there are three copies discovered, one on the Girnār hill in Kathiāwār (or Cutch), one at Shāhbāzgarhi, near Peshawur, and one at Khalsi, or Kālsi, near Mussooree. One king, Antiochus, is mentioned also in the Second Edict, which exists at the same three places, and also at Dhauli and at Jaugada in Orissa. The passage in the Thirteenth Edict is as follows :—[2]

"This is the chiefest conquest, in His Majesty's opinion—the conquest by the Law of Piety; this also is that effected by His Majesty both in his own dominions and in all the neighbouring realms as far as six hundred leagues[3]—even to where the Greek king named Antiochus dwells, and beyond that Antiochus to where dwell the four kings severally named Ptolemy, Antigonus, Magas, and Alexander," etc. These names are read in the original as Aṃtiogo, or Aṃtiyoko; Turāmaye, Turāmayo, or Tulāmaye; Aṃtekena, Antakāna, or Aṃtikini; Maka, Magā, or Mākā; Alikasandale, or Alikasudaro.

The reader of Greek history will remember that Alexander the Great invaded India in the years 329–326 B.C., and returned to Babylon only to die—in 323 B.C.—leaving his conquests to be quarrelled over by his generals. In the division which ensued, the Indian province fell to Seleucus Nicator. This prince at first opposed, but afterwards supported the rising power of Sandracottus (Candagutta, the grandfather of Asoka), and it would appear that the Greek rulers of the Bactrian Kingdom maintained a close alliance with the Magadhan dynasty. The names Antiochus, Ptolemy, Antigonus, Magas, were all somewhat common among the successors and descendants of the

[1] Dip. vi. 22–24, Oldenberg's translation.

[2] As translated by Vincent Smith, *Asoka*, p. 131.

[3] "League," *yojana*, a varying measure, commonly taken as equal to seven or eight miles (Note, l. c.).

Macedonian generals; but there was only one period, and that a short one, when four kings of these four names and an Alexander were all reigning at the same time. This was from the year 260 to 258 B.C. Then the five names mentioned in the Edict were borne by Antiochus II of Syria, Ptolemy Philadelphus, Antigonus Gonatas of Macedonia, Magas of Cyrene, and Alexander of Epirus. Unless, therefore, Piyadasi was mistaken in believing all these to be reigning when he wrote, his fourteenth year fell between 260 and 258 B.C. This date does not differ by more than two or three years from that which is obtained, a reasonable correction being admitted, from the "Great History" of Ceylon.

The Rock Edicts, which bear dates, all fall between the eleventh and the eighteenth year of Asoka's reign; one, which is undated, is probably attributed to the eighteenth; while the Pillar Edicts were issued in the twenty-seventh and twenty-eighth.

For the years, therefore, from 260 to 242 B.C. the evidence of the Asoka inscriptions is good; and we come at last to the question, "What picture of Buddhism do we find here?"

It will clear the ground if I say first what we do not find. We do not find those terms, the Three Pitakas, or the Vinaya, or the Sutta Pitaka, which are the titles of the collection of Buddhist "Sacred Books" as we know them. We do not find any allusions to the Four Truths, or the Twelve Causes, or the Eightfold Way, nor the terms Karma or Nirvana; the technical classifications of faults and hindrances are never, or scarcely ever, met with; there is no course of Conduct, Meditation, Knowledge.

If the series had stopped short of the Bairat inscription, we should have had to say that there is no mention either of the Buddha or of the treatises of religion. We should have said, without reserve, that the Buddhism of Asoka is not the Buddhism of the Pitakas. The earliest edicts reveal a system—official guardians of religion or morals, and assemblies for disciplinary purposes—but it is a system of which the Pitakas know nothing.

Further, though the tone and purpose, and to a great extent the language, of nearly all the edicts is thoroughly imbued with the Buddhist spirit, yet the king expresses not only an ample tolerance for various religions but a zeal for the interests of all which cannot be said to be the spirit of the Pitakas.

The Bairat Edict, however, which is unfortunately undated, exhibits the king in a much closer relation to technical Buddhism. It is addressed to the Community of Magadha; the king professes his attachment to the Buddha, the Law, and the Community; speaks of the "utterances of the Buddha" as all good, and commends certain passages, one of which is termed a Sutta, to be especially studied by his subjects, monks and nuns, laymen and laywomen. Of these passages, two bear titles similar to those now found in the Sutta Pitaka, and three others of the seven, besides these, have been identified[1] with passages in the books as we have them.

This Edict is thus translated by M. Sénart:—

"King Piyadasi salutes the Magadhan clergy and wishes them prosperity and good health. You know, my lords, the extent of my respect and my zeal towards the Buddha, the Law, and the Clergy.[2] All that has been said by the Blessed Buddha, it is all well said: and in so far as I can order anything, my lords, of my own will, I wish that this religious Law may be of long duration. Here are, for instance, my lords, some religious pieces: the *Vinayasamukasa* (teaching of discipline); the *Ariyavasas* (supernatural powers? of the Aryans); the *Anāgatabhayas* (dangers to come); the *Munigāthās* (the stanzas relating to the Muni or solitary religious); the *Upatisapasina* (the questions of Upatishya); the *Moneyasūta* (the Sutta on Perfection); and the *Sermon to Rahula* uttered by the blessed Buddha, and beginning with (the subject of) falsehood. These religious pieces I desire the numerous confraternities of bhikkhus and bhikkhunis to hear frequently and to meditate upon; likewise the lay devotees of both sexes. It is for this, my lords, that I have this engraven, that my will may be known."

The peculiar tone of this proclamation may be explained in either of two ways, or in both. It may be that the king used at the same time one tone towards the leaders of the religion to which he was personally attached, and another tone when he spoke as emperor to his subjects of every creed; one tone to the "Community" of a small district, which was entirely Buddhist, and another to the heterogeneous populations of a continent. Or, on the other hand, it may be that the Bairat Edict is later

[1] By Prof. Rhys Davids.

[2] Or, as I should render it, "Community."

than all the other Rock Edicts, was issued on occasion of some particular event, and expresses a new and more definite enthusiasm, consequent on a more definite knowledge. I think the latter explanation is the main one, but that the former is also true, and comes in to reinforce it.

For there is definite and acknowledged advance in the king's attitude towards Buddhism. He tells us with the greatest candour, that up to the eleventh year of his reign he was careless about such matters, and that still later he was less strict about taking life than he intended to be in future. Much later, in the Pillar Edicts of his twenty-seventh or twenty-eighth years, he acknowledged that he had been for several years a lay disciple (upāsaka) but a lukewarm one, but that he had since entered into much closer relations with the Community, or had actually become a monk.[1]

The Sinhalese chronicles, whose account of Asoka has been proved to contain substantial truth, tell us that an assembly of the Community was held in Magadha during his reign, and that at this assembly the canon of the sacred books was finally established. They tell us too—and it is proved by other evidence—that he sent out missionaries to many countries to preach the doctrine of the Buddha. We may decline to believe that the canon was completed, but that the Buddhist literature was at this time attaining a definite structure (to say the least), everything conspires to prove. Is it not reasonable, then, to believe that there were occasions on which the great emperor took a definite part, as a zealous Buddhist, in the proceedings of the Community; while in his public conduct, as the ruler of all India, he laid the chief emphasis on the more general and less technical aspects of religion?

While it is obvious to any reader of the Sinhalese histories that they are full of legend and of exaggeration, yet in my opinion their account of Asoka is to be reckoned as not only gaining confirmation from his edicts but even throwing light upon them.[2]

[1] The highest authorities understand the language of the Rupnath Edict to assert as much as this. I venture to question this; if Asoka had received "pabbajjā," why did he not use the word about himself, as he does elsewhere about others?

[1] It is a blemish in Mr. Vincent Smith's otherwise excellent work on *Asoka*, that he refuses credit far too harshly to the Sinhalese "monkish" writers. Their proved accuracy in certain details, which they could not have known except from authentic records, forbids us to rate them as low as he does.

Let it be admitted, then, that the Buddhism of Asoka was not in his earlier years, and never was in his imperial utterances, the express Buddhism of the Pitakas; we need not thence infer that the Pitakas were then unknown, nor shall we fail to recognize in him the genuine spirit of Buddhism. The discovery (since the first edition of this book) of the two pillars which record his devout pilgrimages to the spot where he believed Gotama Buddha to have been born, and—what goes even further—to the shrine of a "previous Buddha," show him to have been fully imbued, by the twenty-first year of his reign, with the tradition which the Pitakas embody.

There are few more interesting compositions in existence than these short proclamations. They reveal the personality of their author: he takes his vast dominions, and—as it has turned out—the men of twenty centuries to come, into his confidence. He tells us the changes in his attitude towards religion, and laments his former errors and want of zeal.

The first point on which his conscience, to use Christian language, was awakened, seems to have been that of "taking life." He laments the vast destruction of life—hundreds of thousands of animals a day—which used to take place for the royal table; and specifies with the utmost *naïveté* those which it is still usual to kill, two peacocks and one deer, *but the deer not always*, and promises that in future not even these shall be killed. Later on he mentions with deep regret the multitudes of men who had suffered in his wars, particularly in the conquest of Kalinga; and among the sufferers he feels especially for the religious ascetics, who, if not killed, have been distressed. And from his first conversion the king's kindness has led him not only not to kill, but to provide medicines both for men and for animals; and to have such trees planted, both in his own and in neighbouring countries, as were useful for medical purposes.

The great duty of almsgiving is also among those earliest insisted on, and comes out more and more into prominence; almsgiving, especially to ascetics, to Brahmans and "Samanas" (two titles which latterly distinguished the Brahman and the Buddhist monk, but were at first used alike for any religious ascetic).

The other characteristic Buddhist virtues—pity, purity, truthfulness, and kindness in words—are earnestly commended, the emphasis laid on gentle speech being peculiarly in accord with the teaching which we meet with in the books.

In his admirable lessons on respect for parents, kindness towards slaves, and care for the spiritual interests of condemned criminals; and in what he says of the duty and advantage, not merely of tolerance, but of mutual respect, between differing sects, the royal teacher rises perhaps to a higher level than the Pitakas attain.

He seldom speaks of alms without urging that the inner essence (sāro) of conduct, kindness, that is, and goodness, is worth more than alms and that the best of all gifts is the gift of the true doctrine, and the promotion of religion in those whom one would benefit.[1]

His one desire is for the good of his people, every one of whom he looks on as a son; that they may be as happy here as possible, and enjoy heaven hereafter. Good deeds ensure heaven; they not only bring the high satisfaction here of consciousness of virtue, but much more, they secure an infinite crop of merit. The infinite crop of merit ensuring heaven, is the often-repeated expression for the *summum bonum*. There is nothing here of "Nirvana," but it is a perfectly just representation of one side of the Buddhist teaching.

Once more, the king's watchword is "effort." This word he repeats over and over again. He acknowledges the difficulty of a consistently good life, but urges that it is worth the effort. He calls on his ministers and officials to do their utmost; it is only by exertion that these high fruits can be obtained. Men must strive and never give up. The one fatal obstacle to moral improvement is idleness and want of perseverance.[2]

All this, as it is read in the original—a dialect in which the words are all Pali words, though terminations and inflections are different—is even more strikingly Buddhist than it sounds in the English. The technical terms of the Pitakas are, as has been said, conspicuous by their absence but there is an agreement in phrase, and terms of expression, as well as in tone and emphasis, which keeps us very near to the language of the books. Asoka's sentences are as clearly in sympathy with the canonical texts as they are certainly not quoted from them.

[1] See above, ch. x., p. 112.

[2] The absence of the *word* "pamādo" is the more remarkable.

But meanwhile, there is a whole region outside the limits and characteristics of Buddhism—a system of overseers of religion, higher and lower functionaries, appointed over provinces and districts, in the city and in the palace, to teach all classes, the king's wives and his sons in particular; a system which seems to have been intended to be independent of the distinctions of creed or religion (as is, in fact, expressly stated in the eighth Pillar Edict), and to have aimed at promoting what the king continually calls that *essence* of religion which all sects have in common. To promote good-will and justice, relieve the oppressed, distribute the royal bounties, these were the liberal aims with which this organization, in which Piyadasi justly took delight and pride, was instituted. He boasts that he has sent his emissaries all over the world, into foreign countries as well as his own dominions; but it was to teach, not Buddhism nor any particular creed, but the *essential sound core* of personal goodness.

In this sketch we have been brought in contact with a well-marked personality; that of a man of the widest possible aims and the widest possible tolerance, yet one whose own mind has received its religious influences in a Buddhist form, from Buddhist sources. Of one thing only he is intolerant or somewhat contemptuous—of outward observances. He means probably Brahmanical ceremonies, for he alludes to such rites as were commonly practised in the several occasions of domestic life. They are of uncertain value at the best; in fact virtually useless. And in one place—the only place where he definitely disparages any form of religion—he says he has made those that used to be the gods of India to be its gods no longer. M. Sénart thinks he means the Brahmans.

At this point the writer may be forgiven for pausing and inviting his reader to reflect with him on the unique position occupied in the history of human thought by the imperial moralist. His was an enthusiasm such as was never reached by any Antonine. In him Buddhism inspired perhaps the greatest effort, in scale at any rate, on behalf of good, that was ever made by man, outside of Christianity. The rules and the books are insignificant in his presence.

Two hundred years at least had elapsed since the death of the founder, to whom the organization of moral effort was attributed. A vast change had passed, since his day, over the face—the political aspect at least—of India. The touch of a strange new civilization—the civilization of their distant Aryan brethren of Europe—had been felt by the Aryans of the Ganges. Aided by the Greek invader, a single monarchy had asserted itself, and claimed all India for its own, and had so far succeeded as to give vividness to a new conception—that of a universal monarch. A great man had arisen representative of the native dynasty, who had assimilated much of the new civilization and felt its stimulating influence. In his person the idea of the world-monarch was embodied. He was a man of vast ambitions and vast designs. And on this man, Piyadasi Asoka, at first a despot as careless as others of the means he used, the teaching of the ascetic community laid its spell. He became much more than its patron; he was its apostle. As his reign went on he was more and more imbued with its spirit; the desire to serve it and extend it moulded his magnificent enterprise. He was not merely the Constantine of Buddhism, he was an Alexander with Buddhism for his Hellas; an unselfish Napoleon, with "mettam"[1] in the place of "gloire."

The world was his that he might protect all lives in it; might teach lovingkindness throughout it; might establish in every part of it the Community of the disciples of the Buddha.

Compared with the solid reality of Asoka, the records which are preserved of the Buddha himself are but a shadowy tradition. And as the great king's history becomes better known men will be tempted to speculate whether Buddhism owes more to Gotama than to Moggali;[2] to ask how far what is definite in the history of Bimbisara's days is a reflection thrown back on the mist of the past from the greater epoch of Asoka.

[1] Strange to say, this *word* does not occur in the Edicts.

[2] The leader of the Community in Asoka's time.

CHAPTER XIX

COLLECTION OF THE LITERATURE

AN attempt will be made in this chapter to set forth some of the considerations which must guide any student who attempts to decide by what sort of process the Buddhist sacred books came to be formed into a definite collection, or Threefold Pitaka, and at what date this process was completed. I shall group these considerations under three heads: the evidence of variety of date and authorship; the indications of a particular date for certain parts; and the value of the tradition which asserts that the whole had been completed by the time of Asoka, and was carried, in its completed form, to Ceylon by Mahinda. The third point involves some discussion of the tradition of the Councils.

That the contents of the Pitakas are of various date and authorship will be admitted by every student, even among Buddhists. As much as this, though it is inconsistent with the literal terms of the tradition of the First Council, is stated by the Buddhist authorities themselves. We read in the Digha Nikaya that the Subha Sutta was uttered by Ananda after the Buddha's decease.[1] The two last books of the Culla Vagga purport to contain the record of the Council of Vesali, which is said to have been held a hundred years after that. Parts of the Therāgāthā were first uttered, the Commentary tells us, in the reign of Bindusara, Asoka's father, and were first admitted into the canon in Asoka's time, at the Council of Patna.[2] The Dipavansa tells us that the Kathāvatthu, a book of the Abhidhamma Pitaka, was first uttered at the same Council, by Moggaliputta.[3] And this is borne out, according to the well-known Sinhalese scholar Sumangala, by the linguistic differences be-

[1] See Prof. Oldenberg, *Therāgāthā* (Pali Text Society), p. xi.

[2] Digh. Nik., p. 204. See Sāmantapāsādikā, p. 286.

[3] Dip. vii. 55.

tween the Pali of that book and the Pali of the other six sections of the Abhidhamma.[1]

In the Patimokkha, as has been said above, an old glossary on the text is embedded; and in many other places comments are inserted in the text; for instance, a geographical note in Maha Vagga, v. 13, 12, and a note on a name in *Ib.* viii. 1, 4.

References are made in one part of the Pitakas to another, or to the collection as a whole. For instance, the sum total of the sayings of the Buddha having been classified under nine heads —a process which would hardly take place till some time had elapsed—these nine kinds of text are often referred to,[2] while the less elaborate division into three—Dhamma, Vinaya, Mātikā —recurs constantly.[3] In Culla Vagga, i. 32, is an enumeration of the various similes which the Buddha has used for "lust." As instances of references from one part of the collection to another I may mention these: In Kūtādanta Sutta it is said, "Here are to be embodied the contents of the Samannaphala Sutta"; a particular section of the Sutta Nipata (Atthakathā) is referred to by name in Maha Vagga, v. 13. The stories of the "Cariyā Pitaka" even take for granted the Jataka Commentary.[4] A distinction is drawn between genuine utterances of the Buddha and later additions.[5]

The books have already become, by the date at which later parts are written, the object of study and research. The phrase "saṭṭham savyanjanaṃ," usually rendered, "with text and with comment," is of constant occurrence; and in any interpretation implies a critical attitude towards the text. Some Suttas, we read, are difficult and likely to be shirked by idle monks.[6] There is danger lest a famous Sutta should be lost, for want of some one to learn it by heart from those in whose memory it survives.[7] A certain verse is quoted and said to be old, but liable to be misunderstood by heretics.[8]

It is further abundantly evident that many of the books were composed when Buddhism had been a definite religion long enough for divisions and sects to have arisen. The degeneracy

[1] Preface to *Bālāvatāra*, p. 11.
[2] Maj. Nik. 22. Angut. iv. 6, 102, 186.
[3] M.V. x. 1. Maj. Nik. 33.
[4] See Prof. Morris's *Preface to Cariyā Pitaka.*
[5] Samyut. xx. 7.
[6] Samyut. xx. 7.
[7] M.V. iii. 5, 9.
[8] Maj. Nik. 75.

of monks from the old standard is often deplored; and so is their falling off in numbers.[1] Secessions to rival sects and schisms are referred to, and rules for dealing with formulated heresies are prescribed.[2]

We may take it, therefore, as certain that there is a wide range of variety of date extending at least down to 250 B.C.

We have next to inquire whether internal evidence furnishes any indication of a particular date for the later portions.

The very important Sutta (Mahaparinibbana) which records the last sayings and doings of the Buddha and his final decease, bears indications, not only of a late date, but, as I think, of a particular date—that of the reign of Asoka.

The first point to be mentioned, whatever it be worth as an argument, is certainly interesting in itself. The Sutta contains a supposed prophecy of Gotama's, that Patali, then a comparatively insignificant place (Pataligama) should hereafter be Pataliputta, a great and important city.[3] To Buddhists, who believe in the Buddha's power to foretell the future, no inference can be drawn from this. But all who are not Buddhists, and many who are, will agree that this passage was written after the city had become a very important and central seat of government. I think we may safely add that it was written when one of the gates was known as Gotama's gate, and the ferry as Gotama's ferry.

There is a tradition of doubtful value that it became the royal residence somewhat before the so-called Council of Vesali;[4] and the Dipavansa says that an earlier Asoka, called also Kālāsoka, reigned there. There is good reason, however, to believe this Kalasoka to be a fictitious person. Earlier kings may have reigned in Pataliputta, but we have no reason to think it could have been very important till the great Asoka made it so. A tradition preserved by the Chinese pilgrim, Hiouen Thsang, says that it was the great Asoka who "quitted Rajagaha and fixed his court at Pataliputta." This cannot be strictly true, as it is certain, from the Greek historians, that his grandfather Candagutta was established at "Palibothra"; but it probably represents the substantial truth that Asoka Piyadasi raised the city to a splendour it had never possessed before.

[1] Saṃyut. xvi. 13, 3.
[2] M.V. x. Culla Vagga, ix., x.
[3] See above, p. 42.
[4] See Prof. Rhys Davids. S.B.E. xi., p. 16.

Further, if we may infer from the passage under discussion that Pataliputta had a "Gotama Gate" when the Sutta was written, we may ask, Who can have given such a name before Asoka was converted to Buddhism? His predecessors were not Buddhists.

Next, it is to be observed that the Parinibbana Sutta has much to say about the character of a "Cakkavatti," or universal monarch, and of the way of burying one with ceremonies like those used for a Buddha. Asoka Piyadasi was the first, so far as we know, and certainly the first for many centuries, who answered to the description: in him the Cakkavatti idea was embodied.

Again, this Sutta orders the erection of dagabas, a thing of which we hear nothing in those books which appear to be the earlier. This Asoka did: from his time and from the succeeding century date most of the great dagabas of India and of Ceylon.

And, what is particularly significant, it is stated in the Sutta that by the advice of Dona (see p. 52) these dagabas were to be erected, not in certain tribal provinces only, but in a great variety of places, so that the religion might be propagated over all the world. This consorts exactly with the aims and proceedings of Piyadasi.

From these considerations, it seems extremely probable that the Parinibbana Sutta, while containing older material, was drawn up in the form in which we have it in the time of Asoka.

But this Sutta does not stand alone: it is closely associated with the Saṃyutta and Anguttara Nikayas,[1] and even some of the discourses of the other collections. Part of its contents are identical with Maha Vagga, vi. 28, and its insistence on the subject of unity in the Order links it with the last book of the Culla Vagga.

The last book of the Culla Vagga records the proceedings which have been called the Council of Vesali, and is therefore confessedly of a date as late as—and possibly much later than—381 B.C. The Vesali proceedings were concerned with the offences against unity of certain Vaggian monks. Now the

[1] Cf. Saṃyut. xxi. 2, on wishing the Buddha to remain; xx. 8, on the effeminacy of the Licchavis; xvi. 7, "trāni yeva patikankhā no vuddhi," and Angut. iv. 23; *ib.* 130 (Cakkavatti) 158, 183, 187, etc. See also Sāmañ. S. on the character and proceedings of a king.

Parinibbana Sutta begins with the discourse on unity suggested by a question as to the conduct of the Vaggians. I venture to think that the misconduct of the Vaggian monks, and the proceedings which followed, took place much nearer the time of Asoka than 381 B.C., and were in fact part of the steps in that reform and unification of the Buddhist constitution which marked his reign.

We must now inquire into the third point—the value of the tradition about the completion of the books in Asoka's time. I will state the tradition; then show what difficulties stand in the way of our receiving it, and finally say why I believe it, in spite of these difficulties, to be substantially true.

It is stated in the Commentary on the Vinaya, as well as in the Mahavansa and the Dipavansa,[1] that Mahinda brought with him, when Asoka sent him as missionary to Ceylon, the Three Pitakas exactly as they have ever since been read and as we now have them. They had been preserved in Magadha unaltered from the time of the Buddha's death. At the First Council held immediately after that event, they had been recited and ratified; at the Council of Vesali, exactly a hundred years later, they had been vindicated from certain heretical alterations; and at the Council of Patna, under Asoka, the canon was finally fixed. From this Council went forth the missionaries, of whom Mahinda was one.

That Mahinda went from Magadha to Ceylon about the time alleged, I shall now take for granted: the reasons for believing it belong to the next chapter. But what had he to bring?

The story of the Three Councils is obviously, as it stands, incredible. The first must be put aside altogether: not only is it improbable—there is nothing approaching to early evidence for it. The proceedings at Vesali are recorded in the Culla Vagga with a detail and vividness which incline us to believe the story; but they are not, as there recorded, a Council—only a meeting, apparently of a local branch of the Community to inquire into a particular question: a Committee was appointed, and by this Committee the matter was decided. It was an application,

[1] Although the Commentary, according to the Sinhalese tradition, is very much the earliest of these three authorities, it is not clear which is really the oldest, or whether they are independent versions of the story.

according to the Culla Vagga itself, of the ordinary rules of business to a local dispute. It is true that a sentence is added at the end to bring it into line with the Council of Rajagaha, but this is a palpable afterthought. This was taken up and repeated in the later tradition; but as far as there is anything approaching to contemporary evidence for the Vesali proceedings they are not represented as a Council. In short, as Dr. Oldenberg says, " the tradition of the Second Council in its authentic form does not bring this council into any authentic relation with the sacred books." [1]

Of the Third Council, Asoka's at Pataliputta, there is no early evidence at all. We know of it only from the Commentary, and from the Sinhalese chronicles. The Commentary, though we are told that Buddhaghosha only retranslated it from the Sinhalese version of a very early Pali original, cannot be regarded as direct evidence earlier than Buddhaghosha himself. The Introduction to it, in which the account of the Council occurs, is almost certainly his work. He adds nothing, therefore, to the Dipavansa and Mahavansa. Of such a Council Asoka himself, who tells us so much, says nothing—at any rate, nothing in the Edicts yet discovered. The story of it, in the Ceylon records, is embedded in a mass of legend, and encrusted with extravagant fiction. Even the statement that Mahinda brought the Pitaka books to Ceylon is associated with the undoubtedly false statement, that he brought also the Commentaries. And to complete this list of arguments against the tradition, it is saddled with all the difficulty involved in the assertion, that Mahinda brought this mass of literature only in his memory, unwritten, and that the people of Ceylon, new to Buddhism and to the Pali language, learnt the whole from his lips!

Yet there is even more to be said on the other side.

First, although it would be too much to demand, that any one who denies that Mahinda carried the Pitakas to Ceylon should show who did bring them; still the fact remains, and

[1] Even in the concluding sentence, which I have called "an afterthought," no word is used which necessarily means a council. The word "saṅgīti," popularly rendered "council," bearing that meaning at a later date (the Mahavansa says "Dhātusena held a 'pitaka saṅgīti'") meant only in its earlier use, what Rhys Davids cautiously renders it, "a rehearsal." It means properly "chanting together." It is used repeatedly, not of any council but of an ordinary recitation; e.g. the substantive, in M.V. i. 77; C.V. x. 22; and the verb, in M.V. iv. 15, 4.

counts for something, that they did get there; and that the chronicles which from the third century onwards, amid a vast quantity of nonsense, certainly record a good many historical facts concerning the Community, make no mention of any later importation of the books. They state that in the time of Vaṭṭagāmini, King of Ceylon, the Pitakas were committed to writing, having been till then handed down orally: a statement which has been generally regarded as historical. This was about a hundred and seventy years after the date assigned to Mahinda. If it be admitted that the books arrived in Ceylon at some time in that period, there is no strong chronological reason for doubting that they came, when they are said to have come, at the beginning of it.

Any one who is inclined to reject all that the Ceylon chronicles say, because they are so full of fiction and extravagance, can hardly have considered in how many points they have been proved correct. There was a time when the "buried cities" of Ceylon were thought little better than mythical. Who believed, till exploration proved it, the Mahavansa account of a splendid city on the top of Sīgiri? It is hardly too much to say that the whole course of inquiry and excavation has tended to show that those extravagant romances have in each case a kernel of truth. That the chroniclers knew a good deal about Asoka, his character and deeds, has already been shown. They knew that his grandfather Sandracottus reigned at Palibothra, as the Greeks have told us he did. How did they know these things? Their own answer is, that they were recorded in the monastery at Anuradhapura, where such records had been kept since Mahinda founded it. The knowledge they possessed of the time of Asoka and Mahinda was not a vague tradition of famous events or names of kings: it extended, in one instance at least, to a detail such as could not have been guessed, and was not at all likely to be remembered, unless it had been preserved in some authentic record. For the Dipavansa states that while Asoka sent Mahinda to Ceylon, he sent one Majjhima, amongst others, to the Himavanta country to teach the doctrine. Who would not have supposed that the "monkish chronicler" had not drawn on his imagination for this detail? Why should a monk of Ceylon remember it? Yet, built into the innermost recesses of one of the relic-domes at Sanchi, a stone box was found by

General Cunningham, on which was inscribed in "Asoka" letters: " (relics) of Majjhima, teacher of the Himavat." The dagaba is assigned to about 200 B.C. This is unquestionable proof that the Sinhalese monks, from whose records the Mahavansa was compiled, knew what Asoka did and whom he sent. It is unreasonable, surely, to set aside, unless on the strongest grounds, what they say about the messenger whom he sent to their own country, and whom they asserted to be their own Founder.

But these monks said about Mahinda many absurd and impossible things: is this, about the books, one of these?

Some one—either Mahinda or some one else—certainly introduced into Ceylon the Asoka letters and the Asoka language, and taught the Sinhalese to carve on stone inscriptions very much like his. Some of these are attributed by scholars to the second century B.C. On the road by which Mahinda may have approached Anuradhapura an inscription may be read to-day—it is in one long line a hundred feet long—recording the donation of the spot to the Community, very much as such donations are recorded in the Cave-inscriptions of Asoka himself.

We are not obliged to believe—or to understand the historian as meaning—that Mahinda quite unaided, and on a single occasion, orally conveyed the whole Tipitaka to Ceylon. He lived and worked there many years, and many came from Magadha to join him. And I cannot but think it unreasonable to doubt that the literature which he brought and taught was substantially that which the Sinhalese have ever since preserved as the Three Pitakas.

No one who admits this will altogether reject the story of Asoka's Council.

The belief that there had been Councils was unquestionably an important part of Buddhist tradition. Something must have suggested it: it would hardly have arisen if there had never been any Council at all. Admit that a Council of some sort must somewhere have been held, and it will be felt to be most probable that Asoka held one. Admit that the Sinhalese had access to records which told them the name of Asoka's missionary to the Himavanta, and it will not seem incredible that they should have known whether he held a Council or not. If he did, it is easy to understand how the proceedings of Vesali were dignified with the same title, and how then a pious imagination made a First Council out of the assembly of the Order around the Buddha's tomb.

It remains strange that such a Council is not mentioned in the Edicts yet discovered. But there is that in the Bairat Edict which shows out of what it might have grown. There Aṣoka addresses the Magadhan Community, and specifies certain parts of the sacred books, and declares that all that the Buddha uttered is well spoken. Then for nearly ten years our Edicts are silent: that interval is blank between the Rock Edicts and those of the Pillars. It is surely a bold thing to assert that between these two periods a Council of Patna was not held!

I conclude that the compilation and arrangement of the Buddhist books, which had been growing and accumulating for two hundred years and more, was brought to something like completion under Asoka in the latter part of the third century B.C.

NOTE TO CHAPTER XIX

NOTE ON THE PITAKAS AND THE RUWANWELI DAGABA.

AN interesting illustration of the Pitakas, in regard to the biography of the Buddha, is found in the twentieth chapter of the Mahavansa, where a list is given of the sculptures with which a great king of Ceylon, Duṭṭhagāmini, is said to have adorned the Ruwanweli dagaba in Anuradhapura, about 160 B C. The subjects include: The events near the Bo-tree (in seven times seven, not four times seven days); the request of Brahma; the setting in motion of the Wheel; Ordination of Yasa; Bhaddavaggiya Princes; Conversion of Jatilas; Visit of Bimbisara; Entrance into Rajagaha; Acceptance of Bamboo-park; the Eighty Disciples; Journey to Kapilavatthu, and golden ambulatory; Admission of Rahula; Acceptance of Jetavana. So far all are almost exactly in accord with the Vinaya.

Then follow a number of events which either are not in the Pitakas, or occur under other titles. There are four events concerned with the Visit to the Tavatimsa heaven; seven occasions of the delivery of celebrated Suttas; and one event from the Culla Vagga account of Devadatta.

From this point the tradition of the Parinibbana Sutta is followed almost exactly: The Determination to decease in three months; Cunda's offering; Pukkusa's gift; Drinking the Kukuttha water; the Decease; the lamentation of the Devas; the Homage of Mahakassapa; Self-ignition of Pyre; Division of relics by Dona.

It is evident that this passage, if it could be relied on, would prove the existence of our present Pitakas in Ceylon in 160 B.C.

In view of the sculptures on the rails around the Sanchi Dagaba, carved probably just about that time, it is by no means improbable that Dutthagamini did adorn the circumference of his Dagaba in this way. Nor can any one who has seen these Sanchi carvings, or the Sigiri paintings, feel confident that they might not have survived for the writer of the Mahavansa to see. But from that writer's description of the dagaba itself it is pretty clear that he wrote from imagination, not from what he had seen. He tells us that within the dagaba was a relic-box, composed of six slabs of alabaster, each eighty cubits square by eight inches thick: into the inside of which King Vattagamini at a later date (ch. xxxiv.) was mysteriously conveyed, after hearing beatified beings chanting within it.

This is a case in which the want of truth in one part of the story discredits the details in every part of it, and prevents us from using it to prove that the complete Pitaka was known in Ceylon in 160 B.C. It proves only that it was known in A.D. 400.

PART V

BUDDHISM IN CEYLON: THE PAST

CHAPTER XX

MAHINDA AND THE CONVERSION OF CEYLON

OUR history is now to cross from India to Ceylon, and to trace the fortunes of Buddhism in the island, after its establishment there by Mahinda in the third century. But first we may not entirely pass over the account which is given —though of course fictitious, and I believe late—of the preparations made for this in the Buddha's own time. The historians of Ceylon, whether the authors of the primitive monastery archives, or the original compilers of the Dipavansa and Mahavansa, or their later continuators, desired, not unnaturally, to represent the Buddha as having visited their island. They have not for that purpose either contradicted or interpolated the sacred text. They have found, within the statements of the Tipitaka, opportunities recorded, which the Buddha used (as they say, and as the sacred text does not deny) for visits to Lanka.

The Mahavagga records, among the marvels which preceded the conversion of Kassapa the Jatila, that the Buddha, aware of Kassapa's jealousy of his influence, made a point of withdrawing on the day of Kassapa's festival. He obtained his meal that day from Uttarakuru, and withdrew to eat it to the mystic lake Anotatta in the Himalaya. This was of course completed before midday. The Vinaya says that he rested by the lake in the heat of the day; but it does not mention how he spent the latter part of the afternoon. He returned, we read, before night. The gap is supplied by the Mahavansa. On that very afternoon, being the ninth month of his Buddha-hood, at the full moon of the constellation Phussa, "unattended he visited Lanka, for the purpose of sanctifying Lanka."

The purpose of this visit was to clear the island of the "yakkhas" (demons; forest, or savage beings), who were not likely to make good followers of the Buddha. Taking advantage of one of their assemblies, when they were gathered together in a beautiful garden in the centre of the island, the Buddha appeared unexpectedly in the air above them; terrified them by storms and rain and cold and darkness, till they offered to him the whole island. He then dispelled their terrors and seated himself on the earth among them; but soon caused flames to extend in every direction from the carpet on which he was sitting, till the yakkhas were driven to the shores. He then caused a delightful island called Giri, quite as attractive as Lanka, and prepared in every way for their reception, to approach alongside: the yakkhas stepped on to it, and it returned to its former place in the ocean. Thus, without difficulty or discontent, the undesirable population was disposed of.

The island of Lanka was now occupied by local deities in inconceivable numbers, and these were soon converted. The chief of them, Sumana, the deva of Adam's peak (then Sumanakuta or Sumana's peak), begged for something worthy of worship, and the Buddha gave him a handful of his pure blue (hyacinthine ?) locks, which the deva enshrined in an emerald casket. After the Nirvana of the Buddha, as the Mahavansa tells us with less regard for the Parinibbana Sutta, the thorax-bone was brought from the pyre by an elder named Sārabhu, and deposited in the same dagaba [1] of emerald, which was enclosed in a larger one of marble. Later kings enlarged this further, and this is the history of the celebrated Mahiyangana [2] Dagaba.

To bring the Buddha to Lanka during the early months of his Buddha-hood was a feat of some ingenuity, since, for those months, the Vinaya record is detailed; no ingenuity was shown

[1] This word, from dā = dhātu, relic, and gaba = garbhaya, receptacle, is generally used of large buildings; but may be strictly used, as here, of a small casket, now called "karanduwa." The shape is the same of small and great.

[2] At Alut Nuwara, in Eastern Bintenne, the low ground on the east of the central mountains, on the banks of the Mahāweligangā. It is as nearly as possible the centre of the island. It is now a very insignificant spot, though it has a large dagaba. As late as the middle of the eighteenth century the Kandian king visited and admired it; pilgrims from Siam also went there (Mahavansa, 99, 100).

in saying that in the fifth year, while residing in the Jetavana, he paid a second visit. At that time Ceylon seems to have been occupied by Nagas (serpents, supernatural beings of serpent form, men connected with serpents and serpent-worship, wild tribes of non-Aryans), and a great quarrel was going on among them. The Buddha pacified it by means not unlike those used at the former visit, and then preached and converted many myriads of the Nagas. The geographical references in this story are the vaguest possible; with one exception, which is probably the motive of the whole tradition. One of the Naga kings, so converted, was the King of Kelani, near Colombo, and to him the Buddha promised a visit. Accordingly, in the eighth year of Buddha-hood, the Buddha's third visit to Lanka took place, and several great centres of his worship were established. The Naga king entertained him at Kelani. He then went to Adam's Peak and impressed his footprint on it. Going thence, he spent some time in meditation at Dīghavāpi, in the east of the island, and afterwards at Meghavana (Anuradhapura), on the spots afterwards occupied by the Bo-tree, the Thuparama, and the Sila Dagaba respectively. These visits are referred to in the fifteenth chapter of the Mahavansa.

We learn nothing more about Buddhism in Ceylon until the days of Asoka. In fact, in the mere jumble of fairy tales which takes the place of a chronicle up to Asoka's time—the arrival of Vijayo (who is said to have been the son of a lion), his reception by a kind of Circe, and the rest—one thing is clear, that the original compiler of these chapters—i.e. of all that precedes in Sinhalese history the date of Asoka—represents the religion of the island in those days as Brahman. We read of Paribbajakas, Niganthas, and of various Brahman rites, but of no Buddhist shrines, monks, or believers. Nor is Mahinda reported to have found, when he came to Ceylon, any traces of the Buddha's visits.

These romantic and inconsistent narratives of the preparations for Mahinda's visit being disposed of,[1] we come to that event itself. Here, I believe, we are on historical ground.

It has been shown that the Pali chronicles, by their specification, as the missionary of Asoka to the Himavanta country, of

[1] The preface about Vijayo, etc., is not referred to again in the original portion of the Mahavansa.

that very Majjhima, whose name is recorded as "Himavanta-teacher" in a monument of a date not much later than Asoka's, have established their claim to be trusted in regard to the history of that time. We cannot give them the benefit of these credentials for the time before that, because for the earlier centuries the monuments are as much against them as from Asoka onwards they are in their favour. But it is certain that their compilers had access to good sources of tradition or testimony about the missions which Asoka set on foot. We cannot therefore easily set aside their statement that Asoka's son Mahinda came as the preacher of Buddhism to Ceylon. The writer who knew that Majjhima went to Himavanta is likely to have known who came to Ceylon; especially when he writes in Ceylon, and with a view to the history of Ceylon. The Dipavansa says: "Mahinda, going with four companies to the most excellent island of Lanka, firmly established there the faith, and released many people from their fetters"; and goes on to give an elaborate, and of course imaginative and highly embellished account of the journey of Mahinda, his arrival at Anuradhapura, the royal city, his reception there by the king, Devānampiyatissa, and the establishment of Buddhism in the island.

The king of Lanka was then the great Tissa. Various wonders had attended his birth. He was a great friend of Asoka; and of the treasures which his kingdom produced, "no one," he said, "but my friend Asoka is worthy." He sent therefore gems, pearls, and a left-handed chank or shell, and three mystic chariot-poles, by the hands of ambassadors, to the great king at Pataliputta. Asoka received them graciously, and conferred high honours on the ambassadors. To Tissa he sent back a great variety of precious gifts, but, in particular, all the things necessary for the anointing and inaugurating of a king. He sent also to his ally this "advice"; "I have taken refuge in Buddha; and do thou also the same." And he gave the ambassadors instructions to anoint Tissa—though he was already king—a second time.

This, in its admirable *naïveté*, agrees accurately with what we read in Asoka's inscriptions. That monarch claims to be supreme over Tambapanni (Taprobane or Ceylon), and to have sent to establish Buddhism in all his dominions. The Ceylon historian gives the Ceylon version of the relation between the two kings.

It was just at this time that the great Council of Pataliputta was held; and when it was over, the wise Moggali, who had presided at it, sent out into many lands the missionaries of Buddhism. The chronicles tell us in spite of what obstacles, and by use of what Suttas, the religion was established in each.[1] The conversion of Lanka was assigned to Mahinda.

Now Mahinda, son of Asoka, was born when his father was as yet a viceroy under his father, Bindusara, in Ujjeni or Ujjain, in Avanti, a province in Central India; and his mother, Devī, still lived at Vedisa in that province; and it was from Vedisa, during a visit to her, and not directly from Patna, that Mahinda, when the destined moment arrived, miraculously took his flight to Ceylon. The moment was that of Tissa's second coronation, and when he was prepared, in consequence of Asoka's message, to welcome Buddhism.

King Tissa had set out on an elk-hunt with a retinue of forty thousand men; and in pursuit of an elk, which was really a deity in disguise, he was led to the place where Mahinda and his companions were. He was delighted at the sight of the yellow robes, and was soon converted to the faith which they represented. But not till his intelligence had been tested by a puzzle, with which readers of Buddhist books are now familiar enough.

"What is this tree called?" asked the Elder. "A mango," replied the king. "Besides this one are there any other mango trees?" "There are many." "Besides this mango and those other mangoes, are there any other trees in the world?" "Yes, sir, there are many trees, but they are not mangoes." "Besides the other mango trees and the trees that are not mangoes, is there any other?" "Yes, sir, this mango." "Well done!" cried the Elder, "thou art wise." When the king had been proved by this, and by another puzzle very like it, to be capable of understanding, the Cūlahatthapādopama Sutta was preached to him, and thereupon he and his forty thousand followers (one is rather disappointed to find them all standing by) attained deliverance.[2]

[1] And incidentally shows what Suttas were held in estimation in Ceylon before A.D. 400.

[2] A translation of this momentous discourse, which is a good specimen of a Sutta, is appended as a note to this chapter.

When Tissa discovered that the Elder was no other than the son of his old friend and ally he was the more delighted.

The occasion was marked, of course, by innumerable wonders: innumerable devas, nagas, and winged serpents were converted. The Princess Anulā, sister-in-law of the king, with five hundred ladies, drew near, and they also entered the "first stage." And by the preaching of the Devadatta Sutta a thousand of the common people were converted. The ladies next day attained the "second stage," and wished to be ordained; but Mahinda said it was not lawful for him to ordain them; his sister Sanghāmittā must be sent for.

A large space in the Mahavansa is occupied by the description of the buildings that were erected in places rendered sacred by some act of Mahinda, in what is now the district of Anuradhapura and Mihintale (Mahindatale). It is natural that this should be so, for the Mahavansa, in its original form, is essentially the history of the Great Vihara, as Anuradhapura was formerly called. The name, Anuradhapura, does not occur in the account of Mahinda's settlement.

The central act of the whole series of dedications was the donation to the Community of the Mahamegha Park, in exact imitation of the donation of the Veluvana by Bimbisara to the Buddha himself. This gift, marking the "establishment" under royal protection of Buddhism in Ceylon, as it had been established in Magadha by Bimbisara, was signalized by several earthquakes. All the previous Buddhas of this cycle (kalpa) had visited and sanctified that spot, under different names. On it were soon to stand the Bo-tree, the Brazen Palace, and innumerable sacred places, and hereafter, in Dutthagamini's time, the Ruwanweli Dagaba.

Such was Tissa's first great work, the Mahavihara of Anuradhapura. He was next led to the hill, Missa, where Mahinda had first appeared to him, and there began the construction of sixty-eight rock dwellings, which constituted the Vihara of the Shrine Hill, long afterwards named Mihintale.

The third in order of his foundations was the Thupārāmā Dagaba. This was the first dagaba erected, as tradition goes, in Ceylon; and that which now bears its name, and which doubtless stands on the spot where the original one stood, has good claims to be considered the oldest building in Ceylon. It may, very probably, be in part the actual original. It had the appearance, a few years ago, of a truly venerable building, but has of late been made ridiculous with the stucco and whitewash of the Buddhist revival. It is, like all Ceylon dagabas, a solid mass of brick, of the shape of a bell, placed on a square base, and surmounted by a circular tower. But before it could be erected, a relic must be obtained to be enclosed in it,[1] and this was accomplished by the boldest supernatural means. Not only did messengers go through the air to Asoka's Court to obtain such relics as the great monarch could bestow, but they were commissioned to go further—to Sakka, the prince of the (lower) gods—and demand of him the right collar-bone of the Buddha. All this was duly executed, and, after many more marvels, the right collar-bone, with a terrific earthquake, took its place under the Thuparama Dagaba.

The next step was the obtaining of the Bodhi-tree branch. The king's nephew and minister, Arittha, was deputed to ask for two things—that Sanghamitta, King Asoka's daughter, should come and initiate the ladies of Lanka, and that she should bring with her the right branch of the great Bo-tree. The princess was immediately ready to obey the summons of her brother Mahinda, but as to the sacred tree, King Asoka was in doubt; it would be profane to cut it. But he was informed that the Buddha, when on the very point of his final decease, had (though the Mahaparinibbana Sutta has omitted to mention it) resolved, amongst other resolves affecting Lanka, that this branch should sever itself from the tree and deposit itself in the vase prepared for it. His anxiety was dispelled; and the goldsmith of the gods, Vissakamma, having made a vase of gold of gigantic size, the branch (to make a long story short) planted itself therein, and was conveyed, amid various miraculous circumstances, to Ceylon. Oriental embellishments are here accumulated to a pitch of exaggeration which is repulsive to an English reader. The effulgences, the flowers, the divine music, and the rest, display no new invention, but they show how immense has been the significance of this Bo-tree branch to the Buddhists of Ceylon. According to the principle of

[1] For there were no relics of the Buddha yet in Lanka. This obviously true statement is contradicted by the story in chap. i. of Sarabhu depositing the "givaṭṭhi" in the Mahiyangana Dagaba.

criticism by which I am guided, the wreaths of flowery fiction in which this central tradition is almost buried do not in any degree discredit the central tradition itself; and I am quite prepared, for my part, to believe that the Bo-tree which stands at Anuradhapura derives its life, without the intervention of any new seed, from the root of the Bo-tree which Asoka was instructed to worship. But for the accuracy of the identification of that tree with the tree under which Gotama the Sakyan was resting when he first felt himself to have attained the truth —for this there is no shadow of security. For there is not a hint in all the earlier literature, so far as I have seen it, that any note was taken in the earlier centuries of this particular tree.

Such is the received tradition of the mission of Mahinda, and of the foundation of the Anuradhapura shrines. It was at this Anuradhapura that the chronicle was undoubtedly composed; and its materials were derived, as the author states in his preface, from materials found in the monasteries there.[1] In a suburb of that city, at what is now called Mihintale, the Elder (as Mahinda was called *par excellence*) was established with a handsome monastic establishment: there he died.[2] The chronicler was therefore in a perfectly good position for knowing all that was to be known about Mahinda, who may be justly called, on his authority, the founder of Buddhism in Ceylon.

Some writers (as Professor Oldenberg, Preface to *Vinaya*, p. l., etc.) have been led by independent courses of argument to doubt the whole story and the derivation of Ceylon Buddhism directly from Magadha. They think Buddhism found its way to Ceylon by way of the continent through gradual intercourse, and was not the result of a sudden conversion at the teaching of an individual. I cannot so set aside the evidence. In regard to the earlier history of the sacred books before Asoka's time, I incline, as I have admitted, to the side of scepticism, and I have shown why; but I cannot see any such reason here. That Mahinda came from Magadha by whatever stages to Ceylon, and established Buddhism by the favour of the king, Tissa, who was an ally or a dependent of Asoka, and that Mahinda's sister Sanghamitta followed him and brought with her a branch of the

[1] On the details, see Oldenberg, Preface to his *Dipavansa*.

[2] But it is not certain that the chief ceremonies in his honour were instituted till after the publication of the Dipavansa.

tree which was held sacred in Bihar—these are, I think, facts of history. They are decorated in the chronicle with innumerable embellishments—the sea was covered with flowers, deities danced before the king, etc. etc.—but these are but decorations which can be dropped out of notice without injury to the substance of the record. In regard even to European history we have come to learn that early stories are not, because they are mixed up with poetical fiction, therefore necessarily valueless to the historian, and still more certainly is it the case in Indian literature, modern as well as ancient, that records adorned, or disfigured, whichever we choose to call it, by wild exaggerations, are yet substantially true. We are not to doubt that a meeting was held because it is said that eighty-four thousand monks attended it, or to doubt that many monks came because it is said that they came through the air. If we doubt the central part, it is on other grounds.

One argument, which at first sight might seem to support the chronicle, cannot be justly alleged on its side; perhaps some will think the facts tell rather the other way. I allude to the name Mihintale, borne by the place where the great Elder is said to have resided. It is sometimes taken for granted that this name, now attached to a place east of Anuradhapura, where several ancient temples and dagabas are, and where Mahinda's bed (or place of meditation) is shown—that the name Mihintale is a witness, if not to the fact of Mahinda's coming, at least to the antiquity of the story. But this is not the case. The name cannot be shown to be an ancient one. It does not occur in the earlier part of the Mahavansa. There (ch. xvi., etc.) the place is called Cetiyagiri (Shrine Hill), which proves nothing. A tank was named by Aggabodhi, about A.D. 1100, Mahindattata Vāpi. This is, I believe, the earliest intimation that Cetiyagiri was getting to be called Mihintale. In later chapters we find a garden of the same name, and a tank, Mahindatalāka (ch. lxxix. v. 28), which is the Pali equivalent of the Sinhalese Mihintale. But in the fourth century A.D. the place had no such name. The fact that the historian gives an explanation of its being called Cetiyagiri (ch. xvii.), and does not allude to—what would have been still more to the point—its being named after Mahinda, seems conclusive proof of this.[1]

[1] It is called in Mahav. xiii. *ad fin.*, the Mount Missa, with peak, Ambatthala.

This throws some doubt on the antiquity of the Mahinda tradition, but does not avail, in my judgment, to set it aside.

The work which Mahinda effected was a thorough one, so far as Anuradhapura, the royal city, was concerned. Tissa attempted to be the Asoka of Ceylon. He had exchanged gifts with the great Indian emperor, and received advice—perhaps more peremptory instructions, perhaps contributions—from him. It was natural that under his encouragement Tissa should prosecute the work with vigour.

Later kings, during the next century and a half, carried on the tradition of royal patronage, and built, we are told, the rest of the great dagabas. But Tissa's work, the Thuparama, as it is called, the shrine which gave its name to the "Shrine Park" *par excellence,* has the best claim to be actually identified with what we see to-day. Of this, and of other dagabas, we read several times in the later history that hostile kings destroyed them, and they were afterwards restored by the next orthodox dynasty. But it is no easy thing to destroy a dagaba. Being a solid mass of brickwork, or of earth enclosed in brickwork, it can be entirely destroyed only by being carted away. A destruction which would be enough to satisfy the hatred of the most fanatical of Tamil invaders, might yet leave enough of each of those gigantic mounds to justify the Buddhist pilgrim of to-day in the conviction that he is worshipping the same heap which was worshipped so many centuries ago.

Being content to believe, then, that Mahinda introduced Buddhism into Ceylon, I have next to try to answer the question, "Did he bring the literature as we have it ?"

The chronicles rather take it for granted than directly assert that he did. They mention the discourses which he recited on different occasions, and sum up by saying (Mahav., ch. xx.) that he made known the religion of the vanquisher, the full text (pariyatti), the rule of conduct (paṭipatti), and the conditions of attainment (paṭivedho).

Of his bringing books they say nothing; nothing of the building of libraries or of any other honours paid to books or provision made for them. It is certain that writing was known in Buḍdhist India in Asoka's time. In view of the Greek influence it was impossible that it should be otherwise; but there is reason to doubt whether, even in India, writing had begun to be used by the Buddhists to perpetuate their literature. That they could have made the classifications and the cross-references which they did make, without written copies to turn to, may seem to us—accustomed to books—difficult to believe; but this is not so difficult as to believe that they had books, and yet that in all their literature and in the inscriptions of Asoka, and, I may add, in the early chapters of the Mahavansa, they never once alluded to them! Directions are given (e.g. Mahavagg. i. 25, 16) about every article used by monks, how each is to be cleaned and taken care of. For the shape and material and preservation of robes and slippers, the Vinaya has elaborate prescriptions. Is it possible to believe that there would not have been some such prescriptions about books if the monks had possessed books? (See Rhys Davids' Introduction to Vol. XI. of *Sacred Books of the East*, p. xxii.)

It is to the credit, then, of the veracity of the Mahavansa, that its compiler never hints at the use of books until he tells us that under the reign of Vatta Gamini Abhaya, about 80 B.C., the sacred literature was committed to writing.

It is there assumed that Mahinda had introduced the complete series. In the thirty-seventh chapter, in reference to Buddhaghosha, it is said that Mahinda had translated into Sinhalese the Commentaries which had been lost (or, at any rate, were not to be found) in India. But that the Commentaries were completed in Mahinda's time is extremely improbable. It is also extremely improbable that Commentaries like these, which have neither brevity nor systematic structure to secure them, could be orally transmitted; and in the face of these improbabilities, the *obiter dictum* of the thirty-seventh chapter—occurring in the narrative of events six centuries later—cannot be received.

We must conclude then that Mahinda, and those who followed him, brought in their memories, and committed to the memory of the Maha Vihara fraternity, the main part of the text of the Three Pitakas as it was settled at the Council of Patna—that is, as we have it now.[1]

The missionaries that Asoka, or Moggali, his guide in matters of religion, sent out to Cashmere, or to Nepal or elsewhere, may

[1] That Mahinda brought the three Pitakas is first, I think, expressly stated in Samantapāsādikā, p. 312.

have effected no lasting result; but it was not so with the embassy to Lanka. The emperor's own son had given up the pride of vice-regal authority, and the prospect of the Chariot of Empire, to be robed among the followers, as he at least believed them to be, of purity and love. This Mahinda must have been a man of extraordinary power. He must have combined the tone and deportment of the calm hermit, the prodigious memory of the trained student, and the active capacities of the statesman. The impression which he made upon the island was a very deep and lasting one; the ideal of Buddhism was embodied in him, as tradition represented him; and if our history is trustworthy at all, he must have really embodied it in no small degree, or he could not have won, even with the authority of Asoka, even from the flattered Devanampiya Tissa, so rapid and complete a success. The zeal of the monarch who sent him, the courage, devotion, and ability of Mahinda himself, the enthusiasm with which he was welcomed—these all stand out as facts to which there are few parallels, and which are in curious contrast to the ordinary tenor of life in India and Ceylon.

Are they facts? we are compelled to ask again; and again we are compelled to accept them. The doings and sayings of Gotama, and the royal enthusiasm of Bimbisara, and the donation of Veluvana, these are perhaps only half substantial. We know them at best only through the gradually accumulated records of one or two centuries; but with Asoka, Mahinda, and Tissa, we are on historical ground: the rock of Girnar, the Mahavihara, the Thuparama of Anuradhapura, are substantial facts.

NOTE TO CHAPTER XX

THE LESSER SERMON OF THE PARABLE OF THE ELEPHANT'S FOOTMARKS

THUS I have heard: Once upon a time the Buddha was residing at Sāvatthi in Anāthapindika's park, the bamboo grove. At that time the Brahman Jānussoni drove out from Sāvatthi about midday in a covered[1] chariot of pure white. The Brahman Janussoni saw the Brahman ascetic Pilotika coming towards him from a distance, and when he saw him he said thus: "Whence is the reverend Vacchāyano coming at midday?" "I come, friend, from the presence of the 'Samana,' Gotama."

[1] Some render this "drawn by mares."

"What think you, reverend Vacchayano, of Gotama's wisdom and power of exposition; do you think him a sage?" "Who am I, sir, and how should I estimate the proficiency in wisdom of Gotama? He, methinks, would be a perfect man who could estimate Gotama's wisdom and exposition." "This is high praise indeed, sir, with which you praise the Samana Gotama." "Who am I, who am I to praise Gotama? My lord Gotama is the centre of all praise;[1] he is the best of gods and men." "What such mighty excellence do you see, reverend Vacchayano, in Gotama, that you are so devoted to him?" "Just as if a clever elephant-tracker were to go into an elephant forest, and saw in that forest an elephant's footmark (pada) of great size, extended in length and wide in breadth, he would come to this certain conclusion: 'Ah! that is a great elephant'; just so, since I saw in the Samana Gotama four points (pada) I came to this certain conclusion: 'The Blessed One is a full Buddha, the doctrine taught by him is well-spoken, the system of his Community is perfect,' and those four points are these:—

"I see, sir, sometimes certain sages of the Warrior caste, subtle, disputatious, hairsplitters.[2] They go about refuting other people's doctrines by their cleverness; they hear it said that the Samana Gotama is coming to such and such a village or town; they prepare a question: 'We will go and ask Gotama this question; if he answers in this way, then we will prove him wrong in this way; if he answers in that way, we will prove him wrong in that way.' As soon as they hear Gotama is come to the place, they set off to visit him. Gotama expounds his doctrine, instructs them with his doctrine, brings the truth home to them, kindles their interest, fills them with satisfaction; under the influence of that instruction, and conviction, and interest, and full satisfaction, they never ask Gotama the question, much less prove him wrong—they inevitably become Gotama's disciples. When I saw in the Samana Gotama this first mark, I came to the conclusion: 'The Blessed One is a full Buddha; the Doctrine he teaches is true; the system of his Community is good.' I see the same with wise men of the Brahman caste, and from this second mark I draw the same conclusion. I see it with wise men of the Cultivator caste, and I draw the same conclusion from this third mark.

"Again, I see it in the case of wise ascetics. They too (under the same influence and conviction, instead of asking the question they had prepared) beg Gotama to allow them to come forth from household life into the homeless, and Gotama accepts their profession. They being thus professed, some of them choosing solitude and living in unremitting zeal and effort, in no long time enjoy the full attainment and conscious intuition, even in this world, of that sublime goal of the religious life, for the sake of which noble youths rightly go forth from house and home to the homeless life. Such men say: 'We had all but perished, we had all but utterly perished; we called ourselves ascetics when we were no

[1] "Praised by the praised." The commentaries explain that like sweet flowers, that need no added perfume from outside, Gotama derives his praise from his own perfections; to speak in his praise is "to gild refined gold," etc.

[2] Not exactly in our sense; they can cleave a minute mark from a distance.

ascetics; we called ourselves Brahmans when we were no Brahmans; we called ourselves saints when we were no saints; now we are ascetics, now we are Brahmans, now we are saints.' And when I saw in the Samana Gotama, I said"—[as before].

When Vacchayano had said this the Brahman Janussoni got down from his pure white covered car, drew his robe over one shoulder, made an obeisance in the direction of the Buddha, and three times uttered this enthusiastic cry: "Glory to the blessed, holy, perfect Buddha!" "Certainly," he added, "I must not fail to come into the presence of that lord Gotama; certainly I must not fail to have conversation with him." So Janussoni the Brahman went where Gotama was; having got there he saluted him, and after the usual words of courtesy had been gone through, took a respectful seat on one side. So sitting, he repeated to the Buddha the whole of his conversation with the Brahman ascetic Pilotika. Thereupon the Buddha said: "That is not a full and complete version, Brahman, of the parable of the elephant marks, so listen, Brahman, and I will tell you the full and complete version of the elephant-mark parable; attend to it well." "I will, sir," the Brahman promised.

"If a skilled elephant-tracker goes into an elephant forest and sees in that forest a large foot-print, long lengthwise and broad across, if he is a skilled elephant-tracker he does not at once conclude, 'That is a great elephant.' Why? There are, Brahman, in an elephant forest female elephants of a dwarf breed whose feet are large; and it may be, he says to himself, the track of one of these. He follows it up; and as he follows it up he sees in the forest a large footprint, long and broad, and with rubbing high up on the trunks of trees; but he does not at once conclude, 'That is a great elephant.' Why? There are, Brahman, in an elephant forest tall she-elephants of the breed called 'the tall dark-tusked,' whose feet are large; and it may be, he says to himself, the track of one of those. He follows it up; and as he follows it up he sees in the forest a large footprint, long and broad, rubbing high up, and trunks of trees scratched by the marks of tusks, but he does not at once conclude, 'That is a great elephant.' Why? There are, Brahman, in an elephant forest tall she-elephants,[1] whose feet are large; and it may be, he says to himself, the track of one of those. He follows it up; and as he follows it he sees in the forest a large footprint, long and broad, rubbing high up, and trunks scratched by tusks, and with branches broken off high up, and he sees the elephant himself under a tree or out in the open, moving, or standing, or sitting, or lying down. Then he is certain: 'there is really a great elephant.' Just so, Brahman, when a perfect one is born in the world, a holy absolute Buddha, accomplished in knowledge and in conduct, one who has reached the perfect grade of beings, seeing through the worlds, the unsurpassed trainer of men, teacher of gods and men—a Blessed Buddha; what he has attained to see by his own supernatural insight, he utters to this

[1] Of the breed named Uccā-kanerukā, whose tusks (or tushes) are short, like the budding flower of the kaneru tree.

world,[1] with the worlds of devas, of Māras, of Brahmas; to all beings, Brahmans and ascetics, gods and men. He expounds a doctrine beautiful in beginning, beautiful in midst, beautiful in end, with the meaning and with the text, and proclaims the religious life in all its fullness and purity. That doctrine is heard by a householder, or one of householder caste, or one born in some other caste. On hearing that doctrine he grasps faith in the Tathāgata. When he has attained that grasp of faith he reflects thus: 'House-living is confined and dusty (with the blinding dust of desire); the hermit life is life in the open air. It is not easy, while living in a house, to lead the religious life in unbroken fullness, in unbroken purity, in flawless perfection. I had better put off my hair, and put on the yellow robes, and go forth from the house into the houseless state.' Soon he leaves his little wealth or his great wealth, as the case may be; leaves his little circle of relatives or his great circle of relatives, as the case may be; puts on the yellow robes and goes forth from house and home into the houseless state.

"Thus gone forth and admitted into the Community, he enters into the rules and way of life of the mendicants. He abstains from destroying life; he has laid aside the stick and the arrow; he is scrupulous, merciful, kind, and compassionate to all things that have life and being.

' He renounces theft, and desists from taking what is not given; takes (only) what is given, desires only what is given, and keeps himself from stealing and guile. He renounces unchastity and lives in chastity and continence, having desisted from all sexual acts and intercourse. He renounces lying and desists from it, being truth-telling, truth-abiding, steady, trustworthy, not ready to deceive his neighbour. He renounces slanderous speaking, and desists from it: what he hears here he does not tell there to divide those from these, what he hears there he does not tell here to divide these from those: and so is a joiner of the divided, and an encourager of those who are at one: unity is his pleasure, his passion, his delight; and the words he utters are words that make for unity. He renounces abusive speaking, and desists from it; he will utter only such speech as is sweet, pleasant to the ear, loving, winning the heart, courteous, giving pleasure and happiness to everybody. He renounces talking nonsense; he speaks in season, speaks of facts, speaks to the purpose, speaks of Doctrine and of Rule; when he speaks, what he says is worth treasuring, full of sensible illustrations, and well divided.[2]

"He abstains from the destruction of any groups of seed or germs. He eats but once, abstaining at night, and abstains from meals at wrong times. He abstains from the sight of dancing, singing, playing (on harp, etc.), and shows. He abstains from wearing garlands, perfumes, ointments, from all means of toilet and adornment. He abstains from high couches and wide couches. He abstains from receiving of gold or silver; of raw corn; of women and girls; of slave men and slave

[1] This is otherwise taken: "Having by his own supernatural insight come to know the whole world of devas, etc. . . . he utters it" (see p. 26).

[2] Technical terms referring to the composition and expounding of Suttas.

women; of goats and she-goats; of fowls and pigs; of elephants, cows, horses, mares, of fields and lands. He abstains from going on errands and messages; from trading and selling, from cheating by false balances, by false metals, by false measures; from fraud, deceit, dishonesty, and roguery; from cutting, striking, binding, robbery, plundering, and violence.

"He is contented with such robes as are sufficient for the body, with such alms-food as suffices for the belly; wherever he goes he takes all he needs with him. Just as a winged bird, whithersoever it flies, carries no other burden than its own wings; so is the monk contented with such robes as are sufficient for the body, with such alms-food as is sufficient for the belly; wherever he goes he takes all he needs with him.

"Having attained to this noble system of conduct, he experiences within him the bliss of faultlessness. When with the eye he sees a form, he does not catch at its characteristics or its details; he practises avoiding that which may be the cause of covetousness, dismalness, and other sinful and evil tempers flowing in upon the man who lives with unrestrained sense of sight; he guards his sense of sight, he attains restraint of the sense of sight. So with regard to sounds which are perceived by the ear, smells by the nose, taste by the tongue, touch by the body, objects of cognition by the mind; he practises restraint of all these organs of sense.[1] Having attained to this noble restraint of the senses, he experiences within himself the bliss of detachment. In going or in coming he acts with recollection, in looking this way or looking that way, in drawing in his hand or stretching it out, in wearing robes and bowl, in eating or drinking, in feeding or tasting, in all the necessary acts of life, in going, standing, sitting, sleeping, waking, speaking, or being silent, he acts with recollection.

"Having attained to this noble system of conduct and this noble restraint of the senses, and this noble state of conscious recollectedness, he chooses a secluded dwelling place, a forest, the foot of a tree, a hill, grotto, mountain cave, burial-ground, uncultivated ground,[2] or open ground, or heap of straw. After his meal, when he has returned from begging he sits down, turning in his legs in the cross-legged attitude, erecting his body straight upright, fixing his consciousness before his face. Then having put away all covetousness, he abides with mind cleansed of covetousness, he purges his mind of covetousness; putting away the taint of malice, he abides with no malice in his mind, with kindness and compassion to all that lives and exists, he purges his mind of the taint of malice; putting away sloth he abides unslothful, with consciousness full of light, thoughtful and recollected, he purges his mind of sloth; putting away pride and querulousness, he abides, not lifted up by pride, his mind calmed down within him, he purges his mind of the restlessness of pride; putting away doubt, he abides on the other side of (the river of) doubt; resting without raising difficulties on right principles, he purges his mind from doubt.

[1] Here and in one or two other places the original has been a little condensed.
[2] The printed text has here Vannapatthaṃ for vanapanthaṃ.

"Then having put away these five hindrances, which obscure thought and weaken insight, apart from desires, apart from principles of evil, he abides in the attainment of pleasure and joy[1] which springs from mental freedom, in which there is still the exercise of reflection and movement of thought—the first stage of meditation. This, Brahman, deserves to be called a Tathāgata mark (or stage of attainment); here we may say is the trace of the Tathagata's presence, his rubbings and the marks of his tusks. But not yet does the noble disciple conclude: 'Bhagavā is an absolute Buddha, the Doctrine proclaimed by Bhagava is true, the practice of the Community is good.'

"Further, Brahman, again, all exercise of reflection and movement of the mind being calmed down, in that internal clearness in which the pure mind moves alone, the mendicant abides in the attainment of that pleasure and joy born of self-concentration, which involves no exercise of reflection or movement of the mind—the second stage of meditation. This, too, Brahman, deserves to be called a Tathagata mark (or stage of attainment); here we may say is the trace of the Tathagata's presence, of his rubbings and the marks made by his tusks. But not yet does the noble disciple conclude: 'Bhagava is an absolute Buddha, the Doctrine proclaimed by Bhagava is true, the practice of the Community is good.'

"Further, Brahman, again, the mendicant, pleasureless and indifferent, abides in conscious recollectedness, and feels through all his bodily frame that joy which the noble ones describe as the joy of conscious indifference —so he abides in the third stage of meditation. This, too, Brahman, deserves to be called a Tathagata mark (or stage of attainment); here we may say is the trace of the Tathagata's presence, of his rubbings and the marks made by his tusks. But not yet does the noble disciple conclude: 'Bhagava is an absolute Buddha, the doctrine proclaimed by Bhagava is true, the practice of the Community is good.'

"Further, Brahman, again, the mendicant, by abandonment of joy and abandonment of pain, those former satisfactions and dissatisfactions gone, abides in the attainment of that painless and joyless purity of conscious indifference, which is the fourth stage of meditation. This, too, Brahman, deserves to be called a Tathagata mark (or stage of attainment); here we may say is the trace of the Tathagata's presence, of his rubbings and tusk-marks. But not yet does the noble disciple conclude: 'Bhagava is an absolute Buddha, the Doctrine proclaimed by Bhagava is true, the practice of the Community is good.'

"When thus the mind is collected, purged, white, without lust, freed from corruption, and become soft and workable, firm and motionless, he bends his mind to the knowledge of the recollection of former dwellings.[2]

[1] "Pleasure" is here used for "prīti," a superficial *movement* of satisfaction, as distinguished from "joy," "sukhaṃ," a deeper-seated *state* of satisfaction.

In the first stage there is mental freedom and movement of thought; in the second unity of mind, but no movement of thought; in the third there is still joy; in the fourth even this is gone.

[2] This is the literal meaning of the word; although the idea "former dwellings of the soul" is alien to Buddhism.

He calls to memory the countless variety of former abodes—that is, one birth and two births and three births, four births and five births, and twenty births and thirty births and forty births and fifty births and a hundred births and a thousand births and a hundred thousand births and many closing cycles and many opening cycles and many opening and closing cycles. He says to himself: 'In such a place (or, in such a birth) I was named so-and-so, of such and such a tribe, such and such appearance, living on such and such food, experiencing such and such joys and pains, with such and such limits of lifetime; when I passed away out of that, I was born in such a place or condition, and then I had such and such a name, was of such and such a tribe, such and such a caste, living on such and such food, experiencing such and such joys and pains, with such and such limits of lifetime; passing thence I was born here.' Thus he calls to memory a countless variety of former dwellings, with the characteristics and description of each. This, too, Brahma, deserves to be called a Tathagata mark (or stage of attainment); here we may say is the trace of the Tathagata's presence, of his rubbings and tusk-marks. But not yet does the noble disciple conclude: 'Bhagava is an absolute Buddha, the Doctrine proclaimed by Bhagava is true, the practice of the Community is good.'

"When thus the mind is collected, purged, white, without stain, freed from obscurations, and become soft and workable, firm and motionless, he bends his mind to the knowledge of the passing away and re-birth of beings. With divine sight, pure, superhuman, he sees beings passing away and being born,[1] high or low, of good appearance or bad, in happy condition or unhappy, he recognizes beings going according to their sum of action (karma). 'Ah! friends,' he says to himself, 'these beings have adopted a wicked course of bodily action, of word and of thought, having been blasphemers of the noble ones, holders of false opinions—these, at the breaking up of the body, after death have been born in an infernal state, in an evil condition, in the place of torment, in hell.' Or, 'These beings having adopted a good course of bodily action, of word and of thought, not blasphemers of the noble ones, holders of true opinions—these, at the breaking up of the body, after death have been born in a happy condition, in heaven or in this world.' Thus with divine sight, pure, superhuman, he sees beings passing away and being born, high or low, of good appearance or bad, in happy condition or unhappy, he recognizes beings going according to their sum of action. This, too, Brahman, deserves to be called a Tathagata mark (or stage of attainment); here we may say is the trace of the Tathagata's presence, of his rubbings and tusk-marks. But not yet does the noble disciple conclude: 'Bhagava is an absolute Buddha, the Doctrine proclaimed by Bhagava is true, the practice of the Community is good.'

"When his mind is thus collected, purged, white, without stain, freed from obscurations, and become soft and workable, firm and motionless, he

[1] The words used here for the cessation of one life and the entrance on another imply, the one, "fading or falling away"; the other, "accidental dropping into" (a new condition).

bends his mind to the knowledge of the annihilation of the forms of moral evil. He recognizes in its reality what pain is, he recognizes in its reality what the cause of pain is, he recognizes in its reality what the destruction of pain is, he recognizes in its reality what the course which leads to the destruction of pain is; he recognizes in its reality what the forms of moral evil are, he recognizes in its reality what the cause of the forms of moral evil is, he recognizes in its reality what the destruction of the forms of moral evil is, he recognizes in its reality what the course is which leads to the destruction of the forms of moral evil. This, too, Brahman, deserves to be called a Tathagata mark (or stage of attainment); here we may say is the trace of the Tathagata's presence, of his rubbings and tusk-marks. But not yet does the noble disciple conclude: 'Bhagava is an absolute Buddha, the Doctrine proclaimed by Bhagava is true, the practice of the Community is good.'

"When he thus knows, thus sees, his mind is released from the evil of lust, and his mind is released from the evil of[1] (love of) existence, and his mind is released from the evil of ignorance. In that release of the mind the knowledge arises, that he is released, that birth is annihilated, the religious course lived out, all that has to be done is done, there is no further any cause for remaining here.[2] This, Brahman, may be truly called the foot-mark, the rubbings, the tusk-marks of Tathagatha. Herein, Brahman, the noble disciple has reached the certainty: 'Bhagava is an absolute Buddha, the Doctrine proclaimed by Bhagava is true, the practice of the Community is good.'

"This, Brahman, is the full and complete form of the parallel of the elephant footmarks."

When this had been said, the Brahman Janussoni thus spoke to Bhagava: "Excellent, Lord Gotama; it is as if, Lord Gotama, one should set up what was overturned, or open what was closed, or show the way to one who was astray, or bring a lighted oil-lamp where it was dark, so that those who have sight may behold the form of things; just so has the doctrine been preached by my Lord Gotama in multiform method. I betake me for refuge to Gotama, to the Doctrine, and to the mendicant Community. May my Lord Gotama take me as a professed follower, for I go to him for refuge from this day forward while I have life."

[1] No single word in our terminology will express what the "Asavas" have in common. They are, lusts of all sorts, love of existence, and ignorance, to which false opinion is sometimes added as a fourth. I have here called them forms of "moral evil"; elsewhere "corruptions."

[2] That is either: "In this world of men," or "In this condition of rahatship."

CHAPTER XXI

FROM MAHINDA TO BUDDHAGHOSHA

AFTER the death of Mahinda, the successors of Devanampiyatissa went on building dwellings for the monks, and extending the domain of the great monastery to Anuradhapura. There was as yet but one centre and one association: no rivalry disturbed the unanimity of the happy children of Mahinda.

The first troubles were those caused by foreign invasion. The Tamils of South India invaded Ceylon, and their heroic leader, Elāra, established himself as king; but he reigned with so much goodness and justice, that, heretic Brahman as he was, his memory has always been held in esteem, almost in affection. But the sacred island was not long to lie under the usurped authority of a Brahman king. The patriot hero Dutthagamini was greater even than Elara, and, in a contest which did honour to both, overcame and slew him, and recovered the throne of Lanka for her own Buddhist kings. The war had been undertaken by Dutthagamini as a religious duty; and when he had conquered, his victory was employed for the service and extension of Buddhism. Aided by supernatural power, and finding at every turn supernatural wealth ready to his hand—such is the light in which the Mahavansa sets the story—he built, as a hall for the monks to meet in, the famous Brazen Palace (or Brass-roofed Palace). It was constructed after a plan brought straight from heaven. Repeatedly destroyed in after times and repeatedly restored, it is represented even now by some sixteen hundred stone pillars; but what the edifice was like, whose seven stories rested on these pillars, antiquarians are puzzled to conjecture. Even more celebrated and far more sacred than the Brazen Palace, the same king erected the "Great Shrine," or Ruwanweli Dagaba; and in it he placed, when he had obtained them from the mysterious Naga world, those relics of the Buddha which, at the time of Gotama's decease had been received—so runs the audacious legend—for the future sanctification of Ceylon! In the description of the circumstances under which this relic-dome was built, and of the treasures employed in its construction, the chronicle exhausts the resources of eastern imagination; and if we hold that where the surroundings are fabulous no kernel of truth can be securely grasped, we might put the whole story aside as a fairy tale. But there at Anuradhapura the great dagaba still stands. It has been defaced and renewed, enlarged and altered, a hundred times; but the substantial mass of that gigantic mound—a pile of brickwork out of which a city might be built—is probably the very same material that was heaped there by the conqueror of Elara. This was about 160 B.C.

For nearly another century the history contains nothing of interest; only the murders by which each king gained the throne, the sacred buildings that secured him merit after he had gained it, and the Tamil invasions by which his reign was disturbed. At length, about 90 B.C., the reign of Vattagamini Abhaya is distinguished by the erection of another of the great dagabas which still astonish us at Anuradhapura, the Abhayagiri. But from this erection dates a rivalry, between the monks of the newer foundation and those of the Great Monastery, which marred, for fourteen centuries, the unity of Buddhism in Ceylon.

From this date for the next three centuries, there is little to record. Tamil influence increased, and "bad men" often had the upper hand; but whenever prosperity revived new shrines were built, and the Brazen Palace, which seems always to have been the first to suffer, was restored. But an epoch is marked, about A.D. 300, by the reign of Mahasena. This king adopted the tenets which were hostile to the Great Monastery and proscribed its monks. They fled to the south-east of the island, and for nine years the ancient foundation was desolate. The Brazen Palace and many other Mahavihara buildings were pulled down, and their materials were used to extend the dwellings and halls of the Abhayagiri monks. Mahasena was persuaded, however, by his ministers to restore them; and he did his best by vast works of merit, of which the Mahavihara monks were the recipients, to balance the demerit he had incurred.

After him, the Rājavaliya tells us, the race of kings degenerated. They no longer boasted the pure blood of the "Solar" race. Of such deterioration the older history admits nothing; though alliances with Indian royal families are recorded. But however that may be, it is the period following Mahasena that is marked by that literary activity, to which the continuity of Ceylon history is due. The national characteristics of the past were carried on into later centuries by the compilation of the Mahavansa, and the religious literature was crowned by the works of Buddhaghosha.

Two important features, which are obviously connected, mark the earlier part of the fourth century: the increase of intercourse with India, and the cultus of Mahinda and of the Tooth.

In Siri Meghavana's reign (*c.* A.D. 304) a Brahman princess brought across from Kalinga the so-called Sacred Tooth of Buddha, and the cultus of that relic began. Under the next king we are told that art flourished, especially sculpture. An image of Mahinda was made about this time, and the custom of carrying it in procession was instituted; a measure directed no doubt to the maintenance of the prestige of the Mahavihara, which Mahasena's early violence had impaired, and which was further threatened by the appearance of a second rival community, that of the Jetavana, an offset, under Mahasena's influence, from the Abhayagiri. The next king, Buddhadasa, was an accomplished physician, and imitated the great Asoka in erecting hospitals. In his reign, it is said, the Suttas were translated into Sinhalese. This movement culminated in Mahanama's reign (*c.* A.D. 412–434) in Buddhaghosha.

Of the increased intercourse with India another interesting illustration is afforded by the visit of the Chinese pilgrim, Fa Hien; not only a devoted Buddhist, but a writer at once picturesque and careful. He visited Anuradhapura early in the fifth century A.D., and his account agrees completely with the native chronicle.

Fa Hien begins the record of his visit to Ceylon by repeating the traditions which he learnt there, just as they are contained in the Mahavansa, about the early inhabitants of the island, and the visits of the Buddha. Then he tells us, very graphically, what he saw. The great dagabas were in their glory; that of the Abhayagiri impressed him most; and he says it was four hundred cubits high, and grandly adorned with gold and silver, and finished with a combination of all the precious substances.[1] In the monastery adjoining it there were five thousand monks. The total number of monks in the island he understood to be sixty thousand. His admiration was greatly excited by an image of the Buddha made of green jade, which was twenty cubits high, and had "an appearance of solemn dignity which words cannot express." He describes the Bo-tree, and mentions the "Vihara of Buddha's Tooth"; and speaks of the whole city of Anuradhapura as stately and well-kept. Of the procession (perahœra) of the Tooth he gives a detailed account; and it is to be noted that it was at the Abhayagiri that the principal ceremonies took place.

Of the Mahavihara he speaks as if it held quite a secondary position, although it had three thousand monks. But a monk had lately died there who was held to be a Rahat, who had attained to supernatural knowledge and powers; and the pilgrim describes his cremation. "Fa Hien," he says, "had not arrived in time (to see him) alive, but only saw his funeral." And the other instance which he mentions of individual distinction is also to the credit of the Mahavihara. At the "Chaitya Hill"—not yet known as Mihintale—was a monk of famous virtue named Dhammagutta.

Fa Hien describes in glowing terms the virtue and the liberality of the king, and gives a minute account of the ceremonies at the granting of a site for a new vihara; an account which agrees perfectly with what the chronicles relate and existing monuments prove. Finally, he gives a long report of a sermon which he heard preached on the Bowl of Buddha.

But of Buddhaghosha, or his literary works, Fa Hien has nothing to say. His visit took place before that of the great commentator.

[1] Legge's Fa Hien, pp. 101–110.

NOTE TO CHAPTER XXI

DATE OF FA HIEN'S VISIT TO CEYLON

THE date of Fa Hien's visit cannot, it appears, be fixed on Chinese authority more nearly than to the period A.D. 317-478. The limits are drawn more closely by a comparison of his statements with those of the Mahavansa.

Since he found the cultus of the Tooth in full force, while yet he does not say that it had recently arrived, his visit must have taken place after, and probably long after, the accession of Sirimeghavana (A.D. 304), in whose reign the Tooth was brought to Ceylon.

In the opposite direction a limit is indicated by his silence about Buddhaghosha, who could not have failed to interest him; and Buddhaghosha came during the reign of Mahanama, A.D. 412-34.

Within these limits there were three kings—Jetthatissa, Buddhadasa, and Upatissa—but none of these corresponds with the king whom Fa Hien describes, so well as Mahanama does.

Jetthatissa was a great promoter of art and sculpture, and the mention of the great statue in jade—a material which must have come from India—without mention of its having been the work of the reigning king, suggests a date later than this king's reign.

Buddhadasa was so celebrated for his extraordinary medical skill that it is most improbable that Fa Hien could have left this unmentioned, if Buddhadasa had been the king on whose merits he dwells so fully.

Upatissa seems to have been a very devoted adherent of the Mahavihasa; but the pilgrim represents the Abhayagiri as being in the ascendant, and enjoying the royal patronage.

Mahanama, on the other hand, is recorded as having supported the Abhayagiri monks in the earlier part of his reign: he gave them three viharas. Fa Hien, who was evidently a guest at the Abhayagiri, describes the king's character in more glowing terms than those of the chronicler.

It may be concluded, therefore, with some confidence, that Fa Hien was at Anuradhapura early in Mahanama's reign. The date which this would imply, if the received chronology of the Mahavansa is correct, is shortly after A.D. 412.

CHAPTER XXII

BUDDHAGHOSHA AND THE "COMMENTARIES"

IT would be hardly too much to say that Buddhaghosha was the second founder of the Buddhism of Ceylon. The Ceylon Buddhism of the present day, as it is professed by its most learned and most earnest adherents, is virtually the religion of Buddhaghosha. The interpretation of the sacred books, which has prevailed since his time and is authoritative now for native scholars, is the interpretation fixed by Buddhaghosha and his school. He lived about A.D. 420; in the interval between the composition of the Dipavansa and that of the Mahavansa. The following is the record of him in the Mahavansa:—

He was a Brahman of Magadha,[1] highly accomplished in the

[1] Mr. Harinath De has kindly communicated to me the following note on the Indian origin of Buddhaghosha:—

"The account given in the Mahāvaṁsa of Buddhaghosha's origin and attainments is as follows:—

'Bodhimaṇḍasamīpamhi jāto brāhmaṇamāṇavo
vijjāsippakalāvedī tīsu vedesu pārago
Sammāviññātsamayo sabbavādavisārado
vādatthī sabbadīpamhi āhiṇḍanto pavādino
Vihāram ekaṁ āgamma rattim Patañjalī-mataṁ
parivatteti sampuṇṇapadaṁ suparimandalaṁ.'

"I venture to challenge the correctness of the statements contained in the above lines. My grounds may be very briefly stated as follows:—

"(1) The references to Northern India which occur in Buddhaghosha's work are few and far between, and appear to me for the most part vague and incorrect. For instance, in the commentary to the Majjhimanikāya Buddhaghosha speaks of Rajagaha and mentions its distance from the Bodhi tree in Gaya. So far as I can recollect he is quite wrong about the distance. It appears inconceivable to me how a man who was brought up in the neighbourhood of Bodh Gaya, as Buddhaghosha is said to have been by the author of the Mahāvaṁsa, could possibly have made such a blunder. It is also noticeable that whenever Buddhaghosha mentions any place in Northern India it is always in connection with some foolish legend which may have been picked up from books. There is, so

Brahman philosophy and religion, and wandered about India "as a disputant eager for controversy." In his wanderings he lodged at a certain Buddhist vihara, where he fell into argument with an elder named Revata, by whom he was converted. He soon became a distinguished disciple, and was called Buddhaghosha, "the voice of Buddha" (or rather, perhaps, "he who has a voice like a Buddha"). In India he composed an original work called "Ñānodaya," and wrote a commentary on part of the Abhidhamma. He contemplated writing in India a concise commentary on the whole of the sacred text, and received from Revata the following advice:—

"The text alone (of the Pitakattaya) has been preserved in this land: the Aṭṭhakathā are not extant here; nor is there any

far as I can recollect, not a single reference to any place in Northern India which looks like a personal reminiscence.

"(2) Buddhaghosha's knowledge of the sacred books of the Hindus, so far as it can be gathered from his commentaries, appears to me to be too superficial for an educated Brahmin of his age, and his informations on this point are in many cases incorrect. The commentary on the Ambaṭṭhasutta in the Sumangalavilāsini contains several instances of an imperfect acquaintance with the sacred lore of the Brahmins. On the other hand Buddhaghosha's knowledge of Sanskrit language is generally very correct, and he appears to have been familiar with the Grammar of Panini (see my note on Buddhaghosha and Panini in the P.T.S. Journal for 1906-7).

"(3) It is equally remarkable that there is no reference to the system of Patañjali in the Visuddhimagga, or, so far as I know, in his other works. On the other hand in the Visuddhimagga and the Aṭṭhasālini there are several references to the doctrines of the Sānkhya philosophy. To me it appears inconceivable that a writer like Buddhaghosha, who has devoted so many pages to *Samādhi* in the Visuddhimagga, should have wilfully omitted to mention the Yoga system in his work, if he was so well versed in the system of Patañjali as the Mahāvaṁsa represents him to have been.

"The facts mentioned above, as well as the great fondness which Buddhaghosha seems to show for the Draviḍas—a fondness which led him in one of his commentaries to hazard the assertion that Pali would be the language spoken by a child born of a Draviḍa father and a Singhalese mother, if the child were left to grow up by itself in a forest far removed from human haunts—make me inclined to believe that Buddhaghosha, if he was not a Singhalese by birth and was of Indian origin, must have come from the south of India (the Draviḍa country) or, if he at all came from Northern India, he must have left his native country at a time when he was too young to acquire mastery over all arts and systems of philosophy as maintained by the author of the Mahāvaṁsa. We all know that the biographers of Mahomedan divines of Indian origin feel a delight in tracing back the ancestry of their heroes to some great men of Mecca or Medina. Might not the author of the Mahāvaṁsa have been tempted by a similar pious desire to place the birth of the great exponent of Ceylonese Buddhism in the Madhyadesha, the Holy Land of the Buddhists?"

version to be found of the various expositions of the teachers. The Sinhalese Atthakatha are genuine. They are composed in the Sinhalese language by the inspired and profoundly wise Mahinda, who had previously consulted the discourses of Buddha authenticated at the three convocations and the dissertations and arguments of Sariputta and others, and they are extant among the Sinhalese. Repairing thither, and studying the same, translate them according to the rules of the grammar of the Magadhas. It will be an act conducive to the welfare of the whole world."

The Mahavansa continues: "Having been thus advised, this eminently wise personage, rejoicing therein, departed from thence, and visited this island in the reign of this monarch, Mahanama (A.D. 412–434). On reaching the Mahavihara, at Anuradhapura, he entered the Mahapadana Hall, the most splendid of the apartments in the vihara, and listened to the Sinhalese Atthakatha, and the Theravada, from the beginning to the end, expounded by the Thera Sanghapāla, and became thoroughly convinced that they conveyed the true meaning of the doctrines of the lord of Dhamma. Thereupon, paying reverential respect to the priesthood, he thus petitioned: 'I am desirous of translating the Atthakatha: give me access to all your books.' The priesthood, for the purpose of testing his qualifications, gave only two gatha, saying, 'Hence prove thy qualifications; having satisfied ourselves on this point, we will then let thee have all our books.' From these, taking two gatha for his text, and consulting the Pitakattaya together with the Atthakatha, and condensing them into an abridged form, he composed the commentary called the 'Visuddhimagga.' Thereupon, having assembled the priesthood who had acquired a thorough knowledge of the doctrines of Buddha at the Bo-tree, he commenced to read out the work he had composed. The devatas, in order that they might make his wisdom celebrated among men, rendered that book invisible. He, however, for a second and third time, recomposed it. When he was in the act of producing his book for the third time, for the purpose of propounding it, the devatas restored the other two copies also.

"The assembled priests then read out the three books simultaneously. In those versions, neither in a signification nor in a single misplacement by transposition—nay, even in the

Thera controversies and in the text of the Pitakattaya—was there in the measure of a verse, or in a letter of a word, the slightest variation.

"Thereupon the priesthood rejoicing again and again, fervently shouted forth, saying, 'Most assuredly this is Metteyya Buddha himself': and made over to him the books in which the Pitakattaya were recorded, together with the Atthakatha. Taking up his residence in the secluded Ganthakara Vihara, at Anuradhapura, he translated, according to the rules of the grammar of the Magadhas, which are the root of all languages, the whole of the Sinhalese Atthakatha into Pali. This proved an achievement of the greatest consequence to all languages spoken by the human race.

"All the Theras and Acaryas held this compilation in the same estimation as the text of the Pitakattaya. Thereafter, the object of his mission having been accomplished, he returned to Jambudipa, to worship at the Bo-tree at Uruvela in Magadha."

A similar account is given from Burmese sources, but there is no reason to think that it is independent. The intercourse has always been frequent between the Buddhists of Ceylon and those of Burma, and as Ceylon has been the learner in the latter centuries from her northern sister, so in the earlier days Ceylon was the source of information. We are compelled to take it, on the authority of the Mahavansa, that the Pali commentaries, as they are now read in Ceylon, are from the hand of Buddhaghosha.

It is impossible to say how far his work was a revival and how far a new departure. Had the Commentaries, which he is said to have imported and translated, in point of fact ever been known in Ceylon before? Were they the old traditions of the Anuradhapura monks held from the days of Mahinda, and variously enlarged, and now rearranged, remodelled by a powerful mind? Or had they been elaborated on the continent of India, during the centuries through which the island had been in great measure cut off from contact with the rest of the Buddhist world? Or is the suspicion to be admitted for a moment of a still greater scepticism, as if Buddhaghosha, and not Mahinda, was the real importer of Buddhism into Lanka?

This last suspicion has been suggested, but there is no place for it. The antiquity of the Buddhist buildings in Ceylon is alone enough to refute it. As to the other two alternatives, it is possible that the truth lies between them. It is certain that there were treatises handed down by the monks in Anuradhapura long before Buddhaghosha's visit. The Dipavansa was written considerably, perhaps more than a century, before his time, and the tradition which it embodies must be older still. The writer of the Dipavansa, which differs from the introductory part of a commentary only by being in verse, says that what he narrates has been " handed down by many generations." And Buddhaghosha certainly derived from the same sources part of the historical introduction to his Commentaries on the Vinaya and Sutta Pitakas.

Whence these materials originally came, or how far they had been invented in the island, it is impossible with our present knowledge to say. The existence in them, wherever they are found, and in whatever form they occur, of that story of the Buddha's visits to Ceylon, which is absent from the Pitakas, marks them off from the original books, and prevents our believing that they were brought over by Mahinda. But neither were they introduced *de novo* by Buddhaghosha.

Buddhaghosha was much more than a mere translator or repeater of texts. The Ceylon monks owed more to him than one of themselves could have brought back from a visit to the monasteries of India. It is clear that his was a powerful mind, which had arranged for itself in a clear and fairly consistent system the various materials of the sacred books and of the monastic customs. Visuddhi Magga is confessedly his work. There is no other compendium of Buddhism known at all like it for consistency and completeness ; and in the absence of any other such, it is just to assume that it was first in Buddhaghosha's mind that the Buddha-system attained its final shape. He identified himself with the Anuradhapura school, became its chief light, and gave to its traditions the form which they have ever since retained.

I have exhibited (in chapters iii.–xvii.), as far as my plan admitted, the contents of the canonical texts of the Tipitaka, and the view which I have given of each point in it, so far as it has purported to be the Buddhist view, is in accordance with the interpretation of the Buddhaghosha Commentaries. I have had access to no others, for this is the source of whatever information I have derived from native scholars or from popular language, as well as (substantially) of that embodied in European works and editions of the Southern Buddhism.

I must now give thé reader some idea of the nature of these books of Buddhaghosha's.

A Buddhist Commentary does not differ much in purpose or contents, widely as it differs in method, from a modern one. The occasion and circumstances under which the text was originally uttered are related, the contents are summarized, terms and expressions are explained and illustrated, moral lessons are enforced by examples, and references are supplied to other books by which the teaching of the text is to be supplemented. The Introduction is extended in the case of the greater Commentaries—as those on the Vinaya Pitaka, on the Sutta Pitaka, and on the Jataka—into a considerable narrative. The Introduction to the Commentary on the Jataka, or doings in previous lives of him who was to be the Buddha, goes back to the date, myriads of cycles ago, when, in the days of the Buddha Dīpankara, he who was afterwards Gotama was first definitely engaged to the career of a future Buddha. It mentions events in the lives which he lived during the intervening cycles under successive Buddhas, till it comes down to mention some of the lives in which, during the present cycle, he perfected his store of merit by heroic exercise of the ten great virtues. Then are narrated the circumstances of his deciding, at the entreaties of deities, to be born for his last, his Buddha-life, and his choice, in exact conformity with the practice of all former Buddhas, of the country, clan, and family in which to be born. His birth and training, the sights which led him to seek religious life, his setting forth, his period of severe asceticism, and the attainment, under the Bo-tree, of full Buddha-hood—this story, now so familiar to us all, forms the immediate introduction; for it only remains to be added, that after becoming Buddha and collecting his first disciples, Gotama went to dwell in such and such a place, and while there, on occasion of such and such an event in the Community, he uttered the first Jataka. Similarly, the Commentaries on the Vinaya and Sutta Pitakas open by an account of the circumstances under which the monks assembled at the first council, led by Kassapa, to fix for ever, by chanting them over together, the words of their Teacher's utterances.

In the one case Upali, and in the other Ananda, was called upon to recite. In Ananda's case we are told the reason for his being chosen, his backwardness in becoming a Rahat, and the exact circumstances of his attaining that full insight during the night before the session, and the miraculous way in which, to prove his attainments, he entered the hall of assembly.

Besides these introductions on a large scale to whole collections, there are small introductions to individual portions, and in these are to be found, besides such events as are narrated in the Pitakas, a great number of traditions about the sayings of the Buddha and his monks. Many of these secondary traditions are life-like and interesting, and have a distinct historical value, not perhaps as part of the biography of Gotama, but as samples of the life and manners of the succeeding centuries.

Throughout the Jataka Commentary, an important element in each birth-story is the record of the circumstances which led the Buddha to tell the story. Some of these are obviously invented to lead up to the story, others give graphic pictures of monastic life, and a few may be true traditions of events in Gotama's history.

A careful study of these picturesque scenes and anecdotes, especially in the Jataka book, would perhaps lead to definite conclusions about their date. As far as I have noticed, there is nothing which necessarily implies familiarity with Ceylon, while allusions to snow, to sandy deserts, and to many other things unknown to the island, prove that the ultimate source of some at least of the traditions was in North India, whatever may have been the place of their compilation.[1]

These introductions ended, the text is illustrated by such notes as these :—

When the Buddha perceived that the monks were engaged in this conversation (as recorded in the text), "What," asks the commentator, "was the Buddha doing?" Then follows a full account of the way in which he used to pass his day and night, watch by watch, with special details about the third watch, and a description of the miracles which accom-

[1] In a passage of the Commentary on the Digha Nikaya, in a list of nations whose language was strange, the first place was given to the Tamils. This may indicate that Ceylon was, as tradition says, the country where the materials of the Commentary were found.

panied his going out on his rounds, the soft winds that cleared his path, etc.

When a certain person is said in the text to have admired the good order of the monks of Gotama as compared with those of other teachers, the commentator gives a very elaborate description of the proper conduct of monks, and accumulates an immense number of comparisons to set forth the splendour which emanated from the Buddha's person.

Another element of a Commentary, though one from the nature of the case not always present, is the enumeration and classification of the contents of the text. This is done very carefully for the Vinaya and Sutta Pitakas, and leaves a believing reader no room for doubt as to what was the "Word of Buddha." The contents in the latter case are classified under a great variety of heads, from a great variety of points of view—from that of literary structure, that of moral purpose, and so on.

Important terms are explained, often at great length, generally with reference to etymology, and a variety of alternative views is given; these being sometimes refuted. Often a particular explanation is quoted as being that of "the ancients," or that of a particular school. These explanations are far from contemptible, though the derivations of words are, as might be expected, often unscientific. The principle is generally assumed, that several derivations may all be true or at least instructive. The explanation of the title of the third Collection, "Abhidhamma," is a favourable specimen. The prefix "abhi," it is stated, implies increase, distinction, honour, division, excess. A sentence is given in illustration of each of these uses; e.g. in the case of "Raja" and "Abhiraja" it implies honour, and so on. Then illustrations are given from the Abhidhamma to show how each of these—"increase," "distinction," etc.—apply to its contents. For instance, in the expression, "precious doctrines" (dhammā), "unlimited doctrines," "unsurpassable doctrines," the meaning is "honoured," "worthy of honour"; in short, "Abhidhamma" means "the sublime and elaborate Dhamma."

The variety of etymology sometimes gives rise to a variety of interpretation. A certain class of sophistical disputants are called "amaravikkhepikā." The commentator says, "Amara" means "not dying"; the evasions of these sophists are endless.

But he adds: another way, "amara" is a kind of fish, which comes up and goes down in the water and cannot be caught; so this kind of argument is an eel-like wriggling.

Various readings are also noticed.

Very often terms are illustrated by anecdotes. On the name of Ajatasattu a long story is told about that king. On the name of a particular form of cheating, the "dish-trick," we are told how it is done. They make one dish of gold and two or three of brass to look like gold. Then they go into the country, and enter some wealthy house, and say, "Buy gold dishes." When the price is asked, they offer the more expensive. The purchasers say, "How are we to know that these are gold?" "Test them," say the sellers. Then they rub the gold dish on the stone, give (sell) them all the dishes, and go.

As a good specimen of the commentator's treatment of moral terms, I may quote the distinction between "Hiri" and "Ottappaṃ." It occurs frequently in nearly the same words, and certainly exhibits the moral method of Buddhism at its best.

"Hiri" is shame at impropriety of act, for which a synonym is modesty, while "ottappaṃ" is shrinking from sin. "Hiri" is excited from within, "ottappaṃ" from without. "Hiri" rests on self-authority, "ottappaṃ" on world-authority. "Hiri" has the nature of modesty, "ottappaṃ" of fear. "Hiri" marks sense of propriety, "ottappaṃ" marks quickness to see the danger of fault.

(1) There are four things by which a man excites within him the internal sense of "hiri": considerations of rank, of age, of strength, and of learning. Of rank, as when he abstains from destroying life and other sins from the reflection, "Such and such a sinful act is not the act of people of rank, it is the act of low-born people and fishers; it is not fitting for a man of such rank to commit this act." Of age, when he thinks, "Such and such a sinful act is what boys would do, it is not fitting for a man of my age." Of strength, when he thinks, "This is what feeble-natured people would do, and not a man of my strength." Of learning, when he thinks, "This is the act of fools, not of wise men; it is not fit for a man of my wisdom and learning." Thus by these four considerations he excites the feeling of "hiri" in himself, and so, having put that feeling into his mind, abstains from the sin; hence it is said that "hiri" is excited within the

P

man's self. "Ottappam," on the other hand, is excited by external considerations. If you do the sinful deed, you will meet with condemnation among the four companies. The wise man will condemn him as the city man does dirt; what will the monk do whom the good reject? Thus "ottappam" is excited from without.

(2) "Hiri" rests on self-authority; a well-born man puts himself under his own authority and superiority, and abstains from sin on the ground that it does not become one so religious, so learned, so ascetic, to commit sin; and thus Buddha said: "Whoso puts himself under his own authority, and rejects demerit and practises merit, and rejects faults and practises what is faultless, he keeps himself pure."

"Ottappam," on the other hand, rests on world-authority. A well-born man puts himself under the world's authority and superiority, and so abstains from sin. Great is this world-assemblage, and there are therein ascetics and monks of super-natural powers and divine insight, who know the minds of others. They see from afar, they see close at hand; with their mind they discern minds; they will look at me; they will know me; look, they will say, at that well-born man; he left home and made a sincere profession of the monastic life, but he is living abandoned in sinful and demeritorious ways; there are deities of similar powers and insight; they will say, etc. (the same). Thus he makes the world his authority and superior, and puts away demerit and (so on); hence "ottappam" is said to rest on world-authority.

(3) "Hiri" is of the nature of modesty, that is, modest shame; and "ottappam" of the nature of fear, that is, fear of hell. These are both shown in the avoiding of sin. Just as a well-born man, performing any of the offices of nature, if he sees a person towards whom modesty is due, feels ashamed and confused—exactly in the same way, one man abstains from sin from a sense of modesty towards himself. Another well-born man abstains from sin from fear of hell. This is to be illustrated thus: Suppose there are two balls of iron, one of which is cold and smeared with filth, the other hot and fiery. In that case a wise man will decline to take up the one from disgust at the filth, and the other from fear of being burnt. Here it is to be understood that the declining to take up the cold but filthy ball

is like abstaining from sin from sense of modesty towards oneself; declining the hot ball from fear of being burnt is like abstaining from sin from fear of hell.

"Hiri" marks sense of propriety; "ottappam," quickness to see the danger of sin. Both these also are displayed in the avoiding of sin. One man by the four considerations—of greatness of rank, greatness of learning, greatness of inheritance, greatness of religious character—excites within himself the inward sense of propriety, and abstains from sin. The other, by the four fears—of his own reproach, of the reproach of others, of punishment, of birth in the unhappy conditions—excites in himself "ottappam," the sign of a quick sense of the danger of sin.

"At this point," ends the commentator, "the four kinds of greatness and the four kinds of fear ought to be explained in detail as they stand in the Anguttara Atthakatha"—into which we cannot follow him.

A final quotation shall be one which, from the nature of the text, ought to give an instructive summary of Buddhist principles.

On the words, "He preaches a doctrine lovely in the beginning, lovely in the midst, and lovely in the end," the commentator writes:—

"This means that the Buddha not only preaches, because of his compassion for all beings, an incomparable doctrine of bliss enjoyed through detachment, but, whether he preaches little or much, preaches it in the method of lovely beginning, and so on; in the beginning he makes what he preaches lovely, good, faultless, and in the middle, and in the end too, he makes what he preaches lovely, good, and faultless.

"This 'beginning, middle, and end' applies to preaching, and also to religion itself. In the case of a sermon which consists of a four-line stanza, the first line is the beginning, the next two lines the middle, and the last the end. In a Sutta of one topic, the introduction is the beginning; 'thus he said' is the end; all between these two, the middle. In a Sutta of several topics, the first topic is the beginning, the last topic the end, those between—one or many—the middle. In religion itself, conduct, meditation, insight, is the beginning; and it is said, 'And what is the beginning of good principles? Pure conduct and right belief.' In the words, 'The Buddha, monks, has attained the perfect knowledge of the Middle Way,' the noble Way is called the middle, and the Fruit and Nirvana are called the end. In the saying, 'Therefore, Brahman, a religious life is the final good,' the Fruit is the end. 'Men live, reverend Visakha, the religious life, of which Nirvana is the basis, Nirvana the aim, Nirvana the end'—here Nirvana is said to be the end. In the text it is the beginning, middle, and end of preaching that is meant. And the Buddha, in preaching the doctrine, at the beginning preaches Conduct, in the middle the Way, at the end Nirvana. Therefore it is said, 'He preaches a doctrine lovely in the beginning, lovely in the middle, and lovely in the end.' Hence another preacher, when he expands the doctrine, at the beginning should set forth Conduct, in the middle should dwell on the Way, and in the end, Nirvana. This is the system of preaching."

I pass to the Visuddhi Magga, or, as it is more often called, Visuddhimarga (in Sinhalese shape, Visuddhimargaya). This is not a commentary on any text, but claims to be a compendium of the whole Buddha-system—conduct, meditation, contemplation, the elements of being, the senses, the Truths, the Chain of Causation, and the rest. The particular Commentaries constantly refer to it. It is considered to be the one book from which the Buddhist system can be best learnt. A famous elder, Dhammapāla, who is said to have lived not long after Buddhaghosha, added a Pali Tīka, or explanation; and late in the thirteenth century, the learned Sinhalese king, Pandita Parakrama, wrote a word-for-word interpretation (sannē) in Sinhalese.

I have said that the Commentaries, as far as I know them (but my acquaintance with them is very imperfect), show no clear indications of a Sinhalese origin, but the Visuddhimagga does. The following story, which stands in the Pali text, is sufficient proof of it: An elder named Tissa, who lived on the Cetiya hill (Mihintale), was going forth thence to Anuradhapura, on his begging rounds. A young bride, who had quarrelled with her husband, was coming out of Anuradhapura in the early morning, to go to the house of her kinsfolk, gaily dressed, and adorned like a celestial maiden. Seeing the elder on the road, she laughed a loud laugh in the wantonness of her heart. The elder looked round to see what it was. He saw her teeth: they suggested to him the thought of the thirty-two impurities of the body, and he at once attained rahatship. So it is said :—

> When he saw her teeth (bones),
> He followed up in thought the hint
> And then and there the wise elder
> Attained to rahatship.

Her husband came along the road after her, and when he saw the elder, he asked, "Did you see a woman, sir?" The elder replied—

> "I know not whether woman
> Or man it was who went by;
> But a bundle of bones
> Is going along the high road."

The Visuddhimagga, as far as I have read it (and I have read several hundred pages), adds little or nothing to the Pitakas, but aims at a systematic arrangement of their contents. The imperfection of even this arrangement illustrates the extreme difficulty of bringing each part of the system into logical co-ordination with the rest. In the details, the methods of anti-thesis and division are carried to their utmost degree. On the basis of the classification, conduct, meditation, insight (or virtue, tranquillity, contemplation), the author says, for instance, "Conduct saves from hell, meditation from the elements of desire, insight from all existence. Conduct corrects vice, meditation corrects lust, insight corrects error. Conduct is the virtue of the beginner (sotāgāmi), meditation of the advanced (anāgāmi), insight of the perfect (rahat)." The qualities of conduct are grouped in so many couples, so many triplets, and so many sets of four.

The merits of the work, besides its completeness, are, I think, its comparative conciseness and its great perspicuity. The Pali is generally easier to understand that the Sinhalese explanation.

Later than the Commentaries, there is a considerable amount of Buddhist literature in Sinhalese, which deserves notice; but I leave this, with regret, to others.

An important earlier work, however, the "Questions of Milinda," cannot be passed over. Of this book an interesting account has been given, with a translation, by Professor Rhys Davids, in the *Sacred Books of the East.* "Milinda" is but an adapted form of the name of Menander, the Greek king of Bactria, who reigned probably from about 149 or 115, or even 110 B.C.; and it is he who asks the questions or propounds the difficulties, which are solved by an elder named Nagasena. How long after Menander's time the work was written, there is no means of ascertaining; but Professor Rhys Davids thinks it was "at, or a little after, the Christian era." From such geographical allusions as it contains, it appears to have been written in the far north-west of India, or in the Panjab itself.[1]

This early and important exposition of Buddhist principles seems to have been little known during most of the centuries of its existence. It is quoted, and with great respect, by Buddhaghosha; but there is no certain trace of it from that date until it was translated into Sinhalese by order of Kirti Sri Rajasinha in the eighteenth century.

The "Questions of Milinda" is important for the testimony which it gives to the early completion of the Buddhist canon. The writer refers to so large a proportion of the canonical books, quoting them abundantly and naming them, both by the large collections and by the separate books, that it may be confidently asserted that he had in his hands the Pitakas as we have them now.

In fact, the book is founded and modelled on the Pitakas. Not only does it consist of a series of dialogues constructed to explain points in the sacred text, or arising out of it, but both the dramatic setting of these dialogues, and for the most part, the arguments which they enforce, are taken from the Pitakas. The dramatic setting, though there is not much of it, is remarkably lively and graceful; but it is taken almost entirely from the older texts. The phrases and entire paragraphs, scenes, and events are reproduced almost word for word. The King says: "It is a fine night; what learned teacher shall we converse with?" The monks are entertained in vast companies, or go out singly to beg; greetings are exchanged, and conversions take place. The arguments and the innumerable similes are often developments of what has been briefly said in the Pitakas, or run on similar lines. But while every page recalls the canonical books, the "Questions" has a vigour and variety which would justify the praise of originality. Professor Rhys Davids considers it "undoubtedly the masterpiece of Indian prose."

As a specimen of the topics discussed, I select one which

[1] See note at end of this chapter.

touches on a difficulty which may even have occurred to the reader :—[1]

(THE BUDDHA'S LAST ILLNESS)

"Venerable Nagasena, it was said by the Elders who held the recitation :—

> When he had eaten Cunda's alms,
> The coppersmith's, thus have I heard,
> The Buddha felt that sickness dire,
> That sharp pain even unto death.

and afterwards the Blessed One said : 'These two offerings of food, Ananda, of equal fruit and of equal result, are of much greater fruit and much greater result than any others.' Now if sharp sickness fell upon the Blessed One, Nagasena, after he had partaken of Cunda's alms, and sharp pains arose within him even unto death, then that other statement must be wrong. But if that is right then the first must be wrong. How could that alms, Nagasena, be of great fruit, when it turned to poison, gave rise to disease, put an end to the period of his then existence, took away his life ? Explain this to me to the refutation of adversaries. The people are in bewilderment about this, thinking that the dysentery must have been caused by his eating too much, out of greediness."

"The Blessed One said, O King, there are two almsgivings equal, of equal fruit and result, and of much greater fruit and much greater result than any others, that of which when a Tathagata has partaken he attains to supreme and perfect Buddha-hood (enlightenment), and that, when he has partaken of which, he passes away by that utter passing away in which nothing whatever remains behind. For that alms is full of virtue, full of advantage. The gods, O King, shouted in joy and gladness at the thought, 'This is the last meal the Tathagata will take'; and communicated a divine power of nourishment to that tender pork. And that was itself in good condition—light, pleasant, full of flavour, and good for digestion. It was not because of it that any sickness fell upon the Blessed One, but it was because of the extreme weakness of his body, and because of the period of life he had to live having exhausted, that the disease arose and grew worse and worse ; just as when,

[1] S.B.E., vol. xxxv., p. 242.

O King, an ordinary fire is burning, if fresh fuel is supplied, it will burn up still more; or, as when a stream is flowing along as usual, if a heavy rain falls, it will become a mighty river, with a great gush of water; or as, when the body is of its ordinary girth, if more food be eaten, it becomes broader than before. So this was not, O King, the fault of the food that was presented, and you cannot impute any harm to it."

"But, Venerable Nagasena, why is it that those two gifts of food are so specially meritorious?" "Because of the attainment of the exalted conditions which resulted from them." "Of what conditions, Nagasena, are you speaking?" "Of the attainment of the nine successive states, which were passed through at first in one order and then in the reverse order."

"It was on two days, was it not, Nagasena, that the Tathagata attained to those conditions in the highest degree?" "Yes, O King."

"It is a most wonderful thing, Nagasena, and a most strange, that of all the great and glorious gifts that were bestowed upon our Blessed One, not one can be compared with those two almsgivings. Most marvellous is it, that even as those nine successive conditions are glorious, even so are those gifts made, by their glory, of greater fruit and of greater advantage than any others. Very good, Nagasena! That is so; and I accept it as you say."

NOTE TO CHAPTER XXII.

THE QUESTIONS OF MILINDA.

THIS book bears clear internal evidence of having been written in that part of the world in which Menander reigned.

The historical matter which it contains is as follows: The king's birthplace is said to have been in the district of Kalasi, in the island of Alasanda; a statement is made about the contemporary king of China, which implies that he was a Buddhist; three allusions are made to common Buddhist traditions—about the great Asoka, about a battle in the time of his grandfather Candagutta, and about a king of Kalinga.

The only definite geographical statement is about the distance of Sagala from Kalasi (200 yojanas,) and from Kashmir (12 yojanas). But the less definite geographical indications are conclusive. In the enumeration of countries (there are two in the book), where the purpose is to express any countries whatever, no acquaintance is implied with any but the north and north-west of India. A few more distant places, south and east, are mentioned as ports to which a ship might sail.

There are other indications decisive against a Ceylon authorship, and in favour of a north Indian. The Himalaya and the Ganges are familiarly spoken of, ice is mentioned; and the sun is said not to be so fierce in summer on account of clouds. And there are references, not only to the lion, tiger, and rhinoceros, which are common in the Pitakas, but also to the hyena and the camel.

The Buddhism of the book is substantially that of the Pitakas, with very few indications of the later developments of doctrine. Of Northern developments, or of "Great and Little Vehicles," there is not a trace.

But the writer does not appear aware of a strongly marked distinction between canonical and non-canonical books. Nor does the word Pitaka occur, I think, in the text itself. It is found in some verses which form the heading of a chapter and are not necessarily contemporary with the text.

For legends and anecdotes, the writer draws largely on traditions such as are contained in the Commentaries. But to the traditions of Gotama's biography, as I have extracted it from the Pitakas, I have noticed only two things added by the Milinda Questions—and possibly these may be in some book of the Pitakas which I have not read—the statements that Gotama was moved to dissatisfaction with home life by the sight of the "disfigured seraglio," and that he was tempted by the promise of universal empire, if he would stay at home, in seven days.

Both in ethical interest and in literary merit, the book is very unequal. If it were judged by the well-known dialogue about the king's chariot, it would be much overrated. It contains few, if any, other discussions at once so searching, so lively, and so pointed as that, which is the first.

The opening has a picturesque and dramatic setting; but this element soon disappears; in the greater part of the book it is entirely wanting. In a few instances, King Milinda is not contented with the first explanation, and presses home his difficulty with genuine force; in one or two, Nagasena admits that no answer can be given, rather in the tone in which parents tell their children "not to ask silly questions." Far oftener there is really no dialogue after the first question; sometimes the original question only introduces a very tedious lecture, which consists, in the worst instances, of an enumeration of the twenty-eight this and the eighteen that, and the ten forms of the other. In the best instances, the difficulty started is a real one; such as, why the consequences of ill deeds are so much more apparent than those of good (iv. 36), or whether any death is untimely (iv. 36); sometimes it is a difficulty arising out of Buddhist traditions, such as: How could it be right for Vessantara to give his children for slaves? (iv. 31). Why did not the Buddha perform a miracle for his own convenience? (iv. 7). How came he, after preparing for Buddhahood through so many lives, to think, when he had attained it, of not teaching? (*ib.*)—several, like this last, being met only by evasion. Some of the questions are merely verbal; some absurd, as: If there are demons, why do we never see or smell their corpses? and a few quite irrelevant, such as: How are dreams produced? or, Why is the sun not equally fierce at all seasons? Two treat of revolting subjects with shocking want of reserve, but none have any impure tendency.

As for originalty, it lies almost solely in the treatment; for most, if not all, of the main arguments and illustrations are enlargements of hints derived from the older books. But the treatment is intelligent; in favourable contrast with the later Suttas, and rich in a certain kind of eloquence. The supply of words is astonishing, and takes the reader's breath away.

For the characteristic of the Pali style, increasing as the literature grew, was the accumulation of synonyms for each word, of parallel phrases for each clause, and of rival illustrations for each simile. One consequence of this characteristic is, that the style is most effective when an accumulation of effects is to be described; as when drops are gathered into streams, and streams meet in rivers, and rivers pour into the sea. An eminent, and, I think, a really magnificent instance of this is the description of the earthquake which ensued on Vessantara's celebrated donation.[1]

As a favourable specimen, remarkable for the moral importance of the question attacked, as well as for the stern severity of the answer, and for a liveliness of dialogue above the average, I give, in an abridgment, what follows:—[2]

Suppose a layman has fallen into one of the four great faults, which in a monk are irrecoverable, and afterwards enters into the Community, and suppose he does not know that he ever was guilty of that fault—is spiritual attainment possible to that man?

No; because the essential condition of spiritual attainment is destroyed in him.

But your teaching says that one of the great obstacles to attainment is remorse. Now this man has no remorse; he is calm; why is attainment impossible to him?

Just as a seed, which would come up well in rich, well-ploughed soil, cannot come up on stony and rocky ground, because in the latter the (vivifying) cause is wanting; or as a stick, which can stand on the earth, cannot stand in the air, because the (supporting) cause is wanting, etc. etc., so the necessary condition of spiritual attainment has been destroyed in the man who has committed one of the irrecoverable faults.

There is a genuine resemblance here to the Gospel Parable of the Sower. But the finest touch of ethical teaching, I think, is in the description of faith: Just as when a stream is running high, ordinary men stand on the bank afraid to cross, then comes a strong and active man and leaps it at a bound; so he who has faith aspires and leaps up to attainments which to others seem impossible, and not only secures them himself but arouses the aspirations of others.

[1] Translated in S.B.E., vol. xxxv., p. 175.
[2] Milindapañho. iv. 18.

CHAPTER XXIII

GENERAL SKETCH OF CEYLON HISTORY FROM BUDDHAGHOSHA TO PARAKRAMA

I PROPOSE in this and the following chapter to review very briefly the history of Ceylon, as it is told in the Mahavansa, from the fourth to the end of the twelfth century, in order to extract from it what may be learnt about the relation of the Buddhist Community to the national government; about the different sects which existed within the Community; about the admixture of Hinduism with Buddhism, and whatever other changes the system may have undergone.

The brilliant period, which saw the work of Buddhaghosha and the conclusion of the original part of the Mahavansa, was followed by a time of depression and defeat. A series of Tamil usurpers reigned over Ceylon, and the sacred edifices fell into decay, till a restorer of the national independence appeared in Dhātusena (A.D. 463). Amid the lists of the great tanks which he made for irrigation and of the dagabas which he repaired or built, occurs a feature which deserves special notice. He erected, we are told, an image of Metteyya (Maitrī), the coming Buddha. This is the first mention of any erection for the cultus of this personage, though he is not seldom referred to by the historian; and King Dutthagamini had a special devotion to him, and is to be—when the time comes—his chief disciple.[1] He is often mentioned in later books, and is even now often on the lips of Buddhists as a kind of ideal; but his cultus has never taken root in Ceylon.

The violence and inhuman cruelty of some kings and the meritorious acts of others occupy most of the succeeding chapters of the chronicle. We read of encouragement given to literature by the younger Mogallāna (A.D. 540) and by Aggabodhi (A.D.

[1] Mahav. xxi.

560), the former himself a poet; and of a literary controversy with the "Vetulla heretics" in the latter king's reign. It would appear that in the century 540–640 the native kings were strong and the Buddhist religion prosperous; though dangerous alliance with the Tamils, who were brought over to help the Sinhalese kings to keep their own subjects in order, was preparing the way for the renewal of the foreigners' ascendancy. The history of this and the following three centuries contains a great deal to interest the antiquarian, and some points, presently to be noticed, that illustrate the influence of Hinduism on the Buddhism of Ceylon. But there are not many passages so touching as that which describes the dutiful love and reverence shown to his mother by a later Aggabodhi.[1]

"He was constant in his attendance on his mother, both by day and night; and he was wont daily to wait on her betimes and anoint her head with oil, and cleanse her body, and purge the nails of her fingers, and dress her in clean and soft clothing. . . . He made offerings of flowers and perfumes to her as at a shrine, and then bowed himself before her three times. . . . Afterwards he fed her from his own hands with dainty food, and himself ate the remnants, whereof he scattered a portion on his own head. . . . He laid out her bed carefully with his own hands. . . . And when he departed from the bed-chamber he turned not his back on her, but stepped back noiselessly till he could not be seen. . . . In this selfsame manner did he serve his mother all the days of his life."

"On one occasion, when he spake disdainfully to his servant and called him a slave, it grieved him so that he himself sought to obtain his servant's forgiveness."

We find something to admire in the historian's flattery of kings, when qualities like these are chosen for praise.

Soon after this king's reign the seat of government was moved from Anuradhapura to Polonnaruwa (in Pali, Pulaṭṭhi), a spot farther to the east, where still are seen, deep in the forest, ruins even more beautiful than those of the older city. It was virtually a retreat from the growing power of the Tamils, who were advancing from the West;[2] and although the chronicle is still filled with the great deeds of the kings, it is clear that they had a constant struggle to maintain their thrones, and were not

[1] Mahav. xlix., li., etc. [2] *Ib.* l. 12, etc.

seldom dethroned; till in the tenth and eleventh centuries king after king asserted his claim, only to be defeated and slain. It is to be noticed that many of them committed suicide on the field of battle; an act which the Buddhist chronicler nowhere, I think, condemns.

At length, exactly at the date when William the Conqueror was taking possession of England, Vijaya Bahu recovered the Sinhalese throne, and established a short-lived prosperity. His restoration of the Buddhist Community, which the Tamil conquest had almost extinguished, forms one of the marked epochs of our history. But after this brilliant episode, civil war and foreign invasion had their way again; and it was nearly another century before the royal race was again triumphant in the person of the illustrious Parākrama.

The story of this hero, in the Mahavansa, almost deserves to be called an epic poem. I sketch the first portion of it at some length, partly for the sake of the likeness which it bears to those descriptions of heroic youth which appear in the later biographies of the Buddha.

His aged parents had been lamenting their sad lot in having no son to raise them from the obscurity into which they had sunk (for King Mānābharaṇa enjoyed but a very limited dominion in the southern part of Ceylon), when a glorious divine being appeared to the father, and foretold the birth of an illustrious son. To both the parents there appeared, on one night, the vision of a beautiful elephant entering the chamber of the queen; and the household Brahman announced that this portended the birth of a son, who would have all the marks of wealth and fortune. The delighted king had "pirit"[1] said by monks, and "Soma" rites performed by his household Brahmans, and applied himself diligently to works of charity and religion. When at length the boy was born, nature rejoiced; cool winds blew everywhere, and all was gladness. And when the Brahmans had examined the marks of the child, they pronounced that he was capable of subduing to his rule not Lanka only, but all Jambudwipa.

The young prince grew up, and was distinguished in all manly and royal accomplishments, riding and the use of the bow, and

[1] The recitation of certain Suttas which speak specially of domestic duty and domestic happiness: it is a kind of benediction, but in some cases a mere charm.

the rest; but what ruled in his heart was the love of glory, and the proud determination to bring all Lanka under one rule again. He thought of the achievements of the Bodhisat recorded in the Ummagga Jataka, and those of the heroes of the Ramayana and Mahabharata. "Life is indeed a boon," he said, "to those who are able to do such mighty deeds above the common. Born of Khattiya race, if I do not something worthy of Khattiya heroism, vain will my birth be." [1] Fearing that in the pleasures of royal state his enthusiasm might fade, and determining to learn the condition of the country and the enemy's strength, he stole forth by night from his father's house to explore the "Upper Provinces."

His adventures in this roving life are told at great length, and not without humour; a gay temper and love of fun and amusement being part of his character. He employed a variety of spies, some pretending to be monks, some snake-charmers, physicians, pedlars, or dancers; and by their means got to know the dispositions of all classes and all individuals in the land. By many wonderful displays of strength and courage he taught the people to look upon him as invincible; and meanwhile he trained and organized a system of local officers and captains, and collected material of war.

On the death of his uncle he became ruler of so much of Ceylon as had belonged to him (apparently what is now Saffragam and part of the Western Province), and set himself to strengthen this territory to the utmost, with a view to recovering the rest. To this part of his career are attributed also vast works of irrigation, and the bringing under cultivation of a great quantity of land, by which he greatly increased the resources of his country. He is represented as biding his time, training the noble youths, exercising his troops, and amassing immense stores of money and of gems.

After such ample preparation the hero entered on a long course of battles, in which he gained possession of the north-central part of the island, including the royal city of Polonnaruwa, and the ruined Anuradhapura; quieted the disaffected portions of the south; expelled the Tamils, and carried his triumphant arms into India itself, and to still more distant countries. Wherever he went his enemies faded away before his victorious drums

[1] Mahav. lxiv. 48.

as the glowworm fades at the light of morning. He consumed all before him as a fire advances through the forest. But in his successes he acted with generosity; and he showed the utmost deference to the religious Community. At their request he gave back, on one occasion, to its former ruler a kingdom which he had made his own.

Having attained to the summit of glory, he employed his power not only for the establishment and purification of the Buddhist system, and for the erection of innumerable temples, dagabas, and monasteries; but also for the construction of gigantic works of irrigation, and the wise and beneficent government of his people. Readers would be tempted to discard as altogether extravagant the multitude and the extent of the buildings, and of the artificial lakes and channels, which the historian attributes to Parakrama, were not the record sufficiently attested by the remains which exist of those immense works—works which it has taxed the resources of the English Government even partly to restore.

Having thus reviewed the general history of this period, I will now put together some of the chief intimations which it contains of the internal history of the Community.

CHAPTER XXIV

THE COMMUNITY IN THE MIDDLE AGES

IT is difficult to extract from the Mahavansa a history of Ceylon Buddhism as a whole, not because the chronicle is in substance untrustworthy, but because its point of view is exclusive. All is written from the point of view of the royal court, and of that dominant branch of the Buddhist Community, which is called the Great Monastery or Maha Vihara.

Of the conduct of any laymen but kings and their generals the Mahavansa gives no picture; and as the kings are the only actors, the givers of all alms, the builders of all temples, we do not learn how far the people at large were influenced. The Community is represented as having been replenished and fed, not by the devotion or by the alms of the people, but by the gigantic gifts of kings and by the revenues of land assigned by kings for the support of monks. It does not follow, because the historian makes no mention of any zeal but that of the Court, that no other zeal existed; but we are left to guess it. On the one hand, such displays of royal enthusiasm, and such magnificent holidays and pageants, as are the historian's favourite theme, cannot have failed to secure some of the popular affection for the system which they adorned. On the other hand, the complete collapse of Buddhism, which seems to have followed every royal defection or Tamil usurpation, indicates that slight hold on the hearts of the people which one would expect to be the result of excessive dependence on a court.

And even for the affairs of the Community, the authority of the Mahavansa is limited by the fact that it is the record, and was for years the "organ," of the exclusive Maha Vihara fraternity. Its estimate of the merit of kings, of the prosperity of religion, of the importance of events, is not impartial. It is possible that at times when the Maha Vihara had nothing to record, there may have been signal triumphs in the "Abhayagiri" or the "Jetavana" fraternity. Those centres may possibly have cherished customs or produced literature of which no report has remained. This exclusiveness must be taken into account, from the date of the first recorded secession, early in the second century B.C., to that of the final reunion of the chief sects at the end of the twelfth century A.D.

But within the restricted field covered from this limited point of view there is a good deal that is instructive and that deserves fuller treatment than I can give it here.

The close relations between the Court and the monastery have been already alluded to. They are characteristic of Buddhism both in Magadha and in Ceylon.

The power of the kings was exerted not only for the protection of the religion, but also to no small extent for interference in its affairs. Kings are frequently said to have reformed what was defective in the discipline of the Community. Kassapa V, we read, "purged the religion by enforcing the rules of discipline, and appointed new priests to fill up the vacant places in the Viharas."[1] And many after him did the same. Many of them even presumed to preach. This same Kassapa was well read in the Three Pitakas, and "was a preacher of the law as well as a doer."[2] Sena IV took his seat on one occasion in the Brazen Palace and "expounded the Suttanta in the presence of the brethren."[3] Many kings held "councils" also, in imitation of those which had been held, or were believed to have been held, in ancient days by kings of Magadha.

On the other side, the political power of the monks was great, and seems to have increased as time went on. The more illustrious patrons of Buddhism professed themselves the slaves of the Community; repeatedly dedicated themselves and their kingdom to the Buddha; offered to the monks their royal insignia, and received them back from their hands; they sometimes transferred, or pretended to transfer, to the Community for a fixed period all the prerogatives of the throne.[4] It was Sena II, about A.D. 866, who made it a custom for kings to be anointed at the Ruwanweli Dagaba.[5]

Long before this the monks had made their religious authority

[1] Mahav. lii. 44. [2] *Ib.* lii. 82. [3] *Ib.* liv. 4.
[4] *Ib.* xxxix. 31, etc. [5] *Ib.* li. 82.

felt by the kings, and punished them for disregarding it. They inflicted on Hatthodātha the "inversion of the bowl," the censure which takes away from a layman the privilege of putting alms-food in a monk's bowl; and in a short time he died, as we read, of a sore disease. Other like warnings are recorded, of the speedy death of kings who protected heresy and the like.

It has been intimated already that there existed, during the greater part of the period we are considering, well-marked distinctions between different branches of the Community. These differences amounted at times to fierce hostility.

The Great Monastery, or Maha Vihara of Anuradhapura, was the original foundation of Devanampiya Tissa, who erected for it the Thuparama. For the same monastery, and within the same limits, the "Brazen Palace" and the Ruwanweli (called "the Great") Dagaba were built by the heroic Dutthagamini; and these three erections are always treated in the Mahavansa as the most sacred of the Anuradhapura shrines.

The Mahavansa does not allude, in the earlier or more nearly contemporary chapters to the secessions which gave rise to the other great fraternities; but at a much later date it is incidentally stated that the Abhayagiri secession occurred in Vattagamini Abhaya's reign (*c.* 100 B.C.), and that of the Jetavana, an offset from the former, in Mahasena's reign (*c.* 300 A.D.).[1] Vattagamini built the Abhayagiri Dagaba, but how far the sects were identified with the shrines whose names they bore is not clear.

The secession of the Abhayagiri is said to have been caused by the reception, into the establishment connected with the new dagaba, of the pupil of a monk who had been expelled from the Maha Vihara. This may have been the occasion, but we may suspect a deeper cause. Two facts throw light on it. One is, that the Abhayagiri monks "taught the Vetulla Pitaka and other writings as the words of Buddha";[2] the other, that it was about this time that the sacred texts were first committed to writing. The Mahavansa tells us that "the profoundly wise monks" (doubtless those of the Maha Vihara), foreseeing the perdition of the people, assembled; and in order that the religion might endure for ages, recorded the same in books."[3] If it be the case, as may be inferred from these two passages, that, before the canonical books were committed to writing, in

[1] Mahav. lxxviii. 21. [2] *Ib.* 22. [3] *Ib.* xxxiv. *ad fin.*

90–80 B.C., a monastery could still, without ceasing to be a part of the Community, hold a "Vetulla Pitaka" to be the words of Buddha; and if, as may be less certainly but probably concluded, the Maha Vihara acquired its characteristic position at the date when the "recording in books" took place, then there is serious reason to suspect that the final settlement of the canon took place, for the Ceylon school, at the date of its committal to writing. But this is a digression.

In Silameghavanna's reign (A.D. 614) the Abhayagiri monks were in very bad order; and even after the most wicked had been expelled, it was in vain that the king tried to induce the Maha Vihara monks to join with them in the fortnightly ceremonies. Indeed, through his attempt to bring this about, and his being provoked to use hard words of the orthodox fraternity, and not seeking their forgiveness, he died of a sore disease.

All "three fraternities," however, were tolerated; although that of the Abhayagiri was known as "Dhammarucika," and that of the Jetavana as "Sagalika."[1] Parakrama Bahu, as well as Gaja Bahu, treated them all with great respect, and made earnest efforts to unite them. Parakrama put an end to the divisions which existed within the Maha Vihara itself, and expelled the bad monks; and then, it is said, he "restored unity"; but this was achieved, it would seem, rather by expelling the irreconcilable members of Abhayagiri and Jetavana than by reconciling all. In another place[2] he is said to have united the two (the Maha Vihara and the nonconformists) by the influence of learned monks brought over from Southern India.

From Parakrama's time onwards, we meet with no more indications of the division. All three establishments, so far as they were localized in Anuradhapura, soon fell into the complete ruin in which they have been only recently rediscovered.

Besides the "three fraternities," we read also of "forest-monks" ("arannika") and of "dust-heap-robe wearers" (paṃsukulika). The two terms do not seem to refer to the same persons. The term "forest-monks" need not mean anything more distinct than such as had gone out from either

[1] These terms are used, without disrespect, in the ninth century. Possibly they imply a foreign connection. Sāgala was Milinda's city in N.W. India.

[2] Mahav. lxxxiv. 9.

monastery to a forest life. Such are often alluded to in the Pitaka books. The Pamsukulikas were more definitely a special class. They went out, we read, from the Abhayagiri in the reign of Sena II (A.D. 866),[1] and no doubt aimed at greater strictness and closer adherence to the original Rule, which prescribed "dust-heap-robes" as the only essential clothing for the brethren. They seem to have been held in great respect, and the peace of their "sacred forest" was held inviolable.[2]

All these, though divided, were not treated as heretics, though the Abhayagiri brethren must at times have been little better. But the distinction between separation and heresy is recognized in the words which record the thoughts of Parakrama, as he turned to the task of establishing religious unity. "The religion of the great sage has now for a long time been shaken by hundreds of heresies, and broken up by the disputes of the Three Fraternities."[3]

Another and a more serious alteration of Buddhism took place gradually and, perhaps, unnoticed—the intermixture with it of Hinduism. The historical causes of this are obvious. A large proportion of Hindus from South India became mingled with the population of the island. Tamil soldiers were employed as mercenaries by the native kings; alliances in marriage were made repeatedly, almost regularly, with the royal families of the continent. A succession of Tamil conquerors invaded the island and usurped its thrones. All these things, as well as the ordinary intercourse of commerce between neighbouring countries, familiarized the Sinhalese with the Hinduism of the time. Nor was this altogether an alien influence; for it was on a Hindu foundation, we must remember, that all the social system of the Sinhalese had been originally built; and this Buddhism had not destroyed. It was the profession of Buddhism to be tolerant. What at first was tolerated met with something like a welcome, and in process of time was enforced.

In the old books "monks and Brahmans" had sometimes been merely a double description of the same Buddhist brethren. But the two terms are probably meant to be distinguished when we are told of Kassapa III (A.D. 732) that he "enforced on laymen and monks and Brahmans the observance of their

[1] Mahav. li. 52. [2] *Ib.* liii. 22. [3] *Ib.* lxxiii. 56.

respective customs.[1] At any rate there is no doubt what is referred to when we read that Aggabodhi VII (A.D. 780), zealous Buddhist as he was, "repaired many old devalayas" (temples of Hindu deities), "and caused very valuable images of the gods to be made for them. He gave to the Brahmans the best of such food as was meet for kings," etc.[2] Sena I (A.D. 846) gave immense presents to one thousand Brahmans, whom he fed with milk, rice, etc., in polished vessels of gold. Of Vijaya Bahu it is said: "He took not away that which had been granted aforetime to the devalayas."[3]

Nor was this an instance merely of toleration. Vira Bahu, the father of Parakrama I, "caused Brahman priests who were versed in the Vedas and Vedangas to perform the religious rites," etc.[4] After making great offerings to the three sacred objects of Buddhism he "concluded the ceremony with the help of Brahmans," etc.[5] Parakrama Bahu went further still, for he built, besides all his Buddhist buildings, "a beautiful house of Vishnu, for the Mantra ceremonies."[6] And the chronicler, imbued with the same tone, called a later Parakrama an "earthly Siva."[7]

In short, the presence of Brahman ministers and astrologers became, as it had been before Buddhism arose, a necessity of the royal court; and the references are increasingly frequent to magic and astrology. These had never been successfully discountenanced by Buddhism, but they came more and more to the front.[8]

The period under consideration appears to have witnessed the gradual decline in Ceylon of the institution of the Community of Nuns. In the fabulous description of the days of Duttha-gamini and Vattagamini (first and second centuries B.C.) the nuns are constantly mentioned as attending, and as being provided for, in enormous numbers bearing no inconsiderable proportion to those of the monks. On these legends little can be founded, except that the institution was believed some centuries later to have been flourishing in those earlier days. But much later on, the notices of the female Community are specific.

[1] Mahav. xlviii. 23.
[2] *Ib.* lx. 77.
[3] *Ib.* xlvii. 143.
[4] *Ib.* lxii. 33, 43.
[5] See also *Ib.* lxiv. 14; lxvii. 29.
[6] *Ib.* lxxiii. 71.
[7] *Ib.* xci
[8] *Ib.* lvii. 48; lix. 34; lxii. 15, etc.

Aggabodhi II's queen became a nun, and he built a convent for her (*c.* A.D. 600).[1] Jetthatissa's queen retired to a convent (*c.* A.D. 623), and became a "preacher, perfect in the Abhidhamma and the Commentaries."[2] Convents for nuns were built by Mahinda I (A.D. 768),[3] who made his daughter take the yellow robe; by the queen of Dappula II (A.D. 807;[4] by Hangasena, a captain of Kassapa's (A.D. 912),[5] when nuns were placed in charge of the Bo-tree itself; and by the wife of the commander-in-chief under Kassapa IV (A.D. 939).[6]

After these dates we hear little or nothing more of nuns or convents. They are not included among the institutions of the great Parakrama.[7] And if there is one reference to the "five ranks"[8] (monks, nuns, novices, laymen, laywomen), this is probably only the conventional use of an old expression. When the ranks are expressly enumerated, only four are mentioned, nuns being omitted.[9]

Having altogether died out in the decay from which the Buddhism of Ceylon was rescued by Parakrama, this institution was not included in the revival, and never again obtained a footing in the island.

[1] Mahav. xlii. 49.
[2] *Ib.* xliv. 114.
[3] *Ib.* xlviii. 36.
[4] *Ib.* xlix. 25.
[5] *Ib.* lii. 24.
[6] *Ib.* lii. 63; see liv. 47, etc.
[7] *Ib.* lxxiii. 74, 138; lxxv. 35; lxxxi. 46.
[8] *Ib.* lxxxi. 68.
[9] *Ib.* lxxxiv. 20.

CHAPTER XXV

FROM PARAKRAMA TO THE ARRIVAL OF THE DUTCH

WE have seen that a great revival, both of the national independence and of the Buddhist religion, was begun by Vijaya Bahu in the eleventh century (A.D. 1065) and carried to completion in the twelfth (A.D. 1164) by the great Parakrama. But the prosperity which the latter attained lasted but a little while. With the history of his achievements, no less than eighteen chapters of the Mahavansa are occupied; but the short chapter which follows these is entitled, "The Reigns of Sixteen Kings," and describes a pitiable course of disaster and disgrace.

The great monarch's nephew, an accomplished prince, was murdered after a reign of one year, and the throne was seized by one adventurer after another. Some of them are credited with the erection of sacred buildings; but their opportunities must have been small, for the Tamils were continually coming down upon them, and after a few vicissitudes utterly defeated the Sinhalese, and overran the whole country. "Like the giants of Mara, they destroyed the kingdom and the religion of the land. Alas! alas!" cries the historian.

This state of desolation lasted till about A.D. 1240, when, after a second Vijaya Bahu, a second Parakrama came to the throne. His record is an echo of the earlier hero's fame. Splendid things are said of him, but his greatness was displayed in a diminished domain. The pressure of the Tamils, who were now no longer invaders but occupants of the northern part of the island, had by this time all but finally excluded the native kings from their ancient splendid homes in Anuradhapura and Polonnaruwa. The second Parakrama set up his throne and the shrine of the sacred Tooth—just recovered from the hiding-place in which it had been buried during the Tamil inroads—at Dambadeniya, much farther south, between Kurunegala and Negombo. Thence he removed the Tooth with great pomp to his own native place, Sirivaddhanapura.

This name belonged in after centuries to Kandy, and it was for long the received opinion that Kandy represents the Sirivaddhanapura of Parakrama II. This opinion has lately[1] been shown to be erroneous. Kandy was probably not founded till nearly three centuries later (by Vira Vikkama, A.D. 1542), and the Sirivaddhana of Parakrama II was a place of only temporary importance about seven miles from Dambadeniya.

But the brilliant terms in which it is described might well be thought to favour the old opinion.[1] I select some of the chief features from Mr. Vijesinhe's translation of the Mahavansa, ch. lxxxv.[2] "The city consisted of stately houses and open halls, of high walls and gates," and was adorned with Bo-trees, shrines and dagabas, groves, and image houses. The Tooth was carried to it in procession from Dambadeniya, the whole road being strewn with fine sand, and lined with plantain-trees and flags, and jars full of flowers. All along the way there were royal arches at every five cubits; at every ten, a cloth arch; and at every hundred "a stately house of great size, consisting of three stories and lofty spires, and containing images of the supreme Buddha—all finished with paintings of exceeding great beauty."

Any one who has seen an approach decorated in the beautiful Sinhalese fashion can recognize it exactly, if he will look at the above description through a magnifying-glass reversed. The "stately house of great size," with its three stories and lofty spires, is the "gedigē" (or pandal) that we know so well; and why should not the historian, here and throughout the Mahavansa, describe all that he admires, from flags and plantains to royal assemblies, through his magnifying-glass, and glorify a common scene?

All the inhabitants of Ceylon were summoned to attend;

[1] Shortly before the first edition of this book. See Note I, at the end of this chapter.

[2] The learned translator has unconsciously favoured the identification with Kandy, by introducing the words "for its scenery" into the description of the place. Mr. Vijesinhe writes: "A city that could not be compared *for its scenery*"; but the Pali has simply "incomparable."

and come they did, in their best garments, with flowers of the jasmine and the champak and the iron-wood to offer to the Tooth and to the Bowl. The Vihara was adorned outside with painted arches, with moving images of Brahma and various gods, whose arms moved; with moving figures of horses prancing, and great elephants, and "divers other shows of this kind which delight the world, and are used at feasts."

We need not inquire whether the ancients possessed knowledge, now lost, of automatic machinery. Have we not seen the likenesses of pigeons, and even of dolls and of horses, come out when strings were pulled, and flutter over the heads of royal visitors, even in these degenerate days?

Yellow-robed monks meanwhile, with beautiful fans, sat in various places in pulpits reverently placed for them, and preached the good law; and cries of "Sadhu"[1] went up on every side. And all night long innumerable myriads of lamps with perfumed oil made the whole land shine like a starry sky. Dancers and singers and the blasts of musical instruments added gaiety to the scene; and the crowds "with pleasant shouts went hither and thither, viewing all things with admiration."

The unusual magnificence with which the historian describes this place, is probably accounted for by its having been the birthplace of his king. He was probably a contemporary, and little knew how short-lived the glories of that Sirivaddhana would be.

The extent of this king's actual dominion in the west and south of Ceylon may be inferred from the record of his erecting temples not only at Dambadeniya and Kurunegala, but also at Bentota and at Dondra, the southernmost point of the island. He went on pilgrimage also to Samantakuta, now called Adam's Peak,[2] and, like modern rulers on like occasions, improved the path to that place. In an address to his sons he is represented as claiming to have made the whole island his own, but his sway over the north and east must have been merely nominal. By his minister, he visited all parts of Maya (west and south Ceylon) and constructed bridges and roads. He was a man of great learning and literary ability, and was called by the Community "the omniscient Pandit of the Kali Age."

[1] "Good," the Buddhist equivalent at once of "Amen" and of "Hurrah."

[2] It is natural for the Mahavansa to say that he went there "with his four-fold army." Would you have a king go alone?

To the successors of this king many great donations are attributed, but their power was weakened by renewed Tamil conquests, and the Tooth itself was for a time a prisoner in India. After it was recovered, Parakrama Bahu II installed it with new honours, and instituted a ritual in connection with it. In his time, about A.D. 1300, the Jatakas were translated into Sinhalese.

Over the next two centuries our history passes lightly. The national independence was more and more curtailed, and the national religion lost support, till about A.D. 1550 King Rajasinha apostatized from Buddhism, established Saivism as the Court religion, and persecuted the Community. About the same time (a little earlier) the Portuguese established a footing in the island, and the period of European and Christian influence began.

To the Portuguese a very bad character indeed is given in the Mahavansa. "They were all of them wicked unbelievers, cruel, and hard of heart. . . . They broke into towns and temples and image-houses, and destroyed Bodhi-trees and images of Buddha. They destroyed the country and the religion thereof, and built forts in divers places, and maintained continual warfare." Their advance against Kandy compelled the king, for the safety of the sacred Tooth, to fly; but they were driven back; and after many battles the assistance of the Dutch was invited, and the Portuguese were compelled to withdraw. The Sinhalese king—such was the native view of the event—established the people of "Olanda" in places bordering the sea, that they might guard Lanka and hinder the enemy.

How the Olandas in their turn became as bad as the Portuguese, will appear in the sequel.

NOTE I TO CHAPTER XXV

THE SIRIVAḌḌHANAPURA OF MAHAVANSA

CH. LXXXV

KANDY having been known in later times as Sirivaḍḍhanapura—or, in the more usual Sanscrit form, Sirivardhanapura—the mistake was not an unnatural one, which found in Kandy the Sirivaḍḍhanapura of Parakrama II. That it was a mistake was known to a few scholars, but the facts which put the truth in a clear light have only very recently been brought together.

The facts are these. Sirivardhana, meaning "auspicious and prosperous," is more an epithet than a name, and is given in Sinhalese books to many places, Kurunegala and Yahapaw, for instance, as well as to Parakrama's birthplace and to Kandy. The original name of Kandy seems to have been Senkhaṇḍasela, or the Sinhalese of which that is the Pali form. By this name, with Sirivaddhana added, Kandy is called when it is first mentioned in the Mahavansa (chap. xcii.); but afterwards its proper name is dropped in favour of the auspicious epithet. The birthplace of Parakrama, to which he gave the title, was a place previously and afterwards insignificant, close to the royal city Dambadeniya, in the lowland between Kandy and the sea. Its proper name was probably Nanbambaraya.

How long ago the inhabitants of Kandy began to claim this honour for their own, I cannot tell; but at any rate, about 1833, those who supplied Sir Alexander Johnstone with the books which were placed for editing in Mr. Upham's hands, must have told Mr. Upham that this Sirivardhana was Kandy. For in that author's English of the "Rājaratnācarī," after the words, "the king built the city called Sreewardanam Poora," the words "now called Candy" are boldly inserted, without a hint that they are not in the original (Upham, ii. 104). Neither in the Rājaratnakara (a Sinhalese history completed in the sixteenth century, and largely founded on the Mahavansa), nor in the Rājavaliya (which was written a century or more later, and also follows the Mahavansa closely in this part), is there anything to point to the identification with Kandy.

Turnour, writing a few years later than Upham, placed no confidence in the latter's work, and so escaped the mistake. He does not expressly contradict it, nor does he attempt any other identification: he simply says, "Sirivaḍḍhanapura in the Seven Korles."

Sir Emerson Tennent (i. 414) was more easily misled. Referring to Upham (l.c.), but probably supported also by the popular opinion in Ceylon, he published to the world that Kandy was the birthplace of Parakrama the Second. Knighton, in 1845, and others had already repeated the received opinion; but it was Tennent's popularity and authority that did most to establish it.

The next step is a curious one. In 1877 the learned Sumangala Terunnanse and the late Batuwantudavē Pandit published their Sinhalese translation of the Mahavansa. Into their text, in the passage which states the distance of Sirivaddhana from Dambadeniya, there crept, I know not how, the erroneous reading, "eight yoduns" (ninety-six miles), instead of "half a yodun" (six miles). The Pali for "eight" is "aṭṭha," and that for "half" is "aḍḍha," and the characters are very much alike, but the error is the more surprising from the fact that the translators had already published a Pali text with the reading, "aḍḍha."

It is to be attributed, I suppose, to this oversight that the learned C. Vijesinhe, in his English version, followed the false reading, and removed the place to ninety-seven miles, instead of seven, from Dambadeniya. At the same time, by rendering "atule" as "*incomparable for its scenery*," Mr. Vijesinhe further favoured the identification with Kandy.

The truth seemed now in a fair way to be for ever lost sight of, at any rate by all who should form their opinions from published works and not from direct study of original authorities.

But happily there were still in Ceylon students of the latter class, and among them Mr. K. J. Pohath, Mr. D. M. de Zilva Wickremesinghe (native assistant to the Archæological Commissioner[1]), Velivitiye Dhammaratana Terunnanse (who has kindly helped me with his opinion), and Mr. W. Goonetilleke, the Editor of the *Orientalist*.

Mr. Pohath communicated to the *Orientalist* (Vol. III, p. 218) a note to the following effect: Sir Emerson Tennent has made a serious mistake when he says in his *History of Ceylon* (Vol. I, p. 414) that King Pandita Parakrama Bahu (erroneously called by him Prakrama Bahu III) "founded the city of Kandy then called Siri-vardana-pura." The truth is this king never built a city called Sirivardanapura, much less the city of Kandy. It was to a city in Hat-korale (Seven Korles) called Sirivardanapura, in the neighbourhood of Dambadeniya, that Pandita Parakrama Bahu III (II?) removed the Dalada relic, etc. Mr. Pohath went on to mention some of the authors who had fallen into the mistake. This note attracted little attention in Ceylon, but it was seen and accepted by Professor Rhys Davids, who adopted Mr. Pohath's statement in an "addendum" to Vol. XXX of *Sacred Books of the East*.

It was by Professor Davids' *addendum* that my own attention was drawn to the matter, after I had adopted the mistake in the first draft of my chapter about Parakrama. I consulted Mr. W. Goonetilleke, to whom also the question was then new. His inquiries about the MSS. of the Mahavansa showed that "aḍḍha" and not "aṭṭha," "half" and not "eight," was the true reading. He pointed out also that the tooth was stated, after having been placed at Sirivaddhanapura, to have been

[1] Now of the Indian Institute, Oxford.

carried to Polonnaruwa not from any other neighbourhood but from Dambadeniya. His arguments, based on a careful study of the Mahavansa itself, convinced the learned Sumangala that Mr. Pohath was right.

The argument was carried further by Mr. Wickremesinghe, who, with Velivitiye Terunnanse, had long before this determined that the place was to be sought near Dambadeniya, and had succeeded, as I think, in identifying it still more exactly. The following are the proofs which he has been good enough to communicate to me :—

"The Sirivaddhana, which we are discussing, was confessedly the birthplace of Parakrama, the son of Vijaya Bahu. Now while several books (Daladāpūjāvaliya, Vanne Rājavaliya, and Dambadeṇi-asna) say that Vijaya Bahu lived at Paṭabatgala, in Seven Korles (a place not identified), the Dambadeni-asna says that Parakrama, his son, lived at a place called (and still known as) Nanbambaraya; and that from that place he made a procession-path two 'gows,' or about eight miles, long. The Vanne Rajavaliya also mentions this procession-path. Nanbambaraya is about this distance from Dambadeniya."

But Mr. Wickremesinghe has got nearer than this. He discovered some three years ago at Dambadeniya part of an old poem called "Kalundāpaṭuna," and in this he finds it recorded, that when Parakrama was called to the kingdom he was superintending the cultivation of *his fields at Nanbambaraya, where he had his palace.* This then was in all probability his native place, the place which he would delight to honour, It would be no wonder if he gave to it, when it became the royal abode, the royal and auspicious title.

But even here Mr. Wickremesinghe does not leave us to mere conjecture, for the same passage of the Kalundapatuna says that Nanbambaraya was adorned not only by the king's palace, but by his queen, Sirivardhana Bisawa, "Queen Sirivardhana."

Thus not only is the place with the highest degree of probability identified, but a romantic light is thrown upon its history; while the king's selection of it for honour, and the enthusiasm with which the historian describes it, are abundantly explained. We know not which more to admire, the faithfulness of our ancient historians, or the ingenuity of their modern interpreters.

NOTE II TO CHAPTER XXV

ROBERT KNOX

It was during the latter part of the reign of Rajasinha II, from 1660 to 1680 A.D., that the Englishman Robert Knox was detained, not actually a prisoner but under observation, in the Kandian territory. As a personal record, relating with the simplest modesty his own hardships and dangers, his courage in making the best of his position, the integrity with which he maintained his Christian moral and religious standard under most trying circumstances, and finally the indomitable perseverance with which he at last made good his escape, his *Relation of the Island of Ceylon* is an extremely interesting book. As a sketch of the country and its customs, it is distinguished by an accuracy and sureness of observation which few professed travellers have equalled. And it may be added, that while Knox's veracity is abundantly proved by what residents in the island now see, his testimony gives, on the other side, general confirmation—subject to due allowance for the national pride of the chronicler—to the statements of the Mahavansa. The reader will not complain if I give a somewhat fuller account of Knox's book than my own subject would actually require. He describes the king in terms less favourable than those of the native historian; but one who reads between the lines can see the same strongly marked character in both. Rajasinha was a man of that excessive and revolting degree of pride which is to be found only in tyrants, a man of overbearing self-will and diabolical cruelty; yet not altogether destitute of the capacities, if he had not the virtues, of a ruler. Under the pressure of constant invasions and defeats by the Portuguese and of rebellion among his own people, he seems to have had a policy, and to have acted always with shrewdness and often with courage. He was severe on any injustice on the part of his officers, and on immorality in any but himself. Although his reign was one long watch against conspiracy, he appears to have been as much feared as hated. He had a contempt for those over whom he tyrannized, and a certain admiration for Europeans, of whom, both Portuguese and Dutch, he had a considerable number in his employment. He had also Caffre guards whom he trusted more than his own people. In matters of religion he was tolerant, and inclined to favour Christianity. Though his father was—or had been—a Buddhist monk, he was the son of a "Christian" mother. A Jesuit priest, with whom Knox was well acquainted, seems to have lived an easy life on the outskirts of his Court. The Dutch, by flattering his vanity with inflated titles, and by professing to be only his slaves and messengers and the guardians of his shores, easily secured impunity for their ever-advancing encroachments on the maritime parts of what he called his dominions.

But in fact the country in Rajasinha's days had been impoverished and in parts desolated by Portuguese and Dutch incursions. Kandy was half ruined, having been often burnt by the Portuguese. The condition of Badulla was no better; indeed, all the towns were very small and desolate. Anuradhapura of course was wild forest, but still an object of occasional pilgrimage. Alut Nuwara, on the borders of the wild Bintenne, was a storehouse for corn and salt; but of the once famous shrine of Mahiyangana there Knox does not seem to have heard. And the king intentionally kept the outer portions of his territory uncultivated and without roads, that they might be impassable to invaders. He himself lived, since a serious rebellion which had taken place in 1664, almost entirely at Digili Nuwara, in Hewahette. But Matale, Puttalam, and Badulla were in some sort under his rule.

In all their degeneracy, the Sinhalese of that latter part of the seventeenth century retained much of their skill in the more delicate handicrafts. Knox speaks many times of the excellence of their work in wood, iron, and silver. Nor had they lost their love for gay decorations, processions, and shows. He describes, in an English sailor's way, exactly such splendours as we have been reading of in the Mahavansa, and adds: "*And then they say the palace is adorned beyond heaven.*" He describes the Kandy "perahœra" with great exactness.

Of the morals of the Sinhalese of that day he draws no very attractive picture. Of marriage they had little idea (this was in the Kandian districts), and child-murder was very common. But it is only fair to notice that he gives them credit—which we should not do now—for being very much averse to stealing, and not much given to quarrelling or bloodshed. He says people could travel about with little or no danger.

But it is with what Knox tells us about the state of Buddhism in those days that we are here chiefly concerned. Few or none, he says, were zealous about it. The worship of the (Hindu) gods and of devils was in full force; and the maxim, "Buda for the soul" (so he puts it) "and the gods for this world," shows that the popular superstition was then much what it is now. How it appeared to Knox may best be gathered from a few extracts. He thus begins his account of the religion of the Sinhalese:—

"The religion of their country is idolatry. There are many both gods and devils, which they worship, known by particular names, which they call them by. They do acknowledge one to be Supreme, whom they call 'Ossa polla maupt Dio' (ahasa polowa mœw Deviyo), which signifieth the Creator of heaven and earth; and it is he also who still ruleth and governeth the same. This great Supreme God, they hold, sends forth other deities to see his will and pleasure executed in the world; and these are the petty and inferior gods. These, they say, are the souls of good men, who formerly lived upon the earth. There are devils also, who are the inflictors of sickness and misery upon them; and these they hold to be the souls of evil men. . . . There is another great god whom they call Buddou, unto whom the salvation of souls belongs."

He describes the saying of "pirit" by the Buddhist monks as follows:

"When any man is minded to provide for his soul, they bring one of these priests under a cloth held up by four men, unto his house, with drums and pipes and great solemnity, which only can be done unto the king besides. Then they give him great entertainment, and bestow gifts on him according as they are able; which, after he hath tarried a day or more, they carry for him, and conduct him home with the like solemnities as he came; but the night that he tarries with them he must sing bonna (bana), that is matter concerning their religion, out of a book made of the leaves of tallipot; and then he tells them the meaning of what he sings, it being in an eloquent style, which the vulgar people do not understand."

The Buddhist "priests" he divides into elders (tērunnānsē, which he writes "tirinanx") and ordinary rank and file ("gonni," i.e. ganīn," member of the "gana" or assemblage). "The second order of priests," he says, "are those called Koppuhs (kapurāla), who are the priests that belong to the temples of the other gods; their temples are called 'dewals'"; and he reckons as "the third order the jaderes, priests of the spirits." "When they are sick, they dedicate a red cock to the devil" ("jaccof," i.e. yako).

He devotes a chapter to the description of their worship of planets, and many pages to other superstition, but to "Buddou" (this represents the Sinhalese form of the name, though we should now spell it "Budu") he gives little space; though he says, "it is he, they say, who must save their souls," and "for this god, above all others, they seem to have a high respect and devotion."

(Ribeyro, who was in Ceylon in the earlier part of Rajasinha's reign, and his editor, the Abbé le Grand, are still more ignorant of any serious distinction between the Hindu and the Buddhist elements in Sinhalese religion. Ribeyro has, for instance, this sentence:[1] "The idols are of various forms: some are of man, some of woman, others of monkeys, and others of elephants with many arms, others with bow and arrow, and an immensity of various figures; above all, there is one to which they show much reverence, which is called Bodu; the figure of this is that of a man, and it is made very great, thereby to represent that he was a great saint. I saw it in a pagoda, and it was six cavados (13½ ft.) in height.[2] This, say they, was a great god," etc.).

Of the places of pilgrimage Knox mentions only two, the Footprint on Adam's Peak and the Bo-tree at Anuradhapura. Of the Tooth he makes no mention, and it is almost certain that he had never heard of it. Though this indicates a very complete ignorance or indifference on the part of those among whom Knox moved—and he was familiar with Kandy—it confirms the statement of the Mahawansa, that the Tooth was placed in concealment by Rajasinha's father, and was brought back to Kandy by his son.

Nothing in Knox's evidence is more remarkable, as showing the in-

[1] Literally translated from the original. The Portuguese Ribeyro "passed forty years altogether in the Indies, and eighteen years in the jungles of Ceylon."

[2] Lee renders "thirty-two feet"; but Vieyra (Portuguese Dictionary) makes the "covado" three-quarters of a yard.

difference of the people towards Buddhism, than the position which Christianity held even in the Kandian country. Christians, he says, were looked up to and trusted, and believed to be more conscientious than others. This refers not only or especially to white men, but to native Christians, whose numbers must therefore have been appreciable. They were tolerated, he says, by all, but especially by the king, who preferred them, when he could get them for offices of trust. To Mahommedans also full toleration appears to have been extended.

In spite of the general indifference, the same indications of individual attachment to Buddhism were seen which we see now. The tiny dagaba in the little courtyard of the house—the lay devotees, especially women, begging "in the name of Buddha"—these were not wanting.

I will conclude this notice of a valuable book with an extract which sets the Buddhist temperament in a favourable light:—

"They reckon the chief points of goodness to consist in giving to the priests, in making pudgiahs, sacrifices to their gods; in forbearing shedding the blood of any creature, which to do they call pau boi, a great sin; and in abstaining from eating any flesh at all, because they would not have any hand, or anything to do, in killing any living thing. They reckon herbs and plants more innocent food. It is religion also to sweep under the bogahah, or god-tree, and keep it clean. It is accounted religion to be just and sober, and chaste and true, and to be endowed with other virtues, as we do account it.

"They give to the poor out of a principle of charity, which they extend to foreigners, as well as to their own countrymen. Out of every measure of rice they boil in their houses for their families, they will take out a handful, as much as they can gripe, and put it into a bag, and keep it by itself, which they call mitta-haul ["mettaṃ" rice, or handful-rice?], and this they give and distribute to such poor as they please, or as come to their doors.

"Nor are they charitable only to the poor of their own nation, but, as I said, to others, and particularly to the Moorish beggars, who are Mohammedans by religion: these have a temple in Candy."

PART VI

BUDDHISM IN CEYLON: THE PRESENT

CHAPTER XXVI

THE BUDDHISM NOW TAUGHT IN CEYLON

HOW far will a description of the Buddhism of the Pitakas, such as I have tried to give (chapters iv–xvii) serve for a description of the Buddhism of Ceylon to-day ?

A definite answer can be given to this question if we first draw a broad distinction between the moral system with the theory of human life on which it rests, on the one hand, and, on the other hand, the legendary histories and the theories of cosmogony and geography. The whole being divided into these two groups, we may assert that the first, the moral, is held now with little alteration ; but that the second, the mass of legends and cosmogony, has been so greatly developed and raised to so much greater prominence, as to make the later Buddhism differ widely from that of the Pitakas.

The moral system as taught now differs little from what we find in the sacred books. The aim, indeed, of the leaders of Buddhism at this moment is to teach exactly as the ancient books taught. But whether what was held in Ceylon a hundred years ago, before the European study of the subject began, was as true to the ancient standards, this will be questioned, and the point must be examined.

The Sinhalese, it is sometimes remarked, have been content to relearn their own religion from Europeans. Many people suppose that before European scholars unearthed the Pali language, the sacred books were nearly or quite unknown ; that real Buddhism was recovered for the Sinhalese in the nineteenth century; and that, till this took place, it was almost merged in the Hinduism which had been encouraged by the Tamil kings. This I am convinced is an exaggeration. The tradition had been more faithfully handed down among the Sinhalese themselves than this would imply. Before the Europeans touched the matter, the Sinhalese, if they taught at all, taught substantially what they are teaching now—at any rate, on the side of morality. The sketch that has been given (in chapters xx–xxv) of the contents of the Mahavansa showed, indeed, that Buddhism in Ceylon underwent vicissitudes, and that Hinduism grew up more and more beside it and within it; but it shows also that appeal was made at each revival to the Pitaka books and to the "succession of teachers" (Guru paramparāva); and that there was no complete breach—this the very continuity of the Mahavansa itself proves—with the earlier Sinhalese centuries. We are not entirely without evidence as to the un-Europeanized Buddhism of Ceylon. Knox, who was detained a prisoner in the Kandian country for nearly twenty years, between 1660 and 1680, has left a rough but vigorous sketch of the system as it presented itself to his unprepared but very acute observation. His outlines are not at variance with any feature of the description which a modern visitor would give.[1]

Much later than Knox, but long before any European scholarship had been brought to bear on the subject, the Dutch governor, Falck, in 1766, in cultivating friendly relations with the Sinhalese, put a series of questions to several presumably independent Buddhist authorities; and besides the answers to these questions, he received officially two connected statements about Buddhist tenets, from one of the principal elders, and from an educated Sinhalese official; the latter, on account of his half-European education, being a less valuable witness. These authorities, with many variations in detail, agree substantially in the accounts which they give (1) of the constitution of the worlds of gods and men; (2) of the soul of man; (3) of the nature of good and evil; (4) of reward and punishment; (5) of faith and worship: these being the chief heads, and this the order, under which the questions fall.

(1) Asked whether they believed in gods, they reply to this effect: There are an immense number of inferior gods in Brahma-

[1] See note, Robert Knox, on Chapter XXV.

lokas and devalokas, and in trees, etc., over whom Mahabrahma is supreme (except when a Buddha is in existence), but the Buddha is far superior to them all; on him the gods attend, and from him they receive instruction.

The world came into existence an immense time ago, not by creation but by nature (that is, I suppose, by its *own* nature—swabhāven), but it is periodically destroyed at vast intervals of time. In each such destruction, those beings that are in a certain division of the highest world, called the Abbhassara Brahmaloka, do not perish; and after the reconstruction of the world (which takes place through the surviving action-force of past beings) some of the inhabitants of that Brahmaloka, those of them whose merit is nearly exhausted, find their way to this world, and here, growing by degrees less heavenly and more earthly with the food they feed upon, at last propagate a human race.

(2) Asked whether there is such a thing as a soul, some replied that there is; but this is explained by what others say, that there is some principle called "skandha" (what I have rendered "constituents of being") which live after the body dies, only to be born again according to the actions. As another puts it, all the parts of the man cease entirely; none of the material elements continue, but a mysterious something, "concerning which," as the writer discreetly says, "what appears in the law of Buddha will inform."[1]

(3) Among moral evils, the chief place is assigned to avarice, etc. (the three "Asavas"), and to stupidity or thoughtlessness, etc. (i.e. to the four "Agatis"); or to faults of body, word, and mind; while in moral good the chief value is assigned to giving, purity, and belief in the doctrines of Buddha. All agree when asked that there is a conscience or witness in the heart, some defining it in a way which shows they are thinking of the favourite "hiri ottappaṃ." Above all, recollectedness is necessary.[2] The five, the eight, and the ten "precepts" are enumerated, but not consistently. In no case, among the five "Replies to Questions," is the prohibition of intoxicating drink reckoned as one of the five, or even mentioned at all. It is included and enlarged upon in the statement of the "high priest." In no

[1] Answer of the Galle priests, p. 10. I have been unable to find the Sinhalese original of these documents.

[2] Mudaliyar Rajapaxe, *ib.* p. 29.

case is any reference made to the Buddha as an example of conduct.

(4) In regard to reward and punishment, most of the answerers place as the highest result of good life, Nirvana, "which destroys all errors and acquires all happiness." Some do not mention Nirvana, but only the numerous heavens; all agree about the numerous hells and penal states of being. One reply reckons Nirvana as a local "place of departed Buddhas," situated above the twenty-sixth heaven, and magnificently adorned with gold, silver, and precious stones.[1]

(5) To the question, "In what does your worship consist?" the almost unanimous answer is, "In faith in the Buddha." To the "statement" of Rajapaxe, a Europeanized servant of the Government, and possibly a Christian, I attach very little value. He stands alone in saying that the Sinhalese pray three times a day—at sunrise, noon, and sunset.[2] The statement of the "high priest," which I think the most important, as being probably the least influenced by European thought and language, shows a tendency to emphasize the idea—not much developed even in the later Pitaka books — of suitable retribution, through transmigration, in future human births. The killer of animals, in addition to many births in hells, will, after return to human life, be poor and wretched; the thief will be starved and naked; the lustful will be a hundred times a despised and unmarried woman; the liar will have bad breath and two snake-like tongues, and will never be believed; the drunkard will be subject to disease and delirium. All this illustrates the influence which the Jataka literature has had in forming the Buddhist mind.

Such is an abstract of these documents of 1766. It does not hence appear that the theory at least of Buddhism, as held by the natives of Ceylon before European scholars knew anything about it, differed in any considerable degree from that which such scholars have since elicited from the Pali books; or that the tradition of these books had been lost sight of, or confused with the Hinduism and devil-worship which were going on alongside of it.

I conclude, therefore, that for the moral system of modern

[1] Rajapaxe, *ib.* p. 159.

[2] See note at end of this chapter.

Ceylon—Buddhism, native and not imported—I may refer the reader to my description of the moral system of the Pitakas.

In the regions of history and cosmogony, on the other hand, there is a wide interval between the Pitakas and the later tradition. In those regions, the Sinhalese Buddhist holds, and has long held, as part and parcel of Buddhism, not clearly distinguished from what was more properly called Doctrine, an immense accumulation of romantic and extravagant lore. The life itself of Gotama was early enlarged (probably at different times between 250 B.C. and A.D. 400) by many incidents that had been unknown to the Pitakas, and embellished in every point with enormous numbers, and with flowery and luscious details. Some of the incidents thus inserted, and some of the details of this embellishment, came to be among the most interesting, the favourite parts of the story. The details of the Buddha's birth and of his renunciation, of his visit to his mother in heaven, and of his visits to Ceylon, came actually to take precedence, in interest and in the poetical wealth laid out upon them, of the more authentic incidents in the Vinaya.

The theory, which had its nucleus within the Pitaka cycle, of a succession of previous Buddhas, was developed into the minutest accounts of the life of each such previous Buddha, and of the position which the Bodhisat (he who was to be Gotama) had occupied under each ; till a whole literature had been compiled of the prehistoric biography of the Buddha. One branch of this, virtually embodied already in the Pitakas, the 550 previous births of Buddha—a collection, in fact, of all the fables, proverbs, and Joe Millers of the East—outshone in popularity, as was natural, the less amusing treatises and sermons. Some especially of these "birth-stories"—those which relate the great achievements of virtue on an heroic scale by which the Bodhisat was fitted to become Buddha—acquired the very highest position in sacred lore, and were probably better known than any other part of "bana" (the sacred books as recited). And these tales, which tell how he was to be the Buddha, gave away his eyes in charity, gave his own body to be roasted, gave—greatest of all—his wife and his children to be beaten and enslaved before his eyes—these did probably more than either Vinaya or Sutta to form the Buddhist mind. To us such achievements, as not pretending to have been done in this life at all, are too obviously fictitious to have much interest. To the Sinhalese mind they were not palpably unhistorical. Buddha, in the popular thought, was the hero of the Jatakas.

Similarly around every name to which the Pitakas alluded, the Commentaries had built up a mass of legend of the popular and attractive type; while the native chroniclers, full of the exploits of Sinhalese kings and of their splendid liberality, had added their abundance to the store of food for the national imagination.

In this connection may be mentioned, too, the legendary lists of primeval kings—lists and legends of old Indian, and doubtless pre-Buddhist origin—from Mahasammata onwards. The first eighty-four thousand of these kings had reigned each a million years; King Okkāka, the mythical ancestor of the "Solar Dynasty," comes quite late in the series, and his reign lasted only ten thousand years. The incalculably distant dates assigned to former Buddhas and to the earlier exploits of the Bodhisat find place under these primeval monarchs, and claim their history for Buddhism.

The Sinhalese authors of the fifth and sixth and of the thirteenth and fourteenth centuries worked up this material in a native form. The more romantic of the Jataka tales were told in poetry and drawn out through the "linked sweetness" of innumerable stanzas—stanzas brilliant with the puns, and tinkling with the jingling assonance which is the pride of Sinhalese verse, and overladen with lotus flowers, blue and white and red, and with sandal-wood perfumes and scarlet iron-wood leaves, with swans and honey-bees, with armies and sounding cities and many-storied palaces; a literature crowded with princesses, and magnificent with the march of elephants, and strewn as thick as the floor of a fairy's cavern with gold and precious stones. This, as well as the moral system, is part of what was meant, or is meant, still to the Sinhalese mind by Buddhism.

Then there was the boundless field of cosmogony, with its infinite myriads of cycles of ages, and universes piled upon universes, and vast revolutions and cataclysms—all of which Buddhism had claimed for its own, because all lay open to the Buddha's eye, and all had been illuminated by his innumerable predecessors. It is impossible to ask an English reader to wade through even a short sketch of the geography—Mount Meru and the concentric seas of milk and the rest; the ten thousand worlds, each having its complete apparatus of heavens, earth, continents, and hells, with their presiding deities; or of the chronology of "asankhya-kap-laksha," innumerable myriads of cycles, the least division of which is longer than the period in which the touch of a silk handkerchief once in a century would wear away a mountain! These things are boundless nonsense; but they have for the Indian mind a solemn charm, and though not of Buddhist origin, they lend majesty to Buddhism. Gotama, we are told, discouraged such speculations; but they were not altogether excluded from the Pitakas, and his later followers have emphatically made them their own. How a world cycle comes to an end, by age-long storms and showers and fires; how sun after sun comes into being till the earth is dried and scorched and consumed; the Sutta which describes these catastrophes, and gives the authority of "bana" to such imaginations, is still among those of which copies are oftenest met with in Ceylon, and even of late years has had actual influence in exciting the minds of the Sinhalese.[1] One has only to remember what satisfaction is given to the feelings of a half-educated Englishman, when the lecturer tells him there are probably "some stars whose light has not yet reached us" to appreciate the charm which an asankhya-kap-laksha may have for a Sinhalese.

It is not enough, then, in answering the question, What has been the religion of the Sinhalese? to point to the Pali canon, and to what are logically and historically the fundamental parts of Buddhism. The later and more imaginative portions are truly part and parcel of the Buddhism of the Sinhalese, perhaps the part which is most endeared to them. The Five Prohibitions and the poya days, the duty of sparing life, and the opportunity of giving to the monks, these by themselves could hardly have gained a permanent hold over the hearts of a people; but other attractions besides these have been at work. All their stories of home and childhood, all their national literature, all that was grand to them in history and science; the conquests of their kings, the great buildings of their country, all were engaged in the interests of Buddhism. Not a building but had on it the

[1] Sūriyotgamana Sutta.

lotus or the hare in the moon ; not a ballad but it opened with homage to the Buddha, to the Law, and to the Community. Close to every great tank from which the fields were irrigated shone the white dome of the dagaba.

These are strong roots, everywhere twisted into the soil ; many of them, however, are slowly but surely dying. Education is steadily destroying all belief in Mount Meru and the "Sakwalas" and converting the long range of former Buddhas from an imposing decoration into an encumbrance. The national literature is rapidly being forgotten, not many can even read it, and only a few old people now can say by heart the favourite old stanzas which once were household words. Of the great monuments of architecture, some, it is true, are being repaired ; but by repair they are disenchanted, and the modern Sinhalese prefers an "upstair-house" on an English model to all the palaces of all the Parakramas.

Buddhism, if it lasts, will soon rest entirely on other supports than these : on that which is good and true in its own teaching ; on its alliance with Western scepticism ; and lastly, on that deep root, as yet, alas ! vigorous, which it has struck into the dark places of sorcery and superstition.

CHAPTER XXVII

MODERN MONASTIC LIFE

WHEREVER Buddhism is found in Ceylon[1] it is substantially the same. A monk who goes from the south northward, or from the maritime low country to the central hill country, does not find in any monastery which he may visit much that would strike him as unfamiliar in furniture or customs. If it be a monastery of his own society or sect (samāgama), he meets no difference at all; if it belong to another samagama, the differences are still but slight; at any rate, with one exception, they are such as an outsider might fairly reckon slight.[2]

But the distinction of the four (or three) societies, a distinction internal to Ceylon, is too important to be left unnoticed. It is usual, I believe, to reckon four—those of Siam, Amarapura, Rāmanya (Rangoon), and Kelani. The last, however, is a distinct sect only in the technical sense of a province, having a distinct boundary (simāwa). In every other respect it is one with the Siamese; it is a distinct association or college of monks, but not a separate sect. The other three are more widely distinguished.

The home of the Siam sect is the Kandian country; but it is

[1] Buddhism prevails as the national religion—though side by side with it there is a good deal of Hinduism, some Mohammedanism, and not a little Christianity—over about two-thirds of Ceylon; that is, over the southern and central portions. In the north Hinduism prevails similarly; and in the Hindu parts few Buddhists are to be found. Roughly speaking, if a line were taken (it would not be a straight line) from Puttalam on the west coast, through Vavonia on the north-central road, to Batticaloa on the east coast, very little Buddhism would be found to the north of such a line.

[2] Most of the information contained in this and the following chapter has necessarily, from the nature of the case, been obtained at second hand; but my informants have all been natives of the country, whom I believed to have direct knowledge of the facts.

largely represented also in the low country or maritime provinces, where about twenty per cent of the monks belong to it. The Amarapura and the Ramanya predominate in the low country, but are little by little gaining ground in the Kandian, where they amount together to ten per cent of the whole.

All these represent comparatively recent revivals of Buddhism by successive importations of monks, to revive the Community in the island, from Siam and from Burma.

The Siamese is the oldest, and dates its origin from about A.D. 1750, when Kirti Sri Raja obtained twenty Siamese monks from Siam, under the circumstances described on page 214, to restore the succession which was said to have been lost in Ceylon. The actual Community of Ceylon is, therefore, of late date, though it is believed, and with good reason, to correspond exactly with the former in customs and teaching.

The Amarapura society was founded about A.D. 1800 by men who had been expelled, say the Siamese, from the Siam society; some of their followers being men who had actually been to Amarapura to obtain admission.

The Ramanya is a more recent branch still, and appears to be distinctly traceable to a desire to return to strict conformity with the principles of the books. I go on to state the respective peculiarities of the sects. That of Siam is distinguished from the two others by one marked outward difference—the yellow robe is worn over the left shoulder only, the right shoulder remaining uncovered. The other two sects cover both shoulders. It is curious, considering with what extreme minuteness the Vinaya prescribes every point connected with the monk's dress, that each party should be able to defend its practice by appeal to the sacred literature. But so it is. The Siam party can point to the constantly recurring phrase, "Making the upper robe cover one side,"[1] and can urge that the phrase is used in the very formula under which every one of them—whether of Siam or of Amarapura—has been admitted to the Community, and which is expressly ordered in the record of the original foundation (Maha Vagga, i. 12, 3). But the Burmese claim authority from the same scriptures for the decorous "covering of the whole body" from the phrase, "avasesaṃ karitvā kāyaso."

[1] Uttarasangaṃ ekaṃsaṃ karitvā. See Manu, ii. 193.

But there is a distinction involving a deeper principle than this. The Siamese sect admits to the Community none but members of a particular caste (the Vellala), while the Amarapura and Ramanya profess to admit all. If this were their actual practice, they would justly claim a very honourable distinction, as being the only faithful representatives of a principle which is one of the proudest characteristics of the Buddhism of Gotama. But unfortunately, though they admit members of three other castes—the fishers, the cinnamon-peelers, and the toddy-drawers—even the Amarapura sect refuse to admit the castes which are supposed to be lower than these. They draw a line, though they draw it lower than the Siamese do; and since they draw a line on the basis of caste-distinction, they can hardly be said to differ in principle from their neighbours.

The reader will be curious to know how this departure from the acknowledged theory of Buddhism is justified, and to what texts appeal is made. The answer of the Siam sect is this: "Buddha commanded us to obey kings, and this custom owes its origin to a royal command. The king, Kirti Sri Rajasinha, who introduced the Siam succession, insisted that it should be confined to Vellalas." The other sects, who draw the line lower down, have not this plausible pretext to allege; they would reply, I believe, that in theory their Community is open to all, but that in practice there are never found in the lower castes any people worthy of, or capable of, admission. This would be a mere calumny on the so-called lower castes, for these contain—as notably in my own knowledge the washermen and goldsmiths do—men of ability and character scarcely inferior to any.

The monks of the Siamese fraternity, after receiving alms, utter a short formula in the nature of a blessing—"May you enjoy the merit of this gift" (pin purawanawā); but those of the other two sects, in stricter conformity to the Vinaya rules, depart as they came, in silence.

Another distinction lies in the method of saying "bana," or reading the sacred books in public: it is called the "two-seat custom." In the assemblies collected to hear bana from the monks of the Siamese branch, two seats are placed, and two readers divide the duty, one of them reading out the text, and the other, not when he has finished but concurrently, word after word, or at most phrase after phrase, giving the interpretation. Among the Amarapura and Ramanya one person both reads and interprets, and so only one seat is needed.

The fifth point of distinction turns on a much more curious question, the question, namely, whether the Buddha is or is not at present in existence. There are prescribed in the Dakshina Vibhanga Sutta (of the uparipannāsa of Anguttara Nikaya) seven formulas for giving to the Community, e.g. to the monks only, to the nuns only, to certain monks, to certain nuns, and so on. Six of these are admitted by all, but the seventh, which stands first, is: "To the Buddha, to the monks, and to the nuns" (Tathagate ubhato sanghe denam demi). This formula the Amarapura and Ramanya sects recognize and use; but the Siamese disallow it, on the ground that the Buddha is no longer in a position to receive gifts. It was prescribed, they say, while he was living, but since his Nirvana it is necessarily modified. Whereas the others contend that the absent or deceased Buddha may be taken as represented by his relics. The donor places a casket (karanduwa), supposed to contain a relic, in front of him, the representatives of the Community take seats beside it, and then he offers his gift with the words, "I give this to the Community which is sitting in this hall with the Buddha at its head."

When it has been added that the Siamese cut their eyebrows, but the other two do not, we have exhausted the list of the points of difference—so far as I have been able to learn—between the Siamese on the one hand and both the other sects on the other.[1]

But the Ramanya differs from both the others in points which though less technical, are really more important. This small but influential branch of the Community was confessedly founded as a purer and stricter branch. They aim at a more genuine poverty, possess no lands, use no smart robes or umbrellas, but carry only the native palm-leaf umbrella; they avoid all association with Hindu rites and with the temples (dewala) of Siva, Vishnu, etc., and denounce the worship of all those lower deities (devatā) which occupy in practice so large a part of the field of popular Buddhism. Such a sect is of course a small one, and its influence has depended very much on one

[1] One or two other points are mentioned in a note to Lee's translation of *Ribeyro*, p. 277.

man and one place—Ambagahawatte Unnanse, of a vihara at Payagala, near Kalutara.

It is also more widely separated from the other two than either of them is from the other. The lay followers of the Ramanya monks pay no respect to the monks of the other sects, and Ramanya monks are not admitted, or do not go, to the Tooth Temple in Kandy.

With these exceptions there are few signs of jealousy between the three sects; the division does not much affect the laity. The places of pilgrimage are attended by all alike, though they all belong to the Siam sect, and in each place a donor may give to whichever monk he pleases.

In regard to wealth, the lands belong chiefly to the Siam fraternity, and in their hands, as I have just said, are the lucrative shrines of Kandy, Anuradhapura, Adam's Peak, Kelani, and Tissamaharama. For to them the Kandian king of course assigned all the temple-lands when he restored the succession in A.D. 1750. The possessions of the Amarapura are necessarily of more recent acquirement, but they have acquired, and are acquiring, a good deal of land in the low country. This sect, the Amarapura, is at present the most prominent in controversy, street-preaching, and all that is aggressive. It is among them that the Theosophists have found their chief allies. And their more conservative Siam neighbours, resting in quiet on their ancient temple-lands, are inclined to condemn the Amarapura as making a trade of religion (ayaviyadam læbenawā).

The numerical proportions of the three sects I have no means of exactly ascertaining, but it is guessed that out of the 9598 monks in the island (census of 1891,[1]) about half are Siam, thirty-four per cent Amarapura, and sixteen Ramanya.

Foreign monks who come—and of late years increasingly—to visit the Ceylon shrines, are courteously welcomed; though if a monk from Burma, for instance, visits the Tooth Temple, he is not allowed, I am told, to enter, till he has adjusted his robe according to the Siam custom. As soon as a yellow-robed figure (sramanarūpaya, the "form of a samana") is seen approaching, preparations are made, often very slight, but in a few cases with something like the full ceremony of the books, for his reception. And as long as he is there, he is not allowed

[1] The number in the census of 1901 was given as 7331, a very notable decrease.

to feel himself a stranger; although after he is gone, the conversation is likely to turn, as one of my informants naively said, upon the errors of his sect. A few of the more learned or careful monks, on receiving a stranger, ask him in Sinhalese the series of questions which the Buddha is said to have asked of his monks, whenever they came to see him, about their dwellings and their journey: "In the district in which you live is there facility for getting food?" "Are your dwellings convenient?" and so on. But as a rule the conversation is either about village trifles or about lands and lawsuits. Sometimes the state of monasteries, books, and studies will be discussed; and occasionally a bana book is got out and more directly religious conversation ensues. I have inquired in vain for any favourite stories or jokes of the pansala, corresponding to such as would be current in an English college. If asked, a monk might relate some bit of local tradition, but there does not appear to be now, as a rule, any interest taken in such things.

It was intended, apparently, by the framers of the Vinaya rules, that the members of the Community should move about a good deal from one monastery to another; not that they should be, as the term now is in the Ceylon law-courts, "incumbents" of particular temples or pansalas, and, in fact, life-proprietors of particular properties. But at present it is very rare, though it is not unknown, for a monk to migrate from one monastery to another. The cause is the tenure of property and of customary advantages, which their holder is unwilling to lose or to transfer.

The tenure of temple-property is a very important fact in its bearing on the status of Buddhism in the island, but it is mentioned here only as bearing on the conditions of residence. The properties, having generally been given by kings, not acquired by the monks or given by their immediate lay-adherents, are not as a rule near to the pansalas to which they belong. Some pansalas have villages assigned to them for various services, such as sweeping, horn-blowing, and the like. This is the case with the famous pansalas and temples, like the Dalada Māligāwa (or Tooth Temple) at Kandy, or the Mahiyangana at Alut Nuwara. But many others have lands let out on rent, and cultivated, in some cases by Europeans, as cocoa-nut, tea, or rubber plantations; the monks not hesitating to receive the profits in money. The power to benefit their families, which leading "incumbents" thence derive, is believed to be the cause of enlistment in the monastic life in a large proportion of cases. I am assured by one well able to judge, that if, as the proposed "Buddhist Temporalities Bill"[1] provides, the temple properties are placed in lay hands and administered only for the common benefit, not one in a hundred of those who now join the Community will do so.

The usual number of occupants of a single pansala is two or three. It is rare for only one to occupy a pansala alone, but five is the largest number that is at all frequent; four is a large pansala. To this the great central colleges at Kandy, called the Asgiriya and Malwatta pansalas, are exceptions. The rule for their numbers is twenty in each, but there are now forty or more in each. But in the vast majority of the pansalas which are scattered—in homely villages or in romantic seclusion—through the island, two monks, of whom one is a novice, live alone.

There does not appear to be now any arrangement by which the monks of different monasteries should meet in any sort of periodical assembly or council. The isolation in which as a rule they live, and which must be one of the most undesirable features of the system, is little interrupted; least, where such an interruption would be most useful. For the occasions of meeting depend very much on two conditions, viz. on the reputation and popularity of particular monks, and on the presence in the neighbourhood of wealthy and zealous laymen, or givers, "dāyakayo." Such a giver will invite a specified number of monks to be entertained by him. This "act of merit" on his part (and on that of those who come to hear the monks read) is called—it is a very common and a very popular word in Ceylon—a "pinkama." The invitation is communicated to the chief monk of the pansala that is in, or nearest to, the donor's own village, and by him it is distributed. He carries betel, in sign of the invitation, to as many neighbouring pansalas as will furnish the specified number of guests, and in each of these the invitation is passed down according to seniority. The meal is served by the host and his family, and consists, in accordance with the ancient language of the books and with the regular

[1] Written in 1892. The bill became law, but proved, I understand, ineffective.

practice of Sinhalese dinners, of soft food, hard food, and sweets. At the close there is occasionally the recitation of suitable Suttas, those which praise hospitality to monks and those which describe the characteristics of a good layman's life. But more frequently this recitation is—inevitably, because no one knows or cares for the Suttas—omitted; and a short "blessing," or invocation of merit, by the senior monk concludes the ceremony.

A Bana Pinkama, or merit-act for recitation of the sacred books, is a more important matter. It lasts several days, often fifteen days or a month, and the recitation is a prominent feature. Towards such an entertainment several villages combine, and ask as many monks as they can afford to provide for. The number to be thus invited is sometimes greater than can be found in the neighbourhood, and in that case the leading layman of the inviting villages goes (supposing the case to be in that province) to Kandy, to the central college of the whole Siamese community, i.e. to the Asgiriya or to the Malwatta pansala, and the chief of that central monastery sends the required number of monks. Dinner is served at noon each day to the members of the Community, sitting strictly in seniority, and is followed by the recitation, which is continued into the night, and at full-moon seasons often the whole night long.

Such a pinkama is the great delight and entertainment of the Sinhalese people. Long preparations are made; a preaching-hall (bana maduwa) is erected, often at considerable expense, and the approaches are decorated with arches and lines of arcades, covered, in the beautiful Sinhalese taste, with the pale young leaves of the cocoa-nut, and with flowers and fruit. Globular lamps, which by day, at any rate, are far more beautiful than the paper ones of China, are made of the same delicate leaves, cut in parallel sections like those of which a globe is made, and drawn together at the points. These are hung in the preaching-hall and along the paths which lead to it. In the daytime the roads in the neighbourhood present the appearance of a fair. Crowds in clean bright dresses, in which white and red play the greatest part, pour along the roads in high good humour and with perfect decorum. Large models of ships, steam-engines, houses, and, above all, of gigantic cobras, are drawn along on trucks by oxen. They are accompanied by boys and men dressed up—or undressed and daubed with yellow

—as demons, by dancers, by drummers, and by all the paraphernalia of festivity.

But to return to the monks with whose customs and duties we are now concerned. Their part in these ceremonies is not to give but to receive. They constitute the field in which all this merit is to be sown. To eat what is set before them, to accept the homage of their adorers—a homage which is as far as possible from implying any personal respect—and to receive, on the part of the Community, the gifts of money, robes, etc., which may be brought—these are their primary duties. It is recognized, however, as their bounden duty also to give to the assembled laity the opportunity of acquiring the further merit of hearing, or at least seeing, the sacred books read; the opportunity of acquiring merit by honouring Dhamma as well as Sangha. With this view, far more than with any idea of instruction or of moral influence, the monks who are the guests at a Bana Pinkama take it by turns to read the Pali Suttas, with their Sinhalese comment or explanation. Sometimes, instead of Suttas, they read—what are more popular and are invested by custom with the dignity of bana—the famous Jataka stories. These, by the interpretation, the people are able to understand; and the more because the interpreting monks understand them themselves. The stories are well known to the older country folk, though the younger and the people in towns know little of them; and by the country folk, at least the older, they are genuinely loved, and the well-known favourites are enthusiastically welcomed. To these must be added the Rājavaliya, a Sinhalese history of Ceylon, made up out of the older Pali chronicles and continued down to the beginning of the present century, with accounts of the wars of the Sinhalese against the Portuguese, Dutch, and English. This also is very popular, and takes rank as bana.

Professor Rhys Davids has drawn a pretty picture of such a moonlight scene. His estimate, with which on the whole I agree, must be qualified by the statement that these gatherings are not so far pervaded by genuine Buddhist spirit as to be free from the inroads of caste tyranny. In a recent instance a poor woman had her jacket torn from her shoulders by a lay authority during the very reading of bana, not because she was intruding,

[1] Written in 1892.

but because being of low caste she presumed to wear any such covering in the presence of high-caste people.

But the acquaintance of the common people with the classical Sinhalese, in which the commentaries are most of them written, and that of the monks with the Pali original, is far too small, for any meaning to be conveyed, in the majority of cases, by the reading and interpretation of the Pitaka books.

The spirit in which bana is listened to may be gathered from the following, which represents the statement of an unquestionable authority: In the Kandian country, the Brahmajāla Sutta is often read, and the reading of it is always welcome. A great many people, men and women, flock together to the bana-maduwa, in which this Sutta is to be read. This at first sight seems surprising, for the Brahmajala Sutta is a difficult and a long one. But herein lies the reason of its popularity. As to the difficulty, that is neither here nor there, for no one expects to understand much of any Sutta; but the fun lies in its *length*. The readers have to read very fast; for the fastest readers, beginning at 6 p.m., cannot finish much before half-past seven in the morning. And it is in witnessing their efforts that the pleasure consists. There are two readers, who sit side by side (see p. 240). One reads the Pali original, and the other the Sinhalese commentary or translation. A stranger might expect to hear a paragraph, or at least a sentence, of Pali followed by its translation. But the exchange is kept up much more briskly than this. Each word of Pali, as it is shouted out by the one reader, is followed, with lightning speed, by its echo in Sinhalese from the other. "Evaṃ" shouts the one; "thus" cries the other. "Sutaṃ" cries the first; "heard" shouts his colleague; and so *all night*. "It is exactly like a race," says one who has often heard it, "and the hearers are delighted." Every word carries merit with it, and amusement too.

These pinkamas, as I have said, furnish the chief occasions on which the monks meet together in considerable numbers.

On poya days, i.e. at the four quarters, but especially at the first and third (new and full) of the moon, the monks go to temples (vihara) when laymen are making offerings, and after receiving the offering, preach in a more informal, and, I imagine, more practical way than at the pinkamas; they take some Sutta, or some verse of it as a text, and preach upon it.

It is on the same poya days, generally after the gift-receiving, that confession takes place. At such confessions are assembled only the monks from two or three neighbouring dwellings. From five to ten form a chapter in ordinary places; in the Malwatta as many as fifty may be collected. The form is gone through exactly as in the books (see p. 241). An elder, or any other who knows the Patimokkha by heart, recites it: the monks then by twos make their confession to one another. The assembly is thus taken to be pure. The ceremony takes from two to three hours. The confession, I am told, is merely formal: one who has been at many has told me that he never knew any bad thing voluntarily disclosed. There is not in this any great departure from the principle of the institution as the books present it, for in them also there is no provision for the infliction of penalties for offences made known at the confession. Penalties are imposed by the Community (by "sanghakamma") on other occasions, from information received outside the poya-house, and after a formal accusation.

Besides attendance at these pinkamas and poya days, there are but few occasions on which the monks perform any ministerial rite, or act in any pastoral capacity. To weddings they do not go, either as guests or as ministers, nor is any bana recited at them. On such occasions jayamangalagāthā (stanzas expressing the hope that through certain acts of the Buddha prosperity may accrue to the family) are recited, but by laymen.

At the opening of a new house, one or more monks, if and as invited, go and say a "charm for protection" (ārakshāpiritta). This consists of Ratana Sutta, Mangala Sutta, Karaniyametta Sutta, which are called the three Suttas, and then perhaps Jayamangalagatha. The words of the Ratana Sutta may have had something to do with the habit of calling on the gods or on "God" for protection.

Similarly, when friends and relatives are collected on the day of a child's first eating rice, they invite as many monks as they can afford to feed, and the same pirit is recited. Many monks perform the part of astrologers, and make horoscopes for new-born children; but this they do at home in the pansala. On occasion of death they may go uninvited, and offer the "consolations" of Buddhism. They read to the mourners certain verses (gāthā), especially that which begins "Tirokuddesu tiṭṭhanti") and the short formula, "aniccā vata sankhārā." This last is so common as to be understood by most people.

At the interment, after the body is laid in the grave, wrapped in linen, another cloth is placed over it, and the monk holds up the corner of this cloth; and while another person pours water on the raised part of it, the monk says, "Aniccā vata sankhārā" and—

> "Unnate udakaṃ vattaṃ yathā ninnaṃ pavassati
> Evaṃ eva ito dinnaṃ petānaṃ upakappetu;"

that is, "As water rolling down from higher ground flows over the lower land, so may that which is given in this world benefit the pretas (or, the departed)." The custom of giving offerings to the dead lingers only to this slight extent, though it is recognized in the books. The present theory about it is, that one cannot be sure that the departed are not born as "pretas," a sort of hungry ghoul; and so it is safe to make this act on their behalf. Of course, according to Buddhism, no one who has once entered the first stage (who is a sotāpanno) can ever be born as a preta. But the anomaly is explained by saying that even the most meritorious may, for some small offence, have to be a preta for a week or so. This short purgatory is mitigated or prevented by the recitation.

In a few instances the bodies of laymen, like those of monks, are burned; as in the case of a distinguished headman in the Kandian district a few years ago, to whose funeral rites some forty monks went: offerings, i.e. a dinner, were given to them during the day; at two o'clock the cremation took place.[1]

One of the most important features of the monastic life, in theory at least, is the observance of the retreat of the rainy season or "was." There is not in Ceylon so marked a rainy season as in north India, but the name of this custom bears witness to the latitude in which it originated. The observance of "was" at the present day in Ceylon may be more truly described as the "monks' holiday" than as the "Buddhist Lenṭ." With Lent it has not, as far as I am aware, any feature in common, except that it is a period of time set apart for a religious purpose. The period is three months, roughly coin-

[1] While the proof of this page (in the first edition) was in my hands for correction, my venerable teacher, Batuwantudāwē Pandit, died, and was cremated with great pomp in Colombo.

ciding with the months of European summer. The essential part of the observance is, that the monk remains in one village or place all the time; or, at any rate, may not be absent from it for more than seven days. The place may be either that of his own residence, or some other place to which he has been invited. The majority get an invitation. Those who are known to be able and learned, or who have social influence, always get one; and others according to their merits. Some who are known to be ignorant or bad are never asked.

If a monk gets no invitation, he makes at the beginning of the period a resolution to pass it at home, and having made that resolution he has no occasion to make any change in his ordinary habits: in this case "was" is virtually nothing. But in the more desirable case the order of things is this: the laymen of such or such a village determine, or such or such a rich "donor" determines, to give an invitation or two, or three, or twenty, or even more, monks. If the number wanted is small, he goes to the nearest pansala on a poya day, and tells the monks that he proposes to receive such a number for "was." This is a month beforehand. The invitation is distributed in that pansala, or that and the neighbouring ones. If the number is large, the invitation is managed, as in the case of a pinkama, through one of the central monasteries or colleges. Such invitations to rich villages or houses are of course much desired, and "wheels within wheels" are set in motion to secure them.

When the time arrives, the monks assemble at the place, and are received with more or less state. Rich donors nowadays decorate the roads and the approaches to the place, and the buildings are adorned with white cloths and with the beautiful leaves and fruits of the country. Until of late, the accommodation provided for the monks was simple—"low beds and seats," and the other "requisites" were enough. But now wealthy patrons pride themselves on giving to each monk a separate room, with chairs, tables, and wardrobes, in European style. During his stay the monk is expected to read and explain the bana books, and perhaps to preach in a less formal way. The people on their part make much of him, and do their utmost to have it said, when he goes away, that he has been well entertained.

On the occasions and for the purposes above described, the

monks meet together in more or less number. But these occasions are the exceptions. As a rule, a monk is seen alone. If we meet at times a considerable number, it is because they are travelling probably to a pinkama. In their ordinary life they go abroad alone. In the street of a town, or among the narrow paths which lead, in Sinhalese villages, under the thick shade of cocoa-nut and jak trees, from one low house, in its clean-swept courtyard, to another, the yellow-robed figure moves, in grave and touching solitude. We see him standing, with downcast eyes, holding his bowl with both hands before him, not putting the bowl forward, nor uttering any sound to indicate his presence, nor by any look of impatience, or by any movement, suggesting to a stranger that he is waiting for anything. Such, at any rate, is the attitude and manner which the rules prescribe, and it is strictly conformed to by many, especially by the boy-monks, or novices, of whom there are many. Sometimes, after he has stood thus, like the statue of patience, for some minutes, he moves on, quietly, and to all appearance contentedly, to the next house. There he may be more fortunate. He has already been seen, and the inmates are prepared for him. One of them, generally a woman,[1] brings a ladle full of rice, or of gruel, and pours it into his bowl, or lays in the bowl a few plantains, or a piece of fish—a specimen, more or less liberally chosen, of whatever may be "going" in the house. Having offered it, the woman, if she is a careful Buddhist, makes a low homage or curtsy, herself sitting down and holding up the clasped hands above her head. In some cases no notice is taken of her respectful service, and the impassive visitor moves on to the next house; others, according to the sect, pronounce a short formula of blessing. It is not always that one sees any such respect exhibited. I have often observed a woman place her gift in the bowl with an air of utter indifference, if not contempt, turning away entirely without reverence. And sometimes a woman may be seen, especially in a fruit-shop, where monks, of course, expect to get something, picking out from her bunch of plantains, not the best nor yet the worst, but such as represents a due balance between thrift and religion. But

[1] It was always, probably, chiefly by women that alms were put into the begging-bowl. It is curiously taken for granted that the giver will be a woman, in Culla Vagga, viii. 5, 2.

this is not a temper peculiar to Buddhist donors; in this matter, at least, one touch of nature makes the whole world kin.

These begging-rounds for food (piṇḍapāta yanawā) take place in the morning, and the food has to be taken home and eaten before noon. In the afternoon they go out—or one from the monastery on behalf of all goes out—to collect in the same way such things as are not to be eaten at once, condiments, tobacco, and the like, or other things necessary for the monastery, and in particular, oil.[1]

Of course the mendicant does not go about his rounds day after day through the same street or the same village, without knowing pretty well where he will be successful. It may even be suspected that he has means of conjecturing what is going on in the several kitchens, or at which meal there is salt fish with the rice. In fact, of course, the provision for the village monk is systematically made in certain houses, while others bear a very slight or very intermittent share in the responsibility. And this fact, that the monk, as a rule, walks straight to the place where he knows that he will find his dinner, must relieve the mendicant life of much of its hardship. It is simply a life in which one has not the trouble of keeping house.

But in very poor districts, or where Buddhism is not a power —and there are many such districts—the life of the mendicant is hard. Many monks know well what it is to be hungry, and some, I believe, turn their sufferings to spiritual account, bearing in mind the insignificance of the body, and trying to "have treasure" elsewhere. And, what it surprised me at first to learn, the life is particularly hard in Colombo. Here only a proportion, probably not half, of the inhabitants are Buddhists at all, and of those, most are intent on getting, not giving, so that parts of the town are harder to get a living in by begging than most of the villages. And young men who have come to Colombo to attend the Pali College, have sometimes, if they have no friends in the city, a really hard life, and bear it, I am assured, in some instances, for the sake of learning, with an enthusiasm which is extremely touching.

[1] Obtaining requisites depends on reputation for consistency. See Akank. Sutta, S.B.E., p. 211. To be respected, and so well fed, is claimed as the lowest but earliest of the fruits of being a good monk, in Saman. Sutta, §§ 36, 37. Similarly, keeping well with laymen is given as the object with which a monk is to practise recollection. Culla Vagga, i. 20.

Among the occupations of the monks within their monasteries we may reckon teaching, reading, and whatever other kinds of work are lawful; we might also, from the books, expect to hear of meditation, and of the exercise of those supernatural powers to which meditation is supposed to lead. It may be questioned whether the rules of Buddha do strictly require the monks to teach the young. I do not remember any passage in which it is enjoined. But public opinion seems always to have expected it; and the pansalas are said to have been of old the chief if not the only schools of a nation which was not uncultivated. Of late years in Ceylon, public opinion, which has little respect for unproductive retirement, has demanded that the monks shall justify their existence and their large resources, by contributing effectively to the education of the people. It has begun to threaten that if they do not teach, their revenues shall be applied, either by Government or by committees of their own, to that purpose. At present it is rare, and I believe it has always been rare, for a monastery to offer no teaching at all. One monk in each pansala is nominated by the senior to teach, and the village boys, ten or twelve of them perhaps, come to learn letters. The lessons go on from 7.30 or 8 a.m. to 8.30, and in the afternoon again from 4.30 to 6 p.m. No payment is ever made, nor is any pupil refused. The boys make themselves useful in the courtyard, the flower-garden, and other small works about the monastery.

But besides these village boys there are often novices, "little unnānsēs," as they are popularly called, who live at the monastery to be prepared for the religious life. Lads are thus handed over to the care of the monks at seven or eight years old, though they are not admitted to "pabbajjā" till the age of ten or twelve. In some pansalas there may be four or five such pupils, but one or two is the usual number. They are under the care of the senior monk, who clothes, feeds, and teaches them, while they do the household work, fetch water and wood, cook, and so on. However high their family, they submit to these menial tasks, and are taught to be proud of them. But they do not all go on to adopt the religious life. Out of the boys who are thus entrusted to the monks for education, only some twenty per cent become monks; the rest are mostly lads of low rank who come virtually as servants, to learn their letters and to get fed.

These boys generally leave at about fourteen or fifteen years of age, though of them even some, perhaps ten per cent, stay till they are five-and-twenty. They learn little beyond the alphabet and the "Sattaka Paha." But to the novices a good deal more is taught, as will appear presently.

As regards study on the part of the monks, it is obvious that there must be all degrees, from the ardent student or learned scholar to the rough, coarse peasant who has neither interest in study nor capacity for it. But it may safely be said that anything that deserves the name of study is confined to very few, although the number of genuine students has been increased by the influence of the Pali Vidyodaya College in Colombo. Few monasteries possess a complete copy of the Pitakas, but monks borrow from those which have them. Few leaf-books are now written, for printing has almost superseded them. The Jataka book is a good deal read, not for morals or doctrine, but for amusement. Until of late this was the book most in use at twelve-day pinkamas and the like, but since the revival of the study of Pali, Sutta Pitaka books are often read. In the Kandian country, about which I have learnt most, the Suttas most read are the Dhammacakkappavattana and Satipaṭṭhāna Suttas; after these, Kālakārāma Sutta (of Majjhima Nikāya), Subha Sutta, and Sigālovāda Sutta. And for the rest, those to which there are explanations (sannas), such as the Anguttara and Majjhima Nikaya, are most in use. The Mahāparinibbāna Sutta is not much read. Many who are not Pali students at all can repeat by heart, without understanding, several of the Suttas which form "pirit" (see p. 260), and which are taken chiefly from the Sutta Nipata.

No kind of manual work is done by monks, unless it be a little carpentering or painting, for ornament, about the pansala. Such work is considered to be strictly forbidden by the Buddha. But medicine and astrology, which are also distinctly forbidden, are very much practised. Some of the best native doctors are monks, and of horoscopes they are the chief framers.[1]

As for meditation in any regular form—sitting for the purpose, etc.—it is absolutely unknown; "such things," said one of my informants, "are very non-existent." He had never heard

[1] See both these expressly condemned, astrology with special emphasis, in the Tevijja Sutta. S.B.E., vol. xi., p. 196.

of any one even pretending to practise "samādhi," to use "kammaṭṭhāna," etc. Still less is there any pretence of, or expectation of supernatural powers (iddhi). The Ceylon Buddhists always laugh with utter incredulity at the stories of "esoteric Buddhism," and say, "perhaps there may be such things in Tibet." In fact it is universally believed that the days are altogether past in which the higher walks of Buddhism were trodden. No one takes seriously the system of the "paths," in fact the terms are never heard. In actual life no one is ever heard to profess that he has entered even the first path (sohan maga), or to express a wish to do so. There are no "rahats" now, nor have there been any for many centuries. It is said, indeed, that Buddha prophesied that within no long time rahatship would be extinct. At any rate, in later days, what could not but be admitted as a fact was dignified with the character of a law. In the commentary on the Abhidhamma Pitaka it is said: "Rahatship will not be able to exist more than a century after the Nirvana of the Buddha." There is no reason to think that it was ever, in the Southern Buddhism at least, believed to be possible among contemporaries.[1]

The pretence to supernatural powers is one of the things which make the more genuine Buddhists despise the Theosophists. It is possible that under the influence of foreigners the claim to a revival of "iddhi" may be put forward in Ceylon. If so, it will be a spurious revival, and will be condemned by the more intelligent Buddhists as an instance of the fourth Pacittiya offence, that of falsely pretending to supernatural attainments.

In short, there is little or no idea of even aiming at the standard of monastic life which the Vinaya Pitaka exhibits. In certain points the rule is observed, for instance in the ritual of admission, of full profession (upasampadā), and of confession. But the substance of the rule is ignored, not only in technical details, but in almost all that concerns the practical objects and the higher aims for which the Community professes to exist.

I have said above that boys are received into the viharas to be taught and trained. Such of these boys as are of the proper

[1] In the Mahavansa it is never claimed. The expressions, "like a rahat," "it was as if there were rahats in the world," show that there was no idea of it as a contemporary fact. Mahavansa, 84, etc. Fa Hien, however, refers to a case as having occurred in his time. (See p. 199.)

caste and are satisfied with the life are "admitted," and are then under a particular tutor (or upādhyau wahanse), and are his pupils (atawæsso). They come chiefly from poor families of good rank; very few from among the rich. The ceremony of admission takes place in the monastery, its veranda, or any convenient place; in the presence, if possible, of the boy's parents and friends, to whom it is a great occasion. First his hair is cut; then, if his parents are present, he makes obeisance to them, and asks their permission; then he does homage to his tutor and to any other monks who may be present. He is then washed and ornamented with the complete clothing and ornaments of a layman. From the peculiar arrangement of the turban, which is so put on as to project like a cobra's hood, the lad so dressed and ornamented is popularly called "the cobra boy." About this turban (sumbare) a curious story is told. A Naga or serpent prince, named Divyanāgarāja, applied for admission into the Community. That could not be granted, but in reward for his piety he was promised that in future every monk admitted should wear his badge. The novice is then placed before his tutor, the other monks sitting round, and makes obeisance to him, and sits in the posture of reverence, squatting a little on one side, and receives from his tutor the robe in which his tutor is to invest him. He then asks for admission "for the sake of escaping sorrow," etc., in words like those which we meet in the earliest Pitakas. The robes are then formally given to him, and the girdle is bound on his neck by his tutor, while the novice repeats the words, called "Taco pancake," viz. "Taco, nahaṃ, danta, mamsam, aṭṭhi," etc., the beginning of the list of the thirty-two foul and despicable elements of the body. He then retires and changes the rest of his lay dress for the yellow robes. Then the ten precepts are "given" to him, and this ends the ceremony.

He is then instructed, from six to eight or nine every evening, in the duties of a monk—Herana Sutta, Dinacariyāwa, Satara Sanvara Sīla, Sekhyāwa—which are the main parts of every novice's training. In communicating this knowledge the elder monks are said to spare no pains. But even before this, the principles of deportment (iriyapathā), how to walk, stand, sit, as becomes a monk, are taught by oral instruction and example. It is said that these young monks are not idle, but, in the better cases, are kept hard at work by their tutors. According to the opinion and experience of one who has tried it in a poor Kandian village, it is a hard life, and the boy's spirits are kept up only by the assurance of his parents and teachers that it is a noble life and well worth the suffering. From the poverty of the people, and their less attachment to Buddhism, the life of monks in the Kandian country is harder than in the low country ; but in Colombo, on account of ridicule, disrespect, and the like, it is harder still. But some of these lads, like my informant, are sustained by a genuine desire for learning.

The monks, however, of some of the Kandian monasteries are so well off as not to be dependent on alms ; and so they are without the stimulus, which their low-country brethren have, to a life at least outwardly conformable to their profession. The places where the influences are bad are known and avoided ; but on the whole the lives of two-thirds are bad. More than one whom I have asked has told me that he personally knows three or four places in the Kandian country where theft and forgery go on in the monastery, and supposes there are many more. Very few monks are chaste : many go to women in the villages ; very many are guilty of nameless vices. In the Vidyodaya College, the influence of Sumangala, and of Hewantuduwe (from a Cotta village) is powerful for good : and the lads while at the college for the most part live well ; but most of them return to their bad lives when they get back to their pansalas.

NOTE TO CHAPTER XXVII

PRAYER AND PUBLIC WORSHIP

I. Of prayer, primitive Buddhism knows nothing. There is no room for prayer, properly so called, in a system which admits no Supreme God, nor any being essentially and permanently superior to man. The monk, who claims that the gods do homage to him, cannot pray ; and whatever petition a man may offer to Brahma, Indra, or other deities, is only the petition of one who for the time is out of office to one who is in a position to assist him. But in modern Buddhism the instinct of prayer finds frequent expression, and is probably the more genuine the less it rests on theory. The theory is two-fold. In some cases it is held, that the deities who control earthly affairs are accessible to petition, just as kings are.

The other view, more strictly Buddhist, is this: that merit, one's own or that of another, and especially that of the Buddha, can be brought to bear on one's own needs or on those of others. This may be called the theory, that wishes, when supported by merit, are efficacious.

Four cases of such efficacious wishes may be distinguished.

(1) The assignment of one's own merit to some one else. The book, "Faith of Buddha," described on p. 280, gives, as proper for the assigning of one's own merit to departed friends or kinsfolk, verses which may be thus translated:—

> May this be for the benefit of my kinsfolk:
> May (my) kinsfolk be blessed!

and for assigning it to the gods, these:—

> May the deities and nagas of mighty powers
> Who are in heaven and on earth
> Receive with satisfaction this meritorious act,
> And protect me continually for ever!

(2) The assignment of the merits of the Buddha. This, which I think the nearest approach to prayer, is not common in the books; but I think it may often be in the minds of modern Buddhists. The ignorant peasant, who crouches on the road at Kandy to make obeisance in the direction of the Tooth-relic, comes probably very near to such prayer as the Hindu offers before the image in which he believes the Deity to be present. He is vaguely commending his want to some supposed, or "unknown," Higher Power.

(3) The direction to a particular desired end of the merit of a particular meritorious action of one's own. This is called emphatically a "Wish' (paṭṭhanā, the word elsewhere used for "prayer"). In the introduction to the "Questions of Milinda," a novice obtains, as the consequence of his merit in sweeping out the courtyard of the monastery (reluctantly as he did it), birth as the clever King Milinda; while his senior obtains, apparently as the consequence of his merit in making the novice sweep, birth as the sage Nagasena, who answers all Milinda's questions. These consequences they had expressly claimed or "wished."

(4) The "Act of Truth" or "Truth Procedure." (Saccakiriyā. Kiriyā=kriyā, is an act, legal process, ordeal; in modern Indian languages, an oath.) A person who has acquired merit, may, by the truthful assertion of his past act or course of conduct, command the elements and work miracles. An extreme instance of it is given in the "Questions of Milinda," where a person, who had conspicuously little merit to boast of, yet, by making a truthful assertion of such merit as she had, turned back the flooded Ganges, to the astonishment of King Asoka and all his Court.

The King of China, we are told in the same place (Questions of King Milinda, S.B.E. xxxv. 182), by the like force of truth, every four months used to drive his chariot a league into the sea, and the mighty waves rolled back before him. King Parakrama in like manner (Mahavansa, 70, 209), stopped the rain which threatened to interfere with his march.

This theory is not of Buddhist origin: it is akin to the widespread belief in supernatural power as inevitably acquired by acts of austerity. In the Mahabharata, Damayanti, the wife of Nala, performs an "Act of Truth."

I have not heard of any belief in such powers now.

II. Similarly, for what Christians understand by "public service" there is, strictly speaking, no place in Buddhism. To offer gifts, and to hear the Law, are the only duties for which householders—according to the Pitakas—come to the dwellings (vihara) of the monks. Temples or images, in those days there were none. But after relic-houses and image-houses were multiplied, and "vihara" came to mean not the monks' dwelling but the image-house, something like localized worship necessarily grew up. Very little has ever been done in Ceylon to organize this into public worship; and when we read of Sinhalese kings promoting public religion, it is generally by making arrangements for the reading of the sacred books. There are a few indications in the Mahavansa of the institution of something like a ritual (e.g. Mahavansa, 90, 77); but this never grew to much. But at present we hear of a movement in the same direction. We hear it said, or we read in a guide-book, that at certain hours there are "services" in the Tooth-temple at Kandy. Buddhists have assured me that this only means, that at certain hours especially the laity are invited to do homage to the facsimile of the Tooth (the so-called Tooth itself is shown only on rare occasions). When English visitors say that they have witnessed a kind of ritual, in which the people responded after the manner of a litany, to what was said by the minister, they are describing the "giving" and "taking" of the Three Refuges and of the Precepts. This is a religious exercise, but not of the nature of worship.

CHAPTER XXVIII

PRESENT CUSTOMS AND CONDUCT OF THE BUDDHIST LAITY IN CEYLON

IN attempting to describe the present form and influence of Buddhism in Ceylon, I am met by two great difficulties. One of them is the difficulty which would attend such an attempt under any circumstances on the part of a writer who lived among those whose religion he was to describe. Such a writer cannot be content with mere hearsay or mere generalities ; the matter is real and near to him, and presents itself to his mind in details and in instances. On the other hand, he distrusts his instances and his own impressions, and knows, the more thoroughly the longer he has lived among a people, how little a foreigner can see into their life, how far they are from being all alike, how easily any statement in one direction may be met by contradicting instances. Further, he has personal relations with those of whom he is to write, and feels that any unfavourable feature in his picture may give pain to people whom he esteems or loves. To this difficulty I shall so far yield, as to be much briefer and less decisive in this part of my subject than its importance would suggest. To describe with unhesitating decision the value of a religious system, or the character of an Eastern people, must remain the prerogative of the passing tourist.

The other difficulty is one peculiar to the circumstances of this case, and arises from what is, as I think, the most interesting fact connected with the subject. There are two Buddhisms now in Ceylon : the residuum of the old Buddhism of the past centuries, as it lingers in out-of-the-way places, and as it has shaped the habits and ways of thought of those who are not under European influence ; and a new revival, much more self-conscious and artificial, which aims indeed only at reviving what Buddhism always professed to be, but which has been influenced, in its estimate of that profession, very largely by Europeans. It is easy to distinguish these two Buddhisms in their extremes.

Travelling through the less frequented parts of the Kandian provinces, where the hills begin to rise out of the low country, one may ask a peasant what his religion is. He will reply, "We are Buddhists," but will be surprised at its being expected that he should know anything more of religion than that there is a Bo-tree in such and such a part of the village, before which people lay a few flowers from time to time; he does not know why, but it is the custom. There is a temple with a dagaba a little way off; he has been there now and then, but has no interest in it whatever; the monk who lives there is a man not much respected, but to whom it is the custom to give food when he comes round. He may have taught a few boys their letters; but no one ever heard of his teaching religion to any one, though our informant supposes he says "bana" in his own way. We ask whether the monk does any good in the place; and the answer is, "No. Why should he?"

We go on to the temple, which is half-way up the richly-wooded hill that rises near the village. A path little trodden leads us through the dense jungle, where almost every tree is rich with its own blossom, colourless perhaps, but fragrant, till we climb, with here and there a rude step cut, over steep but rounded surfaces of dark grey stone, between great overhanging boulders, in every cleft of which the wild fig clings, past here and there a narrow cistern for rain-water, made long ago by enlarging a fissure of the gneiss rock. At last signs appear of a path more cleared, and a bit of fence, and a few flowers; and one or two cocoa-nuts, rare at that distance from the sea, stand near a low-roofed hut that nestles close under a vertical face of rock. A yellow robe hangs over the little railing, which encloses a tiny square of well-swept gravel. In this square stands the hut or pansala, the three cocoa-nut trees, and the dagaba, a grey ruined dome, some twelve feet high, on its crumbling base of old hewn stone. A yellow-robed lad comes out and stares at us, and goes away, and soon brings out the old man, whose thin dreary face gains a kind of dignity from the shaven head, which in the boy only adds to the stupidity of his look. The old monk is singularly courteous, and soon insists on sending for a young cocoa-nut for us—perhaps the only one on his trees—and on cutting the end of it with his razor, which he politely assures us can easily be sharpened again. He is pleased by our admiring the place, but except that it is very old, he has nothing to tell us about it; nor can anything whatever, in an intellectual sense, be got out of him. He shows us, with some pride, his two or three books, of two or three leaves each, brown with age and smoke, which he can read but cannot understand. "They are Pali," he says, but he will commit himself no further.

Of the temple or vihara he would apparently not have thought, unless we had asked him where it was, and whether we might see it. "You can," he says indifferently, and leads us along a little path, on the inner side of the enclosure, over which the rock, which behind his dwelling was vertical, leans more and more forward. We come to a little platform of swept gravel, completely overhung by the cliff, against which a low pent-house has been built. A rough narrow door, with a massive lintel of timber, is opened with a key, and we enter a sort of wide but very shallow cave. Nearly in front of us we see a few small figures of Buddha, a brass lamp or two, and an oily little slab of stone, on which some flowers, without leaf or stalk, have been laid; and as our eyes grow accustomed to the dim light, we become aware that the cave extends to some distance on our left; and that up against the rock-wall, partly hewn in the stone, is what was once a recumbent figure of Buddha. "Very ancient," says our guide, but he shows no respect for it whatever.

We are glad to get out of the smell of bats and burnt gums and camphor, and to notice above our head the drip-course, a shallow incision cut in the rock high up over the whole length of the cave building, to throw off the rain, that may run down the surface, before it can reach the pent-house roof. Close to this mark of ancient care we notice a line of letters, unlike the Sinhalese of the present day, and nearly similar to those in which Asoka had his edicts written twenty-one centuries ago. "Very old," says the monk, and adds with pride that the Government Agent once brought a gentleman who read and copied them. They seem, so far as they are legible, merely to record that this cave was given to the Community by some king, the Tissa or Abhaya of his day.

By the time we come away several villagers may have gathered about us, and we learn from them that to the temple we have visited some of the best of the neighbouring fields belong, and that the old monk is supposed to receive a fair return from them. But as far as religion goes, he seems to be scarcely more to them than he is to us—a familiar figure among the immemorial elements of their tiny world.

But if we can lead them to talk of their crops, and houses and illnesses, and of the births and deaths that have occurred in their memory, we shall find that we are in a world of demons, who give trouble and must be driven away, who are sometimes seen, with fatal consequences, in the jungle—a world in which tribute must be paid to the goddess of disease, and to the far-away deity of Kataragama; in which scarcely anything happens by direct human or natural agency, but all by virtue of charms and omens. The old monk up there casts horoscopes, it is true, but for all practical purposes a "kapurāla," an exorcist or devil-priest in the next village, is the pastor of the flock. The whole home life is haunted by a sort of religion, but Buddhism is almost as completely outside it as the British Government.

That is one extreme. Return to Colombo, and go into the Oriental Library at the Museum, and you will see yellow-robed students at work with pen and note-book on Pali manuscripts in Sinhalese or Burmese characters; they are students at the Buddhist College. On the table you may find a copy of the *Buddhist*, an English newspaper as modern in tone as the *Daily News*, full of reports of Buddhist schools, meetings, cremations, and conversions, mingled here and there with a paragraph of abuse of Christianity. If it is the "Birthday of our Lord Buddha," you will find decorations and lamps in half the streets of the city, and meet gay processions and hear "carols" half the night. In the prison you may find a monk preaching to the criminals, or in a hospital visiting the sick; or you will see him holding forth at the corner of the street, exactly imitating, while he denounces, the Christian missionary.

What is clearly fabulous or superstitious in the old system is boldly thrown overboard, and Buddhism claims to be in alliance with modern discoveries and the philosophy of the West. New dagabas are being built, and old ones repaired; books and tracts being printed. The reform of abuses and the improvement of the lives of the "priests" are loudly called for; the Buddhist "schoolmaster is abroad."

Such are the two Buddhisms in the extreme of their divergence. And the questions so difficult to answer are: Is the new of one piece with the old, a true revival of an old stock, or is it a foreign importation, which may replace but cannot revive what went before? And if the answer to this question lies between these alternatives, to what extent has this revival, loud and well advertised as it is, touched the national heart? Is it entirely or nearly co-extensive with European civilization and the English language? Or is it working along native channels, and finding a genuine response in native instincts?

Such questions are very difficult to answer, because between the two extremes I have contrasted there is every intermediate shade.

It is certainly the case that the external and artificial revival has affected not Colombo only, or the Anglicized districts only, but the purely native provinces also, in at least two ways: by the diffusion of education among monks, and by the restoration of ancient shrines.

Since European students incited the Sinhalese to the more frequent study of their sacred "books," Suttas are being read and expounded even in remote villages where, because there was no Sinhalese translation, they had not been heard for centuries. Monks who have some knowledge of the religion they profess, beyond that which suffices for receiving food and seeing the court of the pansala swept, are being sent out in every direction; are living better lives, I believe, and gaining a different kind of respect from that which was paid to their predecessors.

The restored dagabas—though their restoration is due, as at Anuradhapura, to European antiquarian interest, or, as at Tissa Mahārāma, to English irrigation works—are yet attracting pilgrims and promoting an interest in Buddhism, in the remote districts in which they are. Even the obscure and unhealthy Alut Nuwara, its old dagaba being restored, has lately attracted multitudes, who have carried to their villages not cholera only, but, we must suppose, an increased devotion.

These are, both of them, ways in which the educational movement is affecting the general standard, though by an artificial and perhaps temporary effort. But there are directions in which we may see, I think, increased zeal, stimulated by the same causes, but moving more distinctly on the old lines. In some of those places within the maritime provinces, in which Buddhism has long had a strong footing, the new movement has sufficed to develop it. "Donors" are more numerous, and are doing no new thing, but the old on a larger scale—giving to monks in large assemblies, building dagabas, and providing for festivals. One may see along the roads of the southern province twenty monks together, proceeding with some dignity, with very handsome fans and new silk umbrellas, with bowls neatly covered with yellow cloth, and carried by boys well dressed in white, to the place of entertainment. And for miles one may meet companies of gaily-dressed people, women especially, but by no means exclusively, streaming along, cheerful and well-behaved, towards shrines which a few years ago attracted not a tenth of the number. Near such a shrine itself may be seen a hundred or more women, all in white, each carrying in her uplifted hand a piece of the fragrant areca flower, shouting, "Sadhu" from time to time as they march along, and at any rate enjoying the exhilarating sense of procession.

Such a scene strikes one, at first sight at least, as the genuine development of a native custom. On the other hand, one knows that at the back of all this there are subscriptions, often raised by foreigners, and if not by foreigners by representatives of the Colombo school of reformers. The result may be more artificial than at first appears. It may be after all the fruit of a mission from Colombo.

In Colombo itself there are scarcely any Buddhist institutions that are not new. European passengers often ask to see a temple, and for want of any more genuine temple in the town they are taken to one at Kotahena. It is only within the last thirty years that this temple has been heard of. There was a pansala there but no vihara, till one was erected and named (it was completed about 1880) by the energetic controversialist, Mohottiwatte. This man never rose, I believe, to be more than a novice (sāmanera); but he made himself a considerable name, and his cremation, early in 1891, was the occasion of a very large, though not a spontaneous, "demonstration." He started a printing-press, from which a great many tracts against Christianity have issued, and some periodicals. I am told that he erected near the gate of his temple a statue of himself.

Those visitors who think that when they are taken to this place they are visiting a genuine centre of Buddhism, are much mistaken. I am assured that it is not visited by as many as twenty people a day, and that most of the small number are passengers!

What the leaders of the modern school wish the Buddhists of Ceylon now to practise and believe, can be very clearly ascertained from their published manuals; though it is not easy to say whether these books represent a new departure, or continue the tradition of the past. In this respect there is probably a wide interval between the two little books of which I am now to speak.

The first is a short manual in Sinhalese called *Buddha-Faith*, issued from the Kotahena temple, of which I have just spoken, and by the Amarapura sect, some twenty years ago. It is largely used, at any rate in the low country. Most Buddhists who can read, at least in or near Colombo, possess a copy; and some of those who cannot read get it read to them. It contains the rules for "taking Refuge in Buddha," etc.; for "taking," as it is called, or binding oneself to the Five, the Eight, or the Ten Precepts; for the observance of "poya" (uposatha) days, and for meditation on decay, etc.; with short explanations of the doctrine of Karma and of merit and demerit; and of duties towards the dead, towards the gods, and towards the Buddha.

An abstract of some of its contents will show the character of its teaching.

The obligation of the Five Precepts, being universal, may be taken at home, every day or more frequently; or it may be taken more formally in the presence of a monk at a temple. In this case, the person first offers flowers at the temple; he then kneels or prostrates himself before the monk with hands joined together, says three times, "Homage to the Buddha," etc., three times, "I take refuge," etc., and then he repeats after the monk the five precepts (or prohibitions). If he has not time to go to a temple, he can "take sil" before any image of Buddha, or turning himself in the direction in which there is an image or a temple, etc. This is the *minimum* of Buddhist observance; it is practised by the large majority of Buddhists in the more civilized parts of the country, especially in the maritime districts; in the Kandian districts comparatively few do even this; and in the outlying jungle districts it is almost unknown. In such parts the people have, as nearly as possible, no relation with Buddhism but the name.

Taking the Eight Precepts, or " atasil," is more serious. It can only be done before a monk, and on a poya day; the person rises early, and must be fasting, and dressed in a white cloth; and on that day he may not eat after noon. Besides the formulas of " homage " and " refuge," he has to repeat certain stanzas. This is the regular way of observing the poya day, and those who do it are considered regular or devout to a certain extent: they are " upāsakas " of the lower grade. It is often extended to longer periods; sometimes the obligation is renewed continually.

The devotee of the Ten Obligations, or " dasasil," is almost a monk. He is as much bound for life as the monk is, wears a special dress, and shaves his head; and is to undertake no other work than meditation, visiting temples, and giving or doing works of mercy. But he may live in a house, though he must occupy a separate room. He renews his vows every poya day. This is the upasaka *par excellence*. There are very few men of this profession, but a considerable number of women, generally old, are to be seen about the temples, especially in Kandy, or on the way to Adam's Peak. They usually carry bowls as if for begging, and their shaven heads and dirty white dresses give them a pathetic appearance; and one who had read the books would naturally suppose them to be nuns. Female mendicants they are; but they have not been admitted to the Community, and therefore are not called " bhikkunis," but only " upasikas."

The poya days are four in each lunar month, at the four quarters, and are made known by a special almanac, called the " pancanga lita." They are said to be every seventh day; but this, of course, is not strictly the case; if it were, the days would not correspond with the phases of the moon. Nor do they occur, of course, on any particular day of the week. The full moon is much the most observed, and the new moon next; the other two are not recognized except by upasakas. Nor are the poya days fast days in any other sense than this, that the " atasil upasaka " may not eat on those days after noon, or after (the turn of the sun towards) sunset. There is no such thing in Buddhism, either primitive or modern (in Ceylon), as a day on which all eating is forbidden, or on which any degree of abstinence is enjoined on all Buddhists. The word uposatha meant in Brahmanism, whence it was borrowed, a day of abstinence; but as adopted by Buddhism, it means a day of special observances, some of which are accompanied by abstinence for various periods from food, and also from luxuries and amusements.

As regards work, there is no rule forbidding it on the poya day; but upasakas keep away from work, to give themselves to religious occupations; in many cases they shut themselves up altogether. The fact that Buddhist fishermen often refuse to go out on poya days leads Europeans to think that work is forbidden; but it is not the work so much as the taking of life that they avoid.

For it is taught that all the merit of taking the Five Obligations is destroyed by breaking one of them on that day; and it is popularly believed that on poya days Sakra, the chief of the gods who are concerned with human affairs, comes down specially to see who are keeping the precepts. Merit is acquired by offerings, by keeping precepts, and by active works of charity; and is forfeited, according to the "*Buddha-Faith*," not only by breaking the precepts, but by thinking any god greater than Buddha, or by turning Buddhist for the sake of pleasing any god. It is also taught, much to the credit of modern Buddhism, that demerit is incurred *by not doing acts of kindness* or by omitting almsgiving.

The Manual goes on to explain how the merit of a man's acts can be imparted to departed friends or to the gods. It contains stanzas used in the worship of dagabas and in offering flowers; and some of the more popular Suttas, viz. Mangala, Ratana, Karaniyametta; and certain Jayamangalagatha, or stanzas for good luck and prosperity. The latter recite certain actions of the Buddha, and each stanza ends with the refrain, "By virtue of this may your prosperity grow!" It has been said that these verses are not directly religious; but the use of them implies a belief in the Buddha, and their purpose is to obtain for the person congratulated some sort of benefit from the Buddha. It is said that they were once used in welcoming the Governor of Ceylon; but they are no longer admitted on such occasions.

A more recent Manual, published in English, called *A Buddhist Catechism,* was issued in 1881 for use in Buddhist schools, and bears the imprimatur of the learned Sumangala, Principal of the Pali College in Colombo, and High Priest of Adam's Peak.

It consists mainly of a recitation of the principal points in the received biography of Gotama, in a form a little more ornate than that which has been above given from the Pitakas; including the four signs which preceded his leaving home, and the supernatural circumstances which accompanied it, and laying more stress on this renunciation than I have found laid on it in the books. With this is a very favourable and not unfair statement —though in language, of course, coloured by Christian associations—of the Buddhist morality ; and a short, and in my opinion, unsatisfactory statement on the rest of the system. It concludes with the received legends of the Councils, of Asoka, and of Mahinda's mission to Ceylon. Its view of Buddhism differs from that which I have intended to give only in a few details ; the most important, I think, being a statement about the human nature of Gotama. To the question, " Was Gotama a man ? " the answer is, " In form a man, but internally not like other men." The suggestion that Gotama was in any sense not a true man is, I think, quite contrary to the ancient teaching.

In regard to conduct the following may be noted :—

The broad rule is, that if we have an excess of merit we shall be well and happily born the next time ; if an excess of demerit, our next birth will be wretched and full of suffering.

The whole religion of the Buddha is said to be summed up in the verse thus translated :—

> To cease from all sin,
> To get virtue,
> To cleanse one's own heart,
> This is the religion of the Buddhas.

The following are of a very modern colour :—

Q. Do Buddhists consider Buddha as one who by his own virtue can save us from the consequences of our individual sins ?

A. Not at all. No man can be saved by another ; he must save himself.

Q. What, then, was Buddha to us and all other beings ?

A. An all-seeing, all-wise counsellor ; one who discovered the safe path and pointed it out; one who showed the cause of, and the only cure for, human suffering. In pointing to the road, in showing us how to escape dangers, he became our Guide. And as one leading a blind man across a narrow bridge, over a swift and deep stream, saves his life, so in showing us, who were blind from ignorance, the way of salvation, Buddha may be called our "Saviour."

But there is not much that is controversial. A personal God is expressly denied, and creation is said, somewhat more cautiously, to be inconceivable. "Soul" is said to be "a word used by the ignorant to express a false idea." Nirvana is said to be "the total obliteration of everything that goes to make up the physical man"; and the Parinibbana of Gotama is called "the death of his body."

The support of modern science is claimed for Buddhism, inasmuch as the doctrine of the development of the Bodhisats, some quicker, some slower, is substantially in accordance with the theory of evolution. An intelligent student of this "Catechism" will hardly escape the difficulty, which is inherent in the whole system as it now practically exists—the difficulty of reconciling its claim to be scientific with its toleration of superstition and virtual polytheism. In one sentence, the supernatural is denied; in the next, "phenomena-working" power is said to be obtainable by drugs and charms. On the next page, we are told that Buddhists believe that there are such beings as devas, which inhabit worlds or spheres of their own; that they are of three kinds; and some have power to torment the impure.

It is not clear whether these beliefs are among the things of which it is said, "the poetical imagination, zeal, or lingering superstitions of Buddhist devotees, in various ages, have no doubt caused the noble principles of Buddha's doctrines to be coupled more or less with what might be removed with advantage." Certainly if, with these, the belief in planets, charms, and devil-dances can be removed, Christians, at any rate—and surely all good Buddhists—will rejoice.

I am far from wishing—I trust it has been clear throughout this book—to make the worst of Buddhism. I wish Buddhism would make the best of itself. At present it is inconsistent, just where inconsistency does the most harm.

"A personal god," says the *Buddhist Catechism*, "Buddhists

regard as only a gigantic shadow thrown upon the void of space by the imagination of ignorant men." The Buddhist belief is in reality both better and worse than this creed.

A Buddhist mother calls her child, the child that God has given her; a Buddhist says to his friend, God preserve you; in extreme distress Buddhists cry, Are there no gods? And when the modern revival demands that Buddha's birthday should be kept, the motto is constantly exhibited on Colombo walls, God bless our Lord Buddha! To what extent in each instance the thought is of a single supreme God, it is difficult to see. The word used is generally the honorific plural, a grammatical form which is usually, if not always, singular in meaning; but it is possible that it often covers a vague idea, neither definitely singular nor definitely plural. But that the idea is personal, there can be no doubt whatever. The living Buddhist does, as a fact, believe in personal deity, and herein his belief is better than his creed.

But the *Buddhist Catechism*, while it denies what human nature insists on believing, goes on to teach as follows: "Buddhists believe that there are such beings (as devas) which inhabit worlds or spheres of their own." These are certainly thought of as personal. One of the kinds is still subject to passions, and some can torment the impure. Popular belief goes further, and peoples every wood with personal beings, devatās, and demons; identifies every planet with a presiding grahayā; goes to Hinduism for the personal guardians of house and crop, and the personal wielders of luck and pestilence; goes to the basest sorcery for the personal agents of malice and revenge. Here the belief is worse than the creed.

Now I should like to challenge the scientific Buddhist, who thinks himself compelled by science to deny God, openly to deny and denounce and repudiate on the part of Buddhism—I will not say the devas, who open gates to Buddhas, or the Sakra who look after poya days, but at least the devils, Pattinis, Hanumans, and the rest of the more malignant "shadows thrown on the void of space by the imagination of ignorant men."

When I condemn these am I condemning Buddhism?

I have come to the point at which, with all respect for the aims of those who are now, from among the Buddhists themselves, trying to promote what is good by means of Buddhism, I must offer some estimate of the results which, so far as I can learn, Buddhism has effected in Ceylon for virtue. The estimate, unhappily, cannot be a high one.

If it is asked, to begin with, whether the Sinhalese are evidently and unmistakably influenced in their lives by the religion which they profess, as Mohammedans for instance are, the answer must be, No; except in the matter of scrupulousness about taking the life of animals. In other matters, whether a man's conduct were good or bad, he would seldom allege religion as his motive. Religion is a matter of obtaining merit by certain offerings and attendances; not, in ordinary cases, a matter of conduct.

I have taken a good deal of pains to ascertain whether there were men popularly esteemed for their exemplary conduct, and what the instances of that conduct were. Large instances of giving, I have met with; such and such a Sinhalese lady had been a great promoter of building dagabas; another had got the whole Jataka book copied out in a single day; but of conduct, properly so called, founded on religious principle, I have heard very little. A long questioning, of a fairly intelligent man, led me only to the case of a monk who would not allow the conductor of a coach to carry a parcel for him illegally, but insisted on paying for it! Especial inquiries as to the conduct of upasakas, whether they were particularly good husbands, friends, etc., have led only to negative results. I attribute this less to the want of exemplary religious characters than to the absence of any idea that religiousness was to be tested by conduct in ordinary life.

On the other hand, I have found a low standard of conduct acquiesced in as proper to Buddhists as compared with Christians. Instead of the Christian claim which, whether well founded or not, is constantly made, "You can trust me, for I am a Catholic," I have often heard something like this, "What can you expect of me? I am only a Buddhist." It is not expected of an ordinary Buddhist that he will aim high: if he is an upasaka, it is only expected that he will be morose and proud.

I am painfully aware, as I write this, how little Christian conduct often corresponds to Christian standard; but, at any rate, "Christian behaviour" means, in all lips, "good behaviour." I suppose no one ever heard a Sinhalese use "Buddhist conduct" as a synonym for "good conduct."

The lowness of the standard, even in matters on which in theory emphasis is laid, is painfully shown by surprise at an ordinary moral action. An Englishman, driving out from Colombo to a town some twenty miles distant, came up with a little crowd round a woman who had been knocked down by a bullock. As any Englishman would have done, he put her in his carriage, with one or two of her companions to support her, and had her taken slowly towards her home, which was a mile farther on, himself following on foot. He was shocked by hearing one of the women say, "This must be a god; no man would do this." A day or two afterwards he returned, and went a little out of his way to ask after her. He heard his conduct discussed, as he drew near the place, with extravagant admiration; and the expression oftenest repeated was, "No Sinhalese man would have done this!" In case of an accident, it is often impossible to persuade a bystander to help. A man may lie by the roadside and entreat passer-by after passer-by to help him out of the sun into the shade, and not one will stop. When once a poor Tamil girl had died in the hospital at Badulla, no one, Tamil or Sinhalese, could be persuaded to carry her body to the church, because she was of low caste: the Assistant Government Agent and other English gentlemen carried her themselves. It is painful to have to mention these indications of want of humanity, but although I have no doubt that many instances of the contrary could be found, these will be admitted, by those who know Ceylon, to be characteristic, at least of those who have not come under other civilizing influences than those of Buddhism.

The Sinhalese are reported, by a commissioner who came to inquire into the criminal statistics of the island, to stand first on the list of homicides, perhaps in the world. I am not convinced that this represents any very exceptional maliciousness: it is due in part to the knife usually carried; but it certainly shows how little Buddhist theories have formed the conduct of the people. Offences against the precept which forbids taking life, and cruelty, whether to men or to animals, are in no way peculiar to the very ignorant; quarrelling and homicide are probably increased by the early stages of contact with civilization, with the law-court, and the tavern.

In respect of truthfulness and honesty, it is still more distinctly the case, that where there is no restraining force, education, in its superficial forms, and acquaintance with the wealth of others, have a directly vicious effect. Of the half-educated Sinhalese, many are certainly extremely untruthful and thievish; much more so, I believe, than the unsophisticated Buddhist villagers. Buddhism, therefore, has not produced these vices; but it signally fails to prevent them.

In regard to what is sometimes called, in a limited sense, "morality," the case is the opposite to that of honesty; the more civilized are the more moral. The tone and standard among the educated and semi-Anglicised Sinhalese of the maritime provinces is high; marriage is respected among them. Among the ignorant or merely Buddhist Kandians, it is deplorably low; it is hardly too much to say of whole districts that marriage is unknown. It would be unfair to charge this upon Buddhism as a positive result; but it is a result which a higher level of practice among teachers and leaders would have prevented. On the other hand, it is in great measure to three centuries of intercourse with Christian nations that the high standard in the maritime provinces is due.

Such a sketch as I have given does not indicate that Buddhism has been much of a power in favour of virtue. In all these points the Hindu Tamils would compare equally, perhaps favourably, with the Sinhalese. I should be thankful to learn that the case was better than I have represented it. I shall be most thankful if, whether by the labours of Buddhists or by those of Christians, it can be improved.

While I cannot in honesty give a better account than this of the generality, I can heartily say that there are individuals, who, as Buddhists, are setting a good example, and doing their best to teach others what is good. Such ought not to be offended if I reckon them rather as friends of Christianity than as opponents.

As promoters, in the long run, of Christianity, I reckon all who are diffusing knowledge of the true tenets and history of Buddhism; all who are letting light, by whatever channel, into the dark places—and some very dark places exist, and cruel habitations—all who are insisting on what is excellent in Buddhism, when they do so not only to praise Buddhism but to get virtue practised.

If the chosen ground of Buddhism is kindness, and as the Buddhist Catechism adds, justice, it is on that ground that I should like to contend with them ; and let those who are kindest and justest win.

My challenge to my Buddhist neighbours is this : this is what I ask them to do, and what their principles, I believe, would justify :—

Teach the highest possible doctrines of purity, kindness, and justice.

Make the lives of the priests examples of these virtues.

Discourage openly and utterly all demon-worship, charms, astrology, and idolatry.

While using sober argument in the proper place, abstain from all abuse of the faith of others.

Admit that the doctrines of a Creator and Rewarder, of a Saviour from sin, of a helper in the road to Holiness, of an immortal Life, are doctrines characteristic of Christianity.

INDICES

SUBJECT INDEX

INDEX OF PROPER NAMES

INDEX OF PALI WORDS

PROFESSOR MAX MÜLLER'S WORKS.

COLLECTED WORKS. 20 vols. Crown 8vo.

Vol. I. NATURAL RELIGION: the Gifford Lectures, 1888. 5s.

Vol. II. PHYSICAL RELIGION: the Gifford Lectures, 1890. 5s.

Vol. III. ANTHROPOLOGICAL RELIGION: the Gifford Lectures, 1891. 5s.

Vol. IV. THEOSOPHY: or, Pyschological Religion: Gifford Lectures, 1892. 5s.

CHIPS FROM A GERMAN WORKSHOP. 4 vols.

Vol. V. Recent Essays and Addresses. 5s.

Vol. VI. Biographical Essays. 5s.

Vol. VII. Essays on Language and Literature. 5s.

Vol. VIII. Essays on Mythology and Folklore. 5s.

Vol. IX. THE ORIGIN AND GROWTH OF RELIGION, as illustrated by the Religions of India: the Hibbert Lectures, 1878. 5s.

Vol. X. BIOGRAPHIES OF WORDS AND THE HOME OF THE ARYAS. 5s.

Vols. XI, XII. THE SCIENCE OF LANGUAGE: Founded on Lectures delivered at the Royal Institution in 1861 and 1863. 2 vols. 5s. each.

Vol. XIII. INDIA: What can it Teach Us? 5s.

Vol. XIV. INTRODUCTION TO THE SCIENCE OF RELIGION. Four Lectures, 1870. 5s.

Vol. XV. RÂMAKR*I*SHN*A*: his Life and Sayings. 5s.

Vol. XVI. THREE LECTURES ON THE VEDÂNTA PHILOSOPHY, 1894. 5s.

Vol. XVII. LAST ESSAYS. First Series. Essays on Language, Folk-lore, etc. 5s.

Vol. XVIII. LAST ESSAYS. Second Series. Essays on the Science of Religion. 5s.

Vol. XIX. THE SIX SYSTEMS OF INDIAN PHILOSOPHY. 7s. 6d. net.

Vol. XX. THE SILESIAN HORSEHERD ('DAS PFERDEBURLA'): Questions of the Hour Answered. 5s.

CONTRIBUTIONS TO THE SCIENCE OF MYTHOLOGY. 2 vols. 8vo. 32s.

THE SCIENCE OF THOUGHT. 8vo. 21s.

THE LIFE AND LETTERS OF THE RIGHT HONOURABLE FRIEDRICH MAX MÜLLER. Edited by his Wife. With 6 Photogravure Illustrations (three Portraits). 2 vols. 8vo, 32s. net.

MY AUTOBIOGRAPHY: a Fragment. With 6 Portraits. 8vo, 12s. 6d.

AULD LANG SYNE. Second Series. 8vo. 10s. 6d.

DEUTSCHE LIEBE (German Love). Fragments from the Papers of an Alien. Collected by F. MAX MÜLLER. Translated from the German by G. A. M. Crown 8vo, gilt top. 5s.

LONGMANS, GREEN, & CO., 39 Paternoster Row, London, E.C.; New York, Bombay, and Calcutta.